P9-DDC-763

Good Morning, Merry Sunshine

GOOD MORNING,

A Father's Journal of His Child's First Year

MERRY SUNSHINE

BOB GREENE

NEW YORK *Atheneum*

Published simultaneously in Canada by McClelland and Stewart Ltd.

Designed by Kathleen Carey

Printed in the U.S.A.

For my Mother and my Father

Preface

THIS BOOK is the result of looking for other books. When I found out that I was going to become a father, my first instinct was to read everything I could about parenthood. I had no idea of what to expect; I was looking for something that could lead me through the experience—that could tell me what might lie ahead. For me, this was totally unknown territory; I needed to hear from someone who had been there before.

I found many books, some of them excellent. There were medical guides, and pregnancy guides, and child-development guides, and child-activity guides. What I couldn't find, though, was anything that dealt on a human level with what happens when a man and a woman bring a new baby home—when a house that had held two people suddenly holds three.

The problem was that all of the books I read approached the idea of a new baby from the broadest point of view. In their efforts to be encyclopedic, they lost something. They lost the specific sense of what really takes place from the moment a child is born. No matter how much I read, I kept walking away with the feeling that I really didn't know what was about to happen.

All of my professional life I have specialized in writing stories that attempt to capture the humanity of the people and events I am covering. Slowly, it occurred to me that I might have the opportunity here to tell the most human story I had ever encountered—the story of a new life, and how that new life affects the lives of the two people who had helped to create it. It has always been my experience that the freshest, clearest reporting I do is when I am seeing something for the first time; whether a political convention or a Super Bowl, the impressions and sights and sounds and thoughts I have taken away from a story have always been best my first time through.

I decided to keep a journal of my child's first year. It would be the story of her life; it would be the story of her parents' lives now that she was a part of those lives. I had no preconceptions, no expectations; I knew it would be like nothing else I had ever been a part of, and I didn't want to let any of it pass me by half noticed.

I wrote every day. No matter what else I was doing, I made time to fill in that day's entry in the journal. My thinking was that by paying close attention every day to what was happening to my child, and to her parents, I would have the best chance—at the end of the year—of having a precise record of what the first year had truly been like.

This is that journal. It is the story of one year, and of three lives. I have made no attempt to go back over the text and update the opinions or iron out the naïvetés. This is how it happened.

Good Morning, Merry Sunshine

June 11

AMANDA Sue was in trouble. I had yet to meet her; my wife was in her tenth hour of labor, and the fetal monitor attached to her stomach indicated that our baby's heart rate was dipping alarmingly low. We had decided months before that the child would be named Amanda Sue; now, as I stared at the computerized machine that measured the beating of her tiny heart, my insides tightened as I wondered what might happen next, and tried not to think about the possible answers.

There were three doctors and four nurses in the room. We were in the basement of Chicago's Michael Reese Hospital, in Labor Room No. 9. We had left our home at 2:30 a.m.

The cab ride to the hospital was eerie. The city was asleep, and we were almost alone on Lake Shore Drive. We both knew it was unlike any other late-night ride we had ever taken, or would ever take again. The first few hours in the labor room were so easy, they could have been a Lamaze teacher's dream. Every time a contraction would come, Susan would do her breathing, and the pain would pass; it was a breeze. But in the last hours leading up to this moment, the pain had become agonizing. I thought of all the lessons in Lamaze class, from a teacher promising the women that getting through labor would be eminently manageable without drugs; I felt angry, resentful, and helpless as I looked at Susan in the worst pain she had ever experienced. Maybe the breathing exercises were tool enough for some women; but I wished that all of the other expectant mothers in our class could have seen films of something like this, rather than the propaganda of some young mother whizzing her way through labor on a breath and a smile.

An anesthesiologist had given Susan an epidural block with a long needle, after an intravenous injection of Demerol had failed to provide any relief; the insertion of the needle in her back was the only time the doctors had suggested that I leave the room. When I returned she was still crying out; an orangish antiseptic solution dripped down her back, and the table was soaked with blood.

Dr. Allan Charles, Dr. William Alpern, Dr. Martin Motew, and four nurses stood together looking at the printout from the fetal monitor. On the right side of the paper a moving needle charted the intensity of the labor contractions. On the left side another needle recorded the baby's heart. This was accompanied by a steady beeping, keeping time with the heartbeat. I did not have to talk to the doctors to know they were concerned; the very fact that all three of them were huddled here was testimony enough.

Earlier in the day they had joked with me about my nervousness. Every time Dr. Charles would leave the labor room to go into the physicians' lounge, I would follow him in there several minutes later and just sort of hang around. He got the point: I thought he should be in the labor room all the time. "You have to give me a few minutes with my pacifier," he said once, holding up a big cigar. We had laughed. Now that was over.

The doctors conferred quietly. For some reason—they weren't sure why—the baby's heart would beat normally for a few minutes, then slow dramatically. They theorized that something inside Susan was applying pressure on the baby, putting the child in distress and endangering her. They were encouraged that every time this happened, it seemed to correct itself. Still, the graph paper from the monitor was telling a story they really would rather not have been seeing.

And Susan kept crying out. I knew I would rather be here than in the waiting room of my father's generation; the way she kept looking over at me as the pains drove her flat against the table, and as the doctors talked about the baby's heart, I realized that my presence was the only thing keeping her from complete panic. But this wasn't how it was supposed to be. This wasn't some pleasant trip we were taking together; this was trouble of the worst kind, and I could tell that the doctors would have been just as happy without the father in the room.

Just before two-thirty Dr. Charles said he wanted to try to deliver the baby. Outside it was a warm, sunny June afternoon in Chicago; I had not yet seen the day. The doctors, nurses, and I were in scrub suits; now we put on caps and masks, and Susan was wheeled into the delivery room.

I stood at the head of the operating table. The medical personnel surrounded the other sides; Dr. Charles moved swiftly. "You have to help me now," he said to Susan. "You can't tell me how much it hurts. This is it. This is what it's all been about. You have to help get your baby out."

Susan pushed. "That's it," Dr. Charles said. "That's it. Do it again." A nurse took me by the arm and led me to the foot of the table, beside the doctor. "Look at that," she said to me. "Here comes the top of your baby's head."

"Okay, push again," Dr. Charles said. I went back to the other end of the table. I was watching it in a mirror placed behind the doctor.

"It's going to be a tight squeeze," he said. He asked for forceps. They looked like giant, ugly shoehorns. He inserted them and said, "Here comes your baby." In an instant Amanda Sue was there—not crying right away, but waving her arms and legs. She looked fine. A nurse carried her over to a warming table, and a few seconds later she began to cry—and a few seconds after that a pediatrician examined her and said she was in good health. The heartbeat was normal.

The nurse carried her back to Susan and said "Here's your

baby." Susan held Amanda against her chest. Dr. Charles came around and shook my hand. "The problem with the heart came from a low-lying placenta," he said. "It was pressing against the baby, and that's why the heart slowed down. I almost decided to do a caesarean three times. Ten years ago I would have had to, but these new fetal monitors are so sophisticated—the monitor told me that the baby was bouncing back okay every time, so I knew it would be all right to go ahead."

I didn't say anything. I could feel myself shaking.

"You think this was bad," Dr. Charles said. "Wait until she goes on her first date. Now that's bad. My own daughter . . . I tell her to be in at ten o'clock, and she says, 'Dad, what can I do at two in the morning that I couldn't do at ten at night if I wanted to?' "

This was bizarre. We were standing there laughing at the doctor's story, and two feet away Amanda Sue lay moving against my wife's chest. Susan looked up at me and let out a long breath. And then, for the first time, I reached down and touched my daughter.

The nurses let us stay with the baby for fifteen minutes or so before she was taken up to the nursery. Then one of the nurses wheeled Susan into the recovery room, where she would stay for ninety minutes before being taken to her room.

I saw Amanda Sue lying in a heated transport unit in the corridor. Susan must have seen her, too, because in the recovery room she said to me, "I feel funny with her lying there all alone." So I went out and looked at the baby and pretended that I had something to do out there until the nurse came back to take Amanda Sue to the elevator. "That blanket's not going to cut off her breathing, is it?" I said, and the nurse assured me that it would not.

In the recovery room Susan and I sat together behind a curtain. We just kept looking at each other. The moment was full of a new kind of feeling for me—the feeling of family—and then I heard something from the other side of the curtain.

A black woman from Chicago's South Side had given birth perhaps two hours before; she had no husband, and no man had accompanied her to the hospital. She had had her baby alone, and she had lain in the recovery room alone, and now she was leaving alone. I thought of the joy I was seeing on my own wife's face in the moments after the birth of a child, the beginning of a family. And then I looked out to see this other woman being wheeled away, alone.

Her eyes locked with the nurse who sat by the door. The nurse said to her, "You take care of yourself, now." The woman nodded, and then she was gone.

People talk about the emotions that come when a baby is born: exuberance, relief, giddiness, pure ecstasy. The thought that you have seen a miracle in front of your eyes.

I knew I was supposed to be feeling all of those things, and of course I did. But the dominant emotion inside me was a more basic one. I was scared; scared of what I knew was sure to come, and more scared about what I didn't know. I am of a generation that has made self-indulgence a kind of secular religion. I looked down at that baby, and suddenly I felt that a whole part of my life had just ended, been cut off, and I was beginning something for which I had no preparation.

That's what went through me as I watched my baby enter the world; a sense of fear unlike any I have felt in my life. Fear that sprang from the place where the greatest fears have always lurked: fear of the totally unknown.

June 12

I SLEPT fitfully. Alone in the apartment, I kept waking up with a nagging feeling that there was something I should remember. I was groggy from the long day before; it took me several seconds to recall what it was. Amanda had been born. I lay awake and stared at the ceiling, trying to comprehend it.

I had called my parents and Susan's parents within half an hour of the birth. Now, the morning after, I took time to phone other people I wanted to tell. Most of my friends don't have children; their words of congratulations were mixed with a genuine sense of confusion and wonder. Their questions about what it had been like were elementary, not cosmic; this was virgin territory for them as well as for me, and suddenly they were addressing me as if I were the expert.

It was as if, in the last twenty-four hours, I had become a different person. They were asking me things about being a father that they wouldn't have thought to ask just one day before. I told them that I was too new at it to know anything; for all that had changed overnight, the fact remained that Amanda was still less than one day old.

She had microscopic fingernails and a scrawny, funny ducktail hairdo and tiny replicas of a wizened old man's hands. I stared down at Amanda Sue; she lay in a see-through hospital bassinet in room 808 of Michael Reese.

Susan was in bed next to the bassinet. A document had arrived with Amanda's vital statistics. The piece of paper said that she had weighed six pounds, fifteen ounces at birth, and had been twenty-and-one-half inches long.

"She can't be that long," I said.

"Of course she is," Susan said.

"My column's only sixteen inches long, and she isn't as long as the column," I said.

It was true. I write my newspaper column on a computer-generated video display terminal every day, and there is a measuring function in the upper right-hand corner of the screen that tells me how long the story is. When it reaches sixteen inches, the column is finished.

There was a *Chicago Tribune* lying on a chair in the hospital room. I picked it up and carried it over to Amanda's bassinet. I unfolded the paper and opened it to my column. I reached in and placed it next to Amanda. She was, indeed, a little longer than that day's effort.

"Well, she looks shorter," I said.

Susan held her as if she had been doing it all her life. When she handed Amanda to me, I felt like I was trying to balance twenty crystal goblets on my forearms. Every time the baby moved I thought I was going to drop her. I don't see how anyone ever gets used to this.

Amanda started crying. I leaned over the bassinet and said, "Shhh, Helen." Helen is my cat.

The men and women who work in maternity units behave as if they are specially blessed, and in a way they are. My previous experiences with hospitals, both personal and professional, have been unhappy ones—I suspect most people's are—and until you are in a ward devoted to new life, you neglect the fact that this one part of a hospital complex is devoted to happiness.

You could feel it: the doctors and nurses on the floor were used to dealing with people who were glad to be seeing them. I don't know what makes a nurse decide to specialize in newborns instead of, say, cardiac cases; but the people I kept running into were clearly up about their work. They seemed to relish coming here each day.

It made me wish that Amanda and Susan could stay in the hospital a little longer than the standard three days. I felt comfortable and confident with these people around. Once we got home, I didn't know what I'd do if something started to go wrong with that fragile, tenuous baby. Here all we had to do was push a button and help was seconds away. I imagine that kind of fear will be the hardest to kick.

I went outside for a walk and ran into Dr. Charles. He was in a sport coat and tie, and was getting into his car. Our hours with him had been so awesome to me; for the rest of my life I will see him lifting Amanda into the world for her first breath. I had lost sight of the fact that he does this virtually every day. It must be remarkable—to be that important to so many lives.

We shook hands. I asked him if he had been working all day.

"I just came in for a quickie," he said. Another day, another new life. He got into his car and drove off.

A moment for the memory:

Susan had her own room; there were two beds, but the other one wasn't occupied. Amanda had drifted off to sleep, and Susan, exhausted from the past twenty-four hours, was fading, too.

I took my shoes off and climbed up onto the other bed. And in the middle of the afternoon, for the first time, the three of us fell asleep together.

I imagine I'm going to realize all of this through the little things that happen. Late in the afternoon, after my visiting hours were over, I was back downtown. I was walking up the street, and a woman next to me was pushing a little boy in a stroller.

"How old is that baby?" I said.

"Fifteen months," she said.

I have never asked that question before in my life.

June 13

I was visiting Susan and Amanda this afternoon, and the anesthesiologist who had performed the epidural block came in to check Susan out. Her name was Dr. Sunita Rupani, and there was something that I wanted to talk to her about.

It was Lamaze. The more I thought about the pitch we had gotten in the Lamaze course, the angrier I became. I knew that Susan felt vaguely guilty about having "given in" and requested drugs; I had heard stories about other women who—after a successful birth—had actually apologized to their Lamaze teachers because they felt they had somehow failed by needing painkillers.

I started explaining this to Dr. Rupani, and she began to nod in agreement. "The Lamaze teachers tell them it is all in their head," she said. "But the pain is real."

I asked her what she thought about all of this.

"Well, the women need the medicine," she said. "You saw

how it was. They try not to need it, but they do; and when we give it to them, there is such relief. They are so thankful."

I said that, having watched it happen, I saw nothing especially noble about forsaking painkillers. I said that if we had to go through it again, I would recommend that Susan take the drugs much earlier in labor; I asked Dr. Rupani how she thought women would act if Lamaze courses had not become so popular.

"They would ask for medication much sooner," she said.

Amanda threw up and I immediately called for a doctor. Susan laughed at me for being so jittery; but I am going to miss having the comfort of these people being here. If yesterday I was musing about how three days seemed like a short time to stay in the hospital, today it is heavy on my mind. I wish this were like a hotel and you could check out whenever you wanted to. I don't think we're ready.

I have been wondering what this is going to do to my ambition. I have always been a pathologically ambitious person; it is probably the one quality that defines me most clearly. All my life I have been running off on stories; it is what I do, and there has never been any question that I was ready to go anywhere on a moment's notice.

Now I sat in the hospital room, watching my wife hold my baby, and I glanced at the day's newspaper. There was a feature story about Richard Threlkeld, an ABC News correspondent who does a weekly feature called "Status Report" on "World News Tonight." The article told how Threlkeld blocked out a story idea at the beginning of each week, then traveled to the site of the story and got it ready for the Friday show.

I am under contract to "ABC News Nightline"; in March and April I went out on nine stories for the show. In the year previous to that—my first year working for the broadcast—I did thirty-two pieces. This is in addition to my newspaper and *Esquire* columns.

But in the month before the baby was due, I had asked not to travel for the show. I know that I am in no emotional condition to leave Susan and Amanda Sue alone in the immediate future; but how long can this feeling last? What's going to happen the first time the phone rings and it's "Nightline" telling me to meet a camera crew at the airport? If I'm going to be the same person I've always been, I have to live on the run—but in the last forty-eight hours I haven't been able to sit next to a silent phone for more than fifteen minutes without checking the hospital and seeing how Susan and Amanda are doing.

I'm sure this is a dilemma that new fathers have faced over the ages. But that doesn't make it any less new to me. I will hate myself if I give up any of the professional drive that has always consumed me. But already I feel myself changing. This is going to be very difficult.

My first triumph. Amanda had been nursing, and she apparently had some gas; she started to cry, hard, and Susan couldn't make her stop.

I leaned over and started whispering to her and stroking her head. She looked up at me and I kept whispering. And she stayed silent.

Amazing. Forty-eight hours ago she hadn't even been born.

Very late at night I was leaving the hospital. An ambulance was waiting outside the first-floor entrance to the maternity unit. A newborn baby was in a traveling incubator; a doctor and a nurse climbed into the back of the ambulance with the baby, and it sped off—I supposed to another hospital.

Another doctor and nurse, who had been assisting, stood and watched the ambulance race into the night. They stared at the ambulance, with its tiny cargo, until its taillights were out of sight. I don't know what it must be like to have the kind of responsibility that they have. I thought of all the times that I and other newspaper colleagues have called hospital emergency rooms for details on one disaster or another; when they have told us that they are busy, we invariably have come back with our classic demand: "We're on deadline." Deadline. We might miss an edition.

June 14

AMANDA Sue was supposed to come home today. When I got to the hospital to pick her and Susan up, I got into the elevator and found myself pushing the button for the basement—the labor and delivery floor—rather than for the eighth floor where Susan's room was. There was someone I wanted to see.

During the worst part of Susan's labor, a nurse had appeared out of nowhere; she hadn't been assigned to us, but just when things were looking their most ominous she had arrived to help Susan out. She had been terrific; she had known exactly what to say and do, and at the moment of delivery she had placed her hand on my arm as if to share the moment. But then she had disappeared; when I had turned to thank her that day, she was gone.

So I wanted to find her. In the labor corridor, the tension and confusion were the same as they had been three days ago. I heard women moaning, and saw doctors and nurses hurrying into the individual rooms. Of course this goes on every day for the medical people who work here—but coming back, it was nevertheless jarring for me to realize that the feeling of high drama never goes away. To those of us who pass in and out of here it is just a hazy dream, but to these people it's the normal office environment.

A doctor I recognized from that day looked at me quizzically. "Having another one," I said, and then I explained to him why I had really come back. I described the nurse; he went off to find her, and in a second she was there.

Her name was Dee Grodishar; she told me to put on a hospital gown and then to follow her to a place where we could talk.

"I never got a chance to say thanks," I said. "You were there and then you went away."

"Well, it really wasn't my case," she said. "But you were having a terrible time of it, and I wanted to help. I just thought it was best to get lost after everything was okay."

We sat and discussed the whole thing for about fifteen minutes; she asked me how nervous I was, and I said very.

She took a piece of paper and wrote her home telephone number on it. "If you ever have any questions and you can't get to your pediatrician right away, feel free to call," she said. "If I know the answers, I'll tell you, and if I don't I'll tell you where to get them."

She doesn't know what a relief it is just to have that number.

Not that I intend to spoil Amanda Sue, but I popped for sixty bucks and rented a chauffeured Cadillac limousine to bring her home.

I've had enough terrible experiences with Chicago cabbies that I didn't want Amanda's first ride to be in a taxi. I don't have a car in the city; I take cabs everywhere, but in the last few years riding in cabs has combined the speed of a Grand Prix race with the trauma of a Go-Kart track. I didn't need Amanda to risk that at the age of three days.

So as we cruised north on Lake Shore Drive, cars pulled up beside us to look in the back window and try to figure out what celebrity was inside the limo. The curiosity on their faces turned to smiles when they found out that it was a wide-eyed, yawning baby girl.

I took Susan and Amanda up to the apartment; Susan immediately got into bed, put Amanda in a portable carrier, and began to get settled in.

The cat crept slowly into the room. Helen has always been a semi-psychotic cat; we got her declawed a month ago out of fear of what she would do to a baby. She regularly bites at Susan's legs as she walks around the apartment, and we had no idea what she would do to someone who was more nearly her own size.

The jury is still out. She stood at the foot of the bed and yowled at Amanda Sue, letting out hisses and snarls and generally letting it be known that she realized there was a stranger in the house. This I don't need.

During pregnancy, a man is sort of oblivious to how it has taken over a woman's life. Your colleagues at the office are aware that you are expecting a child; but they don't let it get in the way of the work routine.

Today, though, Susan asked me to go to the grocery store where she usually shops to pick up some sandwiches for lunch. I did; as soon as I walked in, the man behind the meat counter said, "I take it this means she had her baby." Some other women who were shopping said, "Susan had her baby?" Bud, the owner, called from behind the cash register: "Boy or girl?"

When I told him, the butcher overheard and said, "I lost my bet."

In the nine months of her pregnancy, I had never been in here; it had never occurred to me that the news meant anything to anyone outside our own home. But of course, everywhere a pregnant woman goes she is advertising the coming event. That's over now; I imagine I'll be a regular at Bud's Grocery in the days ahead.

Another small example of the ways you suddenly change:

I picked up a newspaper. There were two photographs, of two grieving mothers. One had just lost her daughter in a fire; the other had just lost her son in a car accident. The photos were close-ups of faces filled with pain.

For all these years I have looked at pictures like those and thought nothing of them. Today I was outraged at the lack of taste in invading a mother's privacy that way.

In our apartment, Amanda Sue slept while Susan looked down at her.

"We've lived here so long," Susan said. "But all of a sudden the place seems completely different."

June 15

It doesn't matter how many books you read before your baby arrives; nothing gets you ready for that first night when you're out of the hospital and alone, and she's crying and won't stop, and you're holding her against you while her screams rock your chest.

We passed Amanda Sue back and forth. Susan was plainly upset; we knew that on paper it was not unusual for a newborn to cry frantically. But in the hospital she had been perfect; she would eat and then drift off to sleep, with only a minute or two of crying now and then.

Tonight she was howling from midnight to dawn. In a cartoon it's funny to see an open-mouthed baby bawling wildly; when it's happening to you for the first time, though, you simply don't know what to do. Intellectually you have always known that babies cry a lot; but when you're holding your own in your arms, all you can think about is that she's in some kind of pain and that you're totally impotent to do anything about it.

When dawn came after her first night at home, we were still awake, red eyed and exhausted, rocking her and wondering what all of us had gotten into.

Susan's mother arrived. She's staying at a hotel in the neighborhood; she caught a plane here from Ohio and left her bags at the hotel's front desk and came over even before she had checked in.

It's peculiar how you never notice things about people until those matters affect you directly. From the moment Mrs. Koebel walked into the apartment, things calmed down. She picked the baby up and started walking around with her and talking to her; Amanda Sue was crying just as hard, but just watching Mrs. Koebel holding her made me less nervous. I have no idea how to handle a baby, and Susan, although she's better than I, is still brand-new to it.

But Mrs. Koebel had four children of her own, and two grandchildren before Amanda Sue, and she was great at this. It was as if Susan and I were kids who had never driven a car before, and were suddenly put behind the wheel; we lurched, we slammed on the brakes, we looked around nervously, we hesitated. Mrs. Koebel was like someone who had been driving all her life. She didn't even have to think about the process.

In the hours after she showed up, the level of tension in the apartment dropped dramatically. I've asked her if she will stay for two weeks, and she has said yes. I may not have learned anything else useful from this situation yet, but I know this: if you're having your first baby, make sure you get a grandmother there as soon as possible. You may think you know everything there is to know about life, but you can't touch her when it comes to this.

My office at home used to have an old cast-iron UPI teletype machine in the corner, and awards and plaques on the walls, and photographs of such uplifting sights as me standing in a prison cell posing with mass murderer Richard Speck.

No more. The room now has light-blue wallpaper covered with cottony clouds, and a white crib with white ribbons tied to it, and a baby-sized dresser with a statue of an angel on top of it. There is no sign that I ever lived another life here.

Late at night, as Amanda wailed, I asked Mrs. Koebel if she would consider sleeping in the apartment with Susan; I could go use her hotel room. She laughed and said that didn't sound like such a good idea; she said she was sure we'd do fine, and that she'd be back at 7 a.m.

Five minutes after she had left we felt as if we were alone in a dark, forbidding forest again. The forest was full of evil monsters who hid in the shadows, and we didn't know which direction they might attack us from, and the only sound around us was the unceasing, piercing cry from a tiny pair of lungs.

June 16

YOU get so self-centered about how the baby is affecting your own life that you forget for a moment how intertwined her birth is with the greater cycle of human life.

A letter addressed to Amanda arrived in today's mail. It was from my ninety-five-year-old grandmother, who is in ill health and lives in a senior citizens' residence.

The letter read:

"Dear Amanda Sue—

"Welcome to the family. You were a little late in getting here, but oh so very welcome.

"You are blessed with a wonderful mother and daddy who must be very happy that you are with them.

"Wish I were younger so as to hear all about your growing up.

"Bless you darling,

"Great-Grandmother Ethel."

Amanda won't stop crying. Apparently she is having trouble digesting Susan's milk; half an hour after each feeding, she cramps up. She screams in pain, she pulls her legs up to her chest, she pulls at her ears, she tries to stick her little fists in her mouth to allay the hurt. Watching her is horrible; once again, there is nothing to do.

We sat up all night again with her, and in the morning Susan called the pediatrician we will be using, Dr. Herman Scheinberg. I could tell that Susan felt reticent about bothering him; for some reason we are trained to be shy about imposing upon professionals' time, even though that's what they're there for.

He returned the call and said that he would order Amanda some glycerine suppositories from the pharmacy. Susan felt better having talked to him. He said that if things don't improve, she should call back. I know that she'll hesitate next time, too; this is just one more routine that's going to take some getting used to.

A package arrived. Inside were photos of Amanda, taken at the hospital by a company that must have a franchise arrangement with them. A large assortment was included; the deal was that you could send them all back if you wanted—or you could keep any number of them, up to the full pack at thirty dollars.

Naturally we went for the thirty dollars. I'd never thought about it, but I imagine it's easier to get money out of new parents than out of almost anyone else. If some other company had sent me something unsolicited and asked for payment, I probably would have been annoyed. With Amanda Sue's pictures, I was almost grateful that they'd included me on the mailing list.

The crying started again late at night. By 3 a.m. Susan was too exhausted to keep her eyes open; she passed out, and Amanda kept doubling up from her gas pains.

What a new world. At 4 a.m.—the time when the last bars in Chicago close—I found myself sitting in a wicker rocking chair, with a pink-tinted lamp shining over my shoulder. I held Amanda Sue in one arm. With the other hand I held a paperback book and read up on Dr. Spock's advice about colic. Is this really me?

June 17

THE littlest things take on importance. Babies have to be burped; everyone knows that. And yet Amanda continues to have trouble bringing up gas after nursing—and if she can't bring up gas, the pains start anew. I just can't stand the sight of her doubling up and screaming.

So after each feeding Susan, Mrs. Koebel, and I take turns holding Amanda and trying to get her to burp. No one told me this was going to be a problem. If a week ago you had warned me that the failure of a baby to burp would be a crisis in my life, I would have thought you were joking. Now it is starting to consume me.

When you look at your baby for enough hours on end, you run the risk of forgetting what lies just a few years ahead.

I was having a drink at the bar of D.B. Kaplan's this evening. Across the way, having dinner with her parents, was a girl who looked to be about sixteen. She was wearing a miniskirt and a ponytail; she was very pretty and fresh-looking, and as I glanced over at the table my thoughts turned to Amanda Sue, and the world of other little girls she would soon be entering.

The manager of the restaurant was making his rounds, and he stopped at the table to ask the people if everything was all right. When he came to the bar, he was laughing.

He said to the bartender and me:

"Do you know what that girl just said to me right in front of her parents?"

We asked him what.

"She said she was going to tell me a joke. And she said, 'Why is a girl's crotch so close to her butt?' I said I didn't know. And she said, 'So when she gets drunk at night, her boyfriend can pick her up and carry her home like a six-pack.' Her parents thought it was the funniest thing they'd ever heard."

The manager and the bartender laughed and shook their heads. I just looked down into my drink.

It seems that every other person I meet begins the conversation with: "Well, this is going to change your life."

My problem is that I loved my life the way it was. I really enjoyed it. And as happy as I am about all of this, I find myself wondering if changing that life really will be such a great thing. I know I couldn't go on being the eternal traveling kid forever; still, it's never been anything but fun, and sometimes at night I look at the ceiling and wonder if it's gone for good.

June 18

YOU get so tired. In the middle of the night something interrupts your sleep; it is that cry again, and you don't know how you're going to make it out of bed to hold the baby.

The fears are worst in the middle of the night, too. Last night Susan started crying; she had tried everything she could to make Amanda Sue be calm, and nothing was working. Suddenly, she decided that the baby wasn't getting enough milk. Nothing I said could persuade her differently. She said that we had to try formula, right away.

So, groggily, I got the bag we had brought home from the hospital. Inside it were samples of formula; I read the labels to try to figure out how you used them. But by this point Susan was all right; she knew it wasn't her lack of milk; it was just the baby's gas that was causing the problem. And so we rocked Amanda Sue until dawn.

The doctor prescribed an antispasmodic to relax Amanda's stomach. He said to have the pharmacy call him.

When the delivery man arrived with the prescription, we looked at the bottle. On the label was typed: "Amanda Sue Greene. One drop every four hours."

It was the first time I had seen her full name written down. In a funny way it made her seem more real; it verified her existence. Her name on a prescription bottle served the purpose a birth certificate is supposed to serve. The medicine wasn't for us, even though we had ordered it; it was for her. She was a person.

At night I went to a place called Dos Hermanos for a drink. Two nineteen-year-old college women who are working downtown for the summer started a conversation with me.

"Are you married?" one of them asked at one point.

"Yes," I said.

"Do you have any children?" she asked.

It was the first time since Amanda Sue's birth that I had been asked that question by a stranger.

"Yes," I said.

"How old?" she said.

"One week," I said.

The two of them went crazy. They had a thousand questions.

"That must be so beautiful," one of them said. "Making love knowing that you're trying to make a baby."

"Well, I'm not sure. . . ," I said.

"I can't even imagine it," she said. "I just think of all the years of trying not to have a baby."

The other one chimed in:

"Does it make your relationship with your wife that much better?"

"Well, really, things happen kind of quickly. . . ," I said.

The first one again:

"Did you have the baby because the world seemed so bad, and you wanted to make someone new who could help change things?"

"No, I don't think that was exactly it," I said.

"But if you didn't want your baby to change things, then what was it?" she said.

"We just sort of thought it was time," I said.

"That can't be it," she said. "It can't be just because you thought it was time."

"That was pretty much the way it was," I said. "We just thought it was about time."

"I don't believe it," she said. "That can't be it."

June 19

AND one more way things are changing:

Several months ago, ABC gave me a beeper. The beeper, I was instructed, was to be carried with me at all times. Any time

I was away from a telephone, I was to have the beeper switched on; that way, if "Nightline" wanted to reach me, they could get me instantaneously.

For some reason I revolted violently against that. To me, a beeper represented a complete loss of freedom. It was okay with me that I had all these bosses; but a beeper meant being put on a tether; a beeper meant that someone else owned you. Not one second of your time was your own.

I never turned the beeper on. Never. Once I managed to leave it in a cab, but the cabbie returned it to the beeper company (you get a small reward if you turn it in), and the beeper company returned it to ABC, and ABC returned it to me. I kept leaving it turned off. I took pride in the fact that, even if ABC beeped me, they would not be able to reach me.

Now I keep the beeper turned on all the time. There is nowhere I go that the beeper isn't switched to the ready position.

On our refrigerator door at home is the number to call if I need to be reached in an emergency; I have told Susan to have me beeped if anything at all goes wrong. Suddenly having the beeper is a great comfort.

I went to the office tonight to go through the mail; I have been taking some time off, and it was piling up.

When I came back Susan and the baby were asleep; Mrs. Koebel was waiting up for me. When I came in, she got ready to return to her hotel.

"What time did she go to sleep?"

She told me.

"Did she take her medicine?"

She said she had.

"Did she have gas?"

She said a little.

"What time did the baby eat?" I said.

I realized that I sounded like something out of a situation comedy. I never could have anticipated asking those questions; before Amanda Sue was born, they seemed like a worried parent's clichés.

But you don't say them thinking they're clichés. You say them because, all of a sudden, out of nowhere, they are important to you. As soon as they're out of your mouth you know how ridiculous you must sound; but the fact is, for the first time in your life you really want to know the answers to those things.

June 20

The drops seem to be working. Amanda isn't cramping up as much; she is getting some sleep, and when she's awake she isn't so quick to cry.

Sometimes I'll bring her into the bedroom and lay her down on my chest and just breathe with her. That funny little ducktail sticks over her collar, and she makes baby sounds, and outside it's a bright summer day with girls in bikinis on the beaches. I don't want to be anywhere else.

All the manuals we have say how important the closeness of breast-feeding is to the baby; they say that even if a mother chooses to bottle-feed, she should always hold the bottle herself, and never leave it propped for the baby to take. The hours spent in that kind of close contact with the mother are vital, the books say; if a baby is deprived of that closeness, she may even develop psychological problems later in life.

Watching Amanda nurse, I wonder how much this has to do with the way children feel toward their mothers as opposed to their fathers. I assume the books are right; and if nursing is such a paramount thing in molding a baby's trusting personality, is it any wonder that children often feel so much more intimately attached to their mothers? I watch Amanda taking Susan's milk, and I realize that, even before she really knows who we are, the emotional pattern is set in a way that can never be changed.

Susan was walking around the apartment burping Amanda.

"Yes, it is," Susan said in a high, crooning voice. "I know . . . I know. Yes, it is. Yes, it is."

Before Amanda was born, I never heard Susan talk baby-type talk, even in jest. Now it is second nature. She isn't at all self-conscious about it. And I must confess—in the middle of those long nights I have sung a chorus or two of "Rockabye Baby in the Treetop" myself. There's no humorous intent. When you're holding your baby, those sorts of things come out of your mouth. You don't even have to try.

June 21

DURING the final months of Susan's pregnancy, I heard something that I doubted. It turned out to be true.

It was this: in the ninth month, the woman was supposed to begin having vivid, bizarre, Technicolor dreams—dreams so jarring that they made earlier dreams seem placid in comparison. What's more, the man was supposed to go through the same things. The ninth-month dreams, for some reason, were alleged to affect both mother and father.

And they did. During that last month, I had the most startling dreams of my life, every night. Susan, too. She said that hers have stopped—she's not sleeping enough to dream. But mine haven't. Every night, without fail, even when I drift off for only a few minutes, the dreams persist.

I was hungry. I asked Susan when dinner would be ready.

She just stared at me. The baby was crying, and Susan was carrying her around the living room. Her mother had gone back to the hotel to rest.

"How dare you," Susan said.

"All I asked was where my dinner was," I said.

"Where's *your* dinner," Susan said.

This is the first time in our marriage that I haven't eaten as soon as I was hungry. The answer is obvious: I can make my own dinner, or go out. Fact is, though, that I liked getting dinner when I wanted it. It was a nice way to live.

June 22

I'VE been going in to work during the days, just to get out of the house. I'm still technically on vacation, but it's easier to make calls at the office, and it's nice to get away, if only for a while.

There the contrast is stark. Everyone else has the beginning of summer tans; they're rested and work-oriented and pretty normal. I, on the other hand, am exhausted and pale and irritable. I was one of them, and now I'm someone else. All my thoughts are baby thoughts.

It's a distinction I don't like all that much. I knew the baby was going to change my life, but I didn't expect her to define it. I imagine that goes away. Tonight at home I called a man named Neil Weiner. He and his wife had been in our Lamaze class; they had given us rides home every week, and I wanted to tell him that we had had our baby.

When he answered the phone his voice was as tired and as lifeless as mine. In the background, his newborn daughter was howling; he didn't even offer to have Linda come to the phone —she was feeding their baby. From his monotone, I could tell that he was going through the same thing I was. For some reason it made me feel better; I wasn't alone in this.

The fingernails are the thing. Everything about the baby is amazing, but when I look at her fingernails—so small you couldn't even measure them on a ruler, but perfectly formed—that's when the miracle hits home again every time. And it's not just me; when people come into the apartment and see Amanda for the first time, they invariably end up saying, "My God. Look at those fingernails."

I'd take a picture of them, but they wouldn't show up.

Sometimes when I'm asleep, I forget. I think my life is the same as it always was.

Then she will cry, and I will come to wakefulness, and in my confusion I will think that someone is hurting the cat. In a few seconds I will remember. It's not the cat. It's a human being in the other room, and she needs us.

June 23

I HAD to go out to the suburbs tonight, to a Putt-Putt miniature golf course where I was to do some interviews for an *Esquire* story.

I walked around the course, and I stopped a man who was playing the game with his two daughters. The girls jabbered at him, and I made notes, and at the end I asked him how old he was. He said thirty-six.

I'm thirty-five. He seemed much more than one year older. I think that's the essential difference between those of us who elected to wait to have children, and those who went ahead and did it early. For whatever reasons we gave ourselves, the subliminal one was that we really weren't ready to grow up. Career factors and financial factors and personal factors and everything else—what it came down to was that we perceived "parents" to be our mothers and fathers, and we weren't ready to take that role yet.

I think we always had a curious reaction to our contemporaries who had gone ahead and done it. We somehow felt that they were the ones who were missing out on something. This experience they were having—the raising of a family—seemed to us to be a detriment. We saw ourselves as savoring the riches of an exciting, enticing world, while they were locked into something we didn't have to deal with yet.

There's probably some truth to that. But as I talked to the fellow at the Putt-Putt tonight, I sensed in him a kind of solidness that I don't feel in myself. His daughters looked up at us as I took notes; they tugged at his pants and asked him what was going on. He has had twelve years of Putt-Putts and McDonalds and PTA meetings; I have been doing other things during those twelve years. That doesn't make one of us any better than the other; but as I talked to him I felt a dimension that I know I am lacking.

I got the correct spelling of his daughters' names for my story. He asked me if I had any children, and I said yes, one.

When I got home Susan was asleep. Mrs. Koebel was there holding the baby. I have started to take her for granted, but it's going to be tough when she goes back to Ohio. The beeper may always be turned on, but my real reassurance comes from knowing there is always someone there with Susan and Amanda. Once she's gone, I have the feeling that it's going to seem like the middle of the night all the time.

June 24

I SPOKE too soon about those antispasmodic drops. Amanda isn't sleeping. Susan is getting frantic. We know that babies are supposed to cry a lot; but they're also supposed to sleep much of the day, and Amanda doesn't. It takes us three hours to get her calm enough to close her eyes; twenty or thirty minutes later she is screaming again.

Dr. Scheinberg told Susan on the telephone to increase the dosage. I'm confused about all of this; the baby is less than two weeks old, and already she's taking medication as a matter of course. The alternative, though, is to ignore her crying.

June 25

"If she would only settle down for two hours," Susan said.

This was at 4 a.m. We still can't get her to sleep for more than an hour or so. The cartoons about new parents getting up in the middle of the night for feedings don't convey this. I had always assumed that there was supposed to be a down time between feedings, when the baby and the parents slept. It hasn't been like that, though.

I know what wrecks Susan and I are becoming; I can only imagine what this is doing to the baby. Sleep is supposed to be one of the important factors in a newborn's growth and health pattern. Amanda isn't sleeping.

June 26

Susan's father arrived today. He will be driving her mother home tomorrow; this is the first he has seen Amanda.

All the thoughts I've been having about the difference between men and women when it comes to babies were reaffirmed with Mr. Koebel. When Susan's mother first arrived here, her natural instinct was to start talking to the baby and to pick her up. With Mr. Koebel, it was more awkward; he looked at Amanda, and he was clearly moved to see her, but he didn't know quite what to do.

When she started crying he looked around for someone else to do something. While Susan and her mother took turns carrying Amanda around the living room, he sat in a chair and watched. I knew exactly how he felt. When Amanda is crying and won't stop, I do what I can to help—but I know, in the end, that it is Susan's responsibility. That may sound like a pretty archaic thing to say, but there's no getting around it.

When Susan or her mother hold Amanda, it seems right; when Mr. Koebel or I hold Amanda, it seems unwieldy. When she cries and Susan or her mother sit for a few minutes without reacting, it seems as if they are neglecting her; when she cries and Mr. Koebel or I just sit there, it seems as if we merely don't know what to do.

I am aware this is contradictory to what we are being told the world is becoming. Women and men, we read, need to take equal roles in the care of a baby. And I'm not saying that the differences are genetic—not exactly. But when the four of us are in the room, and Amanda cries for attention from the nursery, it is clearly Mrs. Koebel and Susan who instinctively know what to do. It is not an inherent lack of capability on the part of the men. Leave me out for a moment; Mr. Koebel landed fighter planes on aircraft carriers during World War II, and he can take care of himself. But when it comes to a two-week-old baby, there's something that has been passed down through the ages, culturally, that makes women think they can handle it, and men doubt that they can. At least this is what I'm coming to believe.

June 27

I don't know whether this is a measure of our exhaustion, or of how quickly you get used to having a baby in the house.

But last night Amanda was crying again, and we didn't get out of bed. We let her cry until she finally fell asleep.

In the morning we talked about it. Both of us remembered drifting in and out of sleep, and hearing Amanda from the other room. We were vaguely ashamed; no matter how tired we are, we can't imagine it's right to let her cry without trying to do something for her.

It's Sunday. In the morning Susan is going to call the doctor again.

Mr. and Mrs. Koebel left today. We're on our own.

June 28

DR. Scheinberg said that Amanda isn't getting enough milk. Susan had been right in the first place.

She called him to talk about Amanda's not sleeping; he said to bring Amanda in. Susan strapped Amanda to her front with one of those baby-carriers and took a cab to his office. She was convinced that Amanda wasn't sleeping because of gas. But when he weighed her, he found out that she had lost several ounces since her birth, rather than gaining the six or eight ounces she should have.

For whatever reason, Dr. Scheinberg felt that Susan's milk wasn't enough for Amanda right now. He suggested that, twice a day, we supplement the feeding with a bottle of baby formula.

Susan is distraught. I can't really understand the reaction; I know that mothers get crazy when they're told their milk supply is inadequate in any way, but as long as commercial formula is readily available, it doesn't seem like such a big deal. If the natural milk isn't enough, then use the formula.

But Susan is near tears. "I was starving her," she said. "She kept crying, and the reason is I was starving her."

At the doctor's office Amanda gulped down a whole bottle of formula and then drifted off to sleep. As he was examining her, he looked at her navel and said, "Oh, my, what happened here?"

After a baby is born—this was new to me—part of the umbilical cord remains even after it has been cut. The parents are supposed to apply alcohol to the cord regularly; in a week or two it is supposed to drop off, leaving a normal belly button.

We thought this had happened. But the doctor found some pus around Amanda's navel, and had to cauterize it.

"I'm not giving her enough milk, her navel was hurt and I didn't even know it. . . . God, I'm a terrible mother," Susan said. She wasn't trying to be overly dramatic. She felt awful.

I suppose I should have felt like a terrible father, too, but I didn't. I just felt the usual: like I have no idea what I'm doing.

June 29

Amanda will drink the formula, but it isn't a magic sleep potion. She's still crying more than seems normal; she still is awake far longer than seems normal. And every time Susan gives her the formula from the pre-sterilized bottles, I can tell that Susan feels defeated. The formula is a symbol of our troubles.

Tonight I finally had to go to the office and do some real work. As I left Susan was holding Amanda, and she said, "Please don't leave us alone for too long." I realized it was the first time since Amanda's birth that Susan was going to be totally alone with her. First there was the hospital, with the doctors and nurses; then there were the two weeks with her mother and me around all the time. Now the reality of being a mother was setting in.

When I got home several hours later, Amanda was nursing again. If a baby can look tired, she looked tired. "Miss Scraggly," I said to her. She didn't smile, and neither did Susan.

June 30

"Sometimes I wonder if I'm ever going to go out again," Susan said.

It's as if all she can remember is sitting holding the baby. The use of the formula now seems to be working—after Amanda drinks it, she drifts off to sleep. I had thought that this would relieve Susan; at last she has a few hours at a time to sleep herself. But it has left her morose.

I have trouble understanding this; apparently Amanda can't

get as much milk as she needs from Susan, and apparently this was a large part of the cause of her crying and sleeplessness. I can see why it would be a crisis if there weren't such a thing as infant formula available. But there is; after Susan nurses Amanda, she takes out a bottle of formula, snaps a disposable nipple onto it, and lets Amanda drink however much more she needs. To me it's a blessing. Amanda is serene and rested for the first time since we brought her home.

It's clearly a defeat for Susan, though. Every drop of milk that Amanda takes from the bottle is a symbol to Susan of her own perceived failing. I have tried to reason with her; I have told her that there is absolutely nothing we can do about it, and that we should be grateful that we are getting the baby the nourishment she needs. I have told her that the baby can't possibly feel any less love for her; Susan holds the baby close and talks comfortingly when she is giving her the bottle, and this has to be just as good for Amanda emotionally as breast-feeding itself.

But Susan is very, very down. She has said she feels like a "total failure"; any effort by me to convince her otherwise makes her snap or go silent. I had thought that, by giving a child life, a new mother would feel potent enough. But when the bottle comes out and Amanda gulps at the formula, I can see in Susan's eyes that she feels she is letting her baby down in a very basic way—and nothing I say will make her feel any different.

July 1

WHEN you're drawing up your list of life's miracles, you might place near the top the first moment your baby smiles at you.

Amanda had slept well—thanks, I am afraid, to the formula. In the morning Susan fed her, and then went to take a shower.

Amanda was on her back in a carriage in the living room. As I have every day, I leaned over and looked at her. I tickled her stomach and scratched her foot.

Every day since she has been born she has reacted by gurgling or shifting her body. Today, though, she looked right at me. And she smiled.

Her toothless mouth opened, and she scrunched her face up, and it really was a grin. It went away momentarily, and then she did it again—looked me in the eye and smiled in my face.

The sleepless nights, the worries, the crying—all of a sudden it was all worth it. I called loudly to Susan, and she came running from the bathroom—she thought something was wrong. Amanda was still smiling when she got there, and we looked down together, smiling back.

It was the first really human thing Amanda has done—the first thing that tells us that maybe she knows us, and maybe she understands how much we care about her. She's got pimples all over her face now—the doctor says this is normal in very young babies, and should go away by itself—and she's as scraggly as ever. But as she lay there smiling up at us, I felt at last that she had joined us on this journey. She is no longer just something we are nursing and carrying along—somewhere inside, part of her knows what's going on, and that part of her is telling us that she's with us.

July 2

My parents drove to town to see Amanda today.

We have talked to them almost every day, and have sent them pictures, and they have talked to the Koebels. But they couldn't stay away any longer; they drove the eight hours from Columbus, and late this afternoon they arrived.

I have never been a very demonstrative son. It's not something I am very good at; I have always wanted my parents to be proud of me—I suppose that's one of the things that makes me so professionally ambitious—and I always hope that they are pleased with what I accomplish in my life. I didn't know how I was going to handle introducing them to the baby, though.

I answered the door. They were standing there—my father with a camera in his hand, my mother carrying a bag full of presents—and they made their hellos to Susan and me. They walked into the living room. I don't think they were expecting to see Amanda yet, but she was on her back asleep in the carriage there.

They made sounds that I can only describe as animal-like when they saw her. The sight seemed to touch something so basic in them that the sounds came out; it was as if something had squeezed their hearts. I realized instantly that nothing I may ever accomplish in the world of work will possibly affect them in the way the sight of their granddaughter did.

They leaned close to her and talked to her, and there was none of the self-consciousness that sometimes marks our dealings with each other. It struck me that what they were going through was something very close to recapturing what they must have had when I was first born.

A man and woman have a child; for a period of time it is as if they are the only three people in the world. The closeness seems perfect. As the years go by, and the mother and father nurture the child and urge the child toward independence, a distance develops. When they want the best for the child, they automatically deprive themselves of the closeness that was there at first. In the case of my parents and myself, the distance—because of me—at times is great.

But suddenly here was Amanda Sue. And although they didn't express it verbally, I could tell that what my mother and father saw in her were some of the same things that they must have seen in me thirty-five years ago. In that baby they were seeing something they must have assumed they would never see again. They stared at her so fiercely; that had to be it, a sense of time and love recaptured.

Only later at night did I stop to think that the distance will inevitably grow between Amanda and me. And that someday I may have to rely on Amanda's own son or daughter to bring back to me the feelings that run through me during these magical days.

July 3

She has found something she likes. When she sleeps, she manages to pull herself up so that her head is wedged between the soft bumpers in the corner of her crib.

I don't know what it is; perhaps it gives her the illusion of being back in the womb, where she was protected twenty-four hours a day. But Susan will feed her, and we will put her to bed, and when we will come in the room to check on her later, there she will be—sprawled at an angle, her head stuck in that corner, sleeping away in the manner she has decided is best.

July 4

I called Herb Holmes, the ABC field producer with whom I most often work on "Nightline" pieces, to see what he's been up to. I'm just about ready to go back to work full-time, and I'm touching base with my colleagues.

Herb was excited. I had let it be known that I didn't want to travel for "Nightline" in the weeks immediately preceding and following the baby's birth, and during those weeks Herb has been working with ABC correspondent David Garcia on a story about drug traffic into the country.

He told me he has just finished cutting the piece. It is twenty-three minutes long—an extraordinary length for television—and he said that "Nightline" is talking about running an expanded edition of the show to accommodate his story. "It's like a little movie," he said.

I felt good for him, but I also felt jealous and resentful. I love doing stories; whether for the newspaper or for *Esquire* or for "Nightline," doing stories is what has made me happy for all of my adult life. If I've learned anything about the news business at the levels I work, it's that if you're not willing to give it your total effort, there's somebody else who will.

And as amazing as these last weeks have been for me because of Amanda, it eats at me that there was a great piece out there, and that I didn't do it. I have always been the guy who will drop anything and go anywhere for a story. This is really the first time I've voluntarily put anything ahead of that; and if the way I'm feeling right now is an indication of how I'm going to react to these reshuffled priorities, then there may be trouble ahead.

I love being home with Susan and Amanda; I have loved these first few weeks of watching the baby's every move.

But twenty-three minutes on the network?

Those are twenty-three minutes I'd like to have.

July 5

My parents went home, and it's just the three of us again.

I have never liked it when a pen leaks on my shirt, or a newspaper smudges my pants; I'm far from a snappy dresser, but I don't like to dirty up my clothes.

When I hold Amanda, though, and she's just eaten, and she spits up on the shoulder of my shirt—which she invariably does—it doesn't bother me at all. Sometimes I even laugh, and when I go out and there's a spot on the shirt where she's been, that's fine.

She's developed a little blister in the center of her upper lip. It's from nursing; she's been sucking so hard that the skin has swelled up. She doesn't even know the blister is there, but it's a constant reminder of what her full-time job has been.

At night, after Susan has fallen asleep, I will lie awake and listen for Amanda to cry. I don't want to drift off to sleep myself if I sense that she's about to start; it seems worth it to me to stay awake so that if she needs us, there's someone to hear her first cry. Like the blister, she doesn't even know about this. But in a way, we may never be closer than in those minutes when I'm lying there waiting to hear her.

July 6

Whenever I used to go to the homes of people who had babies, the first thing I would always notice was the mess.

It seemed as if even the most meticulously neat families would just give it up as soon as there was a child in the house. No matter how they used to live, the house would suddenly be defined by the presence of the baby.

Now I understand. In our living room, there is a big, low, wooden table in front of the couch. We would sit on the couch and watch TV. On the table would be a few magazines, a few ceramic bowls, and a candle or two.

Now Susan uses the couch to nurse Amanda. There are bottles on that table, and boxes of disposable diapers, and disposable nipples, and soiled towels, and bottles of Amanda's medicine and vitamins. The rest of the apartment doesn't look much better.

If it was distracting in someone else's home, it's just as bad in my own. It used to be a pleasure to come home to a spacious, clean apartment. Now, as much fun as it is to come home to Amanda, I can't help yearning for the days when my home looked like something out of a magazine—or at least like something that was attempting to look like something out of a magazine. Never again, I guess.

She likes to look at books.

In the daytime Susan puts her in her carriage in the living room. She lies on her back and just stares at the multicolored bindings of the books on our shelves. It can't be a coincidence; she does it too often. She has found something that appeals to her, and turns to it for pleasure.

July 7

SHE will hold my hand. Her own hands are tiny; they will only take one of my fingers. But when I extend the finger to her, she will fasten her hand around it and grip.

Susan went to the grocery today, and I was alone with Amanda. I was holding hands with her as usual, and she started to cry. She was hungry. I didn't know what to do; I knew that Susan would not want me to give her a bottle of formula, but would want me to wait for her to return so she could try nursing.

So I picked Amanda up and started walking around with her, trying to calm her until Susan got home. Apparently one of my fingers was near her mouth, because before I knew what was happening she was trying to nurse on it.

I felt so hapless. She lowered her little mouth onto the finger and started sucking as hard as she could, seeking milk. She looked up at me with her blue eyes; I could only shrug and watch as she continued to suck, harder still, in search of something I couldn't give her.

The way she smells is amazing. Susan says she has not used baby powder on Amanda; so I don't know what it is. But there is something about a baby's smell that is the purest, finest thing I have ever encountered.

All you have to do is take one step into her room for it to hit you. And when you pick her up it almost makes you dizzy. It isn't just a clean smell; it's something I can't quite define, other than to say it's a happy smell. Even when she's crying and kicking it's a happy smell.

I asked Susan when the baby smell would go away, and she said, "When she stops being a baby." I will miss it.

July 8

I went to the pediatrician's office today.

When Dr. Scheinberg had seen Amanda last week and recommended the supplemental formula, he had asked Susan to bring her back this week. I was having lunch with Madeleine Nash, a correspondent for *Time* magazine, and when we walked out of the restaurant I realized that Amanda was supposed to be at the doctor's office in fifteen minutes. So I didn't go back to the office; I went to Dr. Scheinberg's.

I got off the elevator at his floor—and there was a line of baby carriages, nose to tail against the wall, all the way from the elevators to the door of his office. I could see why; the waiting area was small, and if the parents had brought the carriages with them there would have been no room for the grown-ups and the babies. Dark blue canvas seems to be the material of choice for carriages these days.

In the waiting room there were more fathers than I had expected. I have a fairly flexible schedule at the office, so it was no big deal for me to get to the doctor's in the middle of the afternoon. But I was surprised to see so many other young men with their wives.

I will say this: the young fathers were doing a lot of staring at their watches. The mothers held the babies and seemed resigned to waiting as long as it took. The fathers clearly didn't want to leave—but just as clearly had places they were supposed to be. This new way of life doesn't come easy.

One baby was yowling loudly. His mother was rocking him, but it wasn't doing any good. Finally, as if to herself, she said aloud: "He's thirsty."

And four young fathers, at the exact same moment, reached into four knapsacks and came out with four bottles. They spoke at once:

"Apple juice?" "Formula?" "Water?" "Orange juice?"

They all laughed, and then went back to their watches.

A mother came out of the inner office carrying her child. The baby had extremely long hair; it was dark and spiky, and stuck up as if the boy had put one of his toes into an electrical outlet.

Another young mother, sitting not ten feet away, said loudly: "Look at the hair on that baby. Oh, my God." She didn't seem at all embarrassed; it was as if she assumed that because the baby was too young to understand her, the baby's mother could not hear, either.

When Susan arrived, she seemed very surprised to see me there—and a little nonplused. I had expected her to be thrilled, but the first thing she said was, "Did you think I was too incompetent to do this myself?" But I think secretly she was pleased.

After a few minutes, a nurse came to the door and said, "Amanda Greene?" It was the same feeling as when I had first seen her name on the prescription; I don't know why, but I had thought they would call *our* names, not Amanda's. But Amanda, of course, was the patient.

The doctor was thorough and careful; he explained everything he was doing as he did it. At first I sat silently, but he turned around and said, "Are you interested in what I'm doing?", and from that point on led me through the examination as he conducted it.

He weighed her; she weighed seven pounds eleven ounces, up from last week, which indicated to him that the formula was working. I think that when Susan heard the news, even she was glad that we had tried it.

We sat in the examining room talking. Amanda was uncomfortable in the strange environment; she was screaming and crying, and through it all Dr. Scheinberg spoke in a normal tone of voice, as if the baby's screams weren't even present in the room. That makes sense, I suppose; if a pediatrician were to try to talk over the cries of every baby he examined, his throat would be raw by the end of each working day.

Still, it was unusual. Susan and I were distracted by Amanda's yelling. But Dr. Scheinberg spoke as steadily and moderately as if he were an attorney and we were in his carpeted office. I wonder if they teach that to pediatricians in medical school? It's a small thing, but I would bet that virtually all pediatricians have it in common. We said good-bye to the doctor and went our separate ways.

July 9

Amanda wears these little terrycloth suits every day; they come up high on the collar, and have feet built into the legs. The dark blue one I can think of only as her Elvis suit; it looks just like a jumpsuit that I saw Presley wear in Las Vegas once. Only Elvis didn't have a little owl embroidered on the chest. And Elvis didn't have cradle cap, as Dr. Scheinberg informed us that Amanda had yesterday. So when Elvis was wearing his blue suit, his hair wasn't slicked down with gooey medicine the way Amanda's is today.

As much as I think Amanda has taken over my life, it doesn't compare to what has happened to Susan's life.

Susan holds her virtually all day long, every day. Only when Amanda is sleeping a sound sleep does Susan put her down. The rest of the time—whether Amanda is feeding or fidgeting or crying aloud—Susan is sitting there holding her close.

In the middle of the night when Amanda cries from the other room, it is Susan who gets up. Usually it will happen around midnight, and then around 2:30 or 3 a.m., and then just before dawn. Susan has told me not to get up; I am back to work now, and she has told me to sleep so I can stay awake at the office in the daytime.

So when I get up every morning, Susan is invariably already in the living room with Amanda, as she has been for much of the night.

"During the two-thirty and the four-thirty feedings, I have to slap myself in the face," she told me. "It's the only way I know to keep from falling asleep. I start to nod off, and I don't want to drift off to sleep and drop Amanda, so I just pick up one hand and slap myself."

Tonight Susan looked at me and said, "Do you think of me in the same way?"

"The same way as what?" I said.

"The same way you did before," she said.

"Of course I do," I said, although I wasn't quite sure what she meant.

"I don't think you do," she said.

"How do you think I think of you?" I said.

"I think you think of me just as Amanda's mother now," she said.

July 10

EVERY time she goes to sleep now, Amanda creeps up to that upper left-hand corner of the bed. She just jams her head into the corner; she really has figured out that it helps her sleep.

"Come in here," Susan called from Amanda's room.

She was changing Amanda's diapers, and when she took her suit off Amanda's navel and all the skin around it was a bright red. It didn't seem to bother the baby, but Susan had turned white.

She called Dr. Scheinberg, and he told her to bring Amanda

in. When she returned from his office, Amanda had a tiny bandage around one of her fingers. The doctor had said that the navel was infected, and had drawn blood to see if the infection had spread.

It hadn't; but now we had still another kind of medicine to give her. We made some jokes about her turning into a little junkie, but I know that at least part of us wasn't kidding.

The amazing thing is that when I hold her—in her little white suit tonight, with the tiny rosebuds all over it—and I think about how she has become the central thing in our lives, and has changed everything, I have to think twice before I realize that as important as she is, she weighs just over seven pounds. So small, so fragile.

July 11

I WENT into Amanda's room this morning, and, as I have every morning, I looked down into her crib and said, "Good morning, merry sunshine." She smiled back.

Today Susan asked me why I was saying it.

"I don't know," I said, and I didn't.

But I started thinking about it, and I figured it out. "Good morning, merry sunshine" is what my mother used to say to me every morning when I was a child. I hadn't heard the words since I was five years old—thirty years ago. But without being reminded, here I was saying the same thing every day. I would tell my mother about it, but I think I'm too embarrassed.

I read in a book somewhere that, before long, a baby figures out that "Dad means fun; mom means work." I think I understand that. When I pick Amanda up or carry her around, it is to play with her and to amuse the two of us. When Susan picks her up, it is usually to feed her or to fix something that is wrong.

Susan has figured that out, too. "What if I hadn't called the doctor yesterday about Amanda's navel?" she said. She knew the truth: that if the infection had spread, it would have been considered her fault for not spotting something wrong. That's not how it should be, but it's how things are. Dad means fun; mom means work.

Susan was sitting on the couch nursing Amanda—who turned one month old today—and I leaned over, took Amanda's hand, and said, "Do you know that you're going to have to take care of us in our old age?"

Then I let go of her hand and pondered the fact that it might even be true.

July 12

We seem to be reaching a benchmark of sorts. When Amanda cries now, we accept it as a signal that she needs us. Nothing more, nothing less.

The great concern that accompanied her crying at first is slowly disappearing. When she starts, we know that something is not right with her, of course. But we've finally settled in to the point where we realize that she has no real voice—and that if she wants our attention, the only way she has to get it is to cry for it.

So when we're in the other room and we hear her crying from her crib, our first thought is not automatically that there's a crisis at hand. It's almost as if we hear her calling our names; we know she wants us, and we go to her.

I have tiny scratches on my neck. When I hold her against me, she reaches out and she unballs her hand and she scratches away. Back at the hospital those first few days, the nurses told us that we should hold off on cutting her nails; even though the nails would grow, the nurses said, they are too fragile to trim.

So Amanda reaches out for my neck and grabs at it; the nails dig in. It doesn't really hurt; it feels like the tiniest pinpricks. Just one more sign that she really is alive and growing.

July 13

BEFORE she was born, I thought that there would be long stretches of time when I would notice no change in her. I had seen babies before, of course; but to me all infants looked alike, and I could not imagine—in the first few months or even the first year—that she would develop in any way that I could see.

But every day there is something new. She turns her head now, for example. In the hospital it seemed that if we let her lie there, she would never budge an inch. But I will watch in astonishment as, in her crib, she will be looking in one direction, and then apparently decide that she wants to look the other way. And she will; with the greatest of efforts she will crane her neck and manage to turn her head around. Something in her body and in her mind has taught her how to do that.

She can't crawl yet, but she is doing something close to it. Susan calls it "creeping"; she manages to scoot around in the crib or in the carriage. She does it every night when she moves herself up to her favorite corner; sometimes, for no apparent reason, she will even turn ninety degrees—when we put her to bed she will have her head toward the top and her feet toward the bottom, but a few hours later she will have her head and feet toward the sides.

And the smile, of course, is amazing. Just a few days ago I was so moved to see it for the first time. Now she is doing it all the time. I will pick her up and say something to her, and her whole face will light up. I will be talking, and the sound of a word will apparently please her, and this toothless grin will just spread over her face. Today I squeezed her foot and said "foot." It was as if I had told her the most hilarious joke in the world. When the smile went away I said "foot" again. Again, that smile. And again and again.

She will never remember any of this, of course. And I will never forget.

In the middle of the night, between feedings, when Susan has drifted off into an exhausted sleep and so has Amanda, I will wake up and wonder if everything is all right.

I will walk into Amanda's room. She will be up in that left-hand corner of the crib, and her head will be jammed between the bumpers, and she will be still.

And, carefully, I will slip my finger under her nose, just to make sure I can feel her breathing. Amanda, asleep, doesn't know I'm doing it. I haven't told Susan, either. But I fall back to sleep better myself, having checked.

July 14

My work world is getting back to normal. My thoughts are still filled with Amanda, but just looking at the columns I have written since I returned to the paper tells me that I have other things on my mind, too.

In the time since I've been back I have written about a woman who is a compulsive letter writer; about a hit novelty record that is the talk of the country; about a man who makes his living by writing chatty letters to the nephews, nieces, and grandchildren of people who can't take the time; about a contest to find the woman with the "hottest legs" in Chicago; about a twenty-one-year-old woman who left her parents' home one day more than a year ago and was never seen again; about notes from 1960s high school study halls that a reader unearthed; about a man who is reading *Decline and Fall of the*

Roman Empire as a kind of protest against the diminishment of serious reading in America; about a woman who took her clothes off and walked stark naked down Michigan Avenue.

So, at least during my working hours, I am preoccupied with the things I am reporting on. And when I get home every night, I learn anew that Susan and Amanda have been preoccupied only with each other.

Tonight I walked into the apartment and called hello; I heard the sounds of the television, but there was no answer. I walked into the living room, and Susan, looking tired beyond tired, was asleep on the couch. In the carriage a few feet away, Amanda slept, too.

When they awakened I could tell that this is getting to Susan. She is beginning to feel the difference—the confining difference—that the baby has brought to her world, and she can tell that, even though my world has changed, too, at least I have the discipline of my work to remind me of how things used to be.

And she feels that she and Amanda will inevitably be closer than Amanda and I. After they woke up, Amanda started hiccuping, as she often does. I said, "Amanda, you get the hiccups all the time."

Susan picked her up to burp her and said to her, "He doesn't know that you used to hiccup all the time in my tummy, does he, Amanda?" Just a little reminder that they have a history together that I was never a part of.

July 15

SHE makes bicycling motions. Yesterday she wasn't yet doing it; today she is. As she lies on her back, she raises her arms and it's almost as if she's trying to swim. At the same time her legs are pumping. Sort of like she's running in a race—but she's not strong enough yet to roll over, so the whole race is run on her back.

And now there are noises. Not just the crying sounds, but noises she makes when she sees something and is curious. I don't know whether this counts as the very first stages of trying to talk. But to sit there and see her look at something and come forth with a quizzical sound—it's something.

July 16

SUSAN went out with Amanda today, and when she returned she had the developed snapshots we'd taken over the last few weeks. She was disappointed.

Something was wrong with the camera, and most of the pictures didn't come out well. Plus, in the close-ups of Amanda, you could clearly see that she was right in the midst of her worst pimply stage—a stage which, as the doctor promised, she seems to be growing out of now.

"We've got to get another roll," Susan said. "We've got to hurry, or we'll never have anything of how she looks now."

I know what she means. We're not picture-taking people; in the eleven years we've been married, I doubt that we've taken five rolls of pictures. But suddenly with Amanda, it's different. We want to remember every stage she goes through.

I remember, when I was growing up, my father would make us pose for pictures at every family dinner and gathering. I would hate it; it would be boring, and it would feel like an imposition, and I would rather have been doing almost anything else.

Now I know what he was feeling. Everything is fleeting, but you don't know it when you're a child. In a way, it's almost as if we put more stock in Amanda than in ourselves; it's probably dumb that we haven't taken pictures of ourselves over the years, but we trust our memories to preserve how things have been. With Amanda, though, it's as if we're saying that this time it's too important to entrust to our memories.

So we'll buy more film and we'll take more pictures; right now the only sign of displeasure that Amanda shows is a fierce blink every time the flashbulb goes off. Soon enough I'm sure she'll despise posing for pictures as much as I did when it was my dad behind the camera. She'll put up with it, though; and, like him, I'll be willing to deal with her temporary petulance if it means having her changing images preserved through the years.

"Do you think her pimples look too bad to keep the pictures?" Susan said.

"Let's keep them," I said.

July 17

SUSAN had to go shopping today. It's the weekend, and I was home, and she asked me to stay with Amanda.

This has only happened a few times. Each time that it does, it makes me crazy. Susan is so used to her now that she can put her down in the crib or the carriage and just work around the house until she hears a cry.

But I find myself acting like a sentry on patrol. I'll roll Amanda's carriage into the center of the living room. At first I'll sit on the couch and pretend to read a magazine. But within seconds I'll be up and pacing, walking in a square around the spot where she rests, looking at her as if maintaining eye contact will assure that everything is okay.

When Susan is around, it sometimes feels as if we've come a long way from those first days in the hospital, when everything felt so tenuous. Susan is so good with her now that I have the illusion of everything being under control when all three of us are in the house. Even when Amanda is crying at her worst—and it still happens a lot—by now I feel that Susan can eventually rock her to sleep.

But when it's just Amanda and me, as it was today, I feel as if I haven't made any progress at all. I'm just as jittery as at the moment Dr. Charles pulled her into the world. What do I do if something goes wrong? Do I wait for Susan? Do I call the doctor? Do I try to figure it out for myself? I'm a person who has considered himself to be pretty self-reliant all his life, but when we're alone those are the things that occur to me.

I don't even turn the TV or radio on when Susan's out of the house; I'm afraid they will either distract Amanda and make her cry, or—even worse—distract me and cause me not to pay enough attention to her. Sometimes when she's smiling as I pace, I think she knows what's going on, and is laughing at my nervousness.

When Susan came back she asked how everything had gone.

"Fine," I said, then went into the other room and collapsed on the bed.

July 18

I got a call from my friend Rob Fleder tonight. Amanda was crying in the background, and he kidded me about that a little bit. Then he said: "What are you going to do when she's fifteen or sixteen?"

He meant it the same way Dr. Charles had meant it when, on the day Amanda was born, he had joked about her first date. And although it's amusing on one level, it's bothersome on another. Because raising a girl in this world just isn't the same as raising a boy.

When I look at her lying in her crib now, it seems as if it will be light years until I have to seriously worry about matters like that. But teenage girls these days are . . . advanced. Advanced in ways I don't remember teenage girls of my generation being advanced. The way I have dealt with this so far is that when people have asked me, "What do you want Amanda to be when she grows up?", I have invariably answered, "A nun."

The problem, of course, is that the attitudes you would smile and wink at in a teenage boy—all the attitudes that go into adventuresome tomcatting—are precisely the attitudes that would cause you sleepless nights when your child happens to be a girl. We live in a changing society—and for a parent who grew up in a less-rapidly-changing society, that is precisely the problem. Today there are supposed to be fewer of the distinctions between the sexes when you're making rules. Girls are supposed to be as freewheeling, as curious, and as experimental as boys.

Which is fine on paper. But I'm already wondering about how I'm going to react when it's three o'clock in the morning and I hear teenaged Amanda coming in the front door from a date. Like I say: a nun would be fine.

July 19

MORNINGS are the time. I have always been in a rush in the morning; I am up and in the shower and out the door as fast as I can manage; I can't wait to get to work and get started on the day's column.

Until now.

Mornings are the time that I almost can't believe how lucky we are to have Amanda here. I'll wake up—Susan will be asleep from having fed her just before dawn—and I'll go into Amanda's room, and she will just be stirring awake. Good morning, merry sunshine.

I'll pick her up, and she will blink and look around; she will just be coming out of sleep, too, and she won't know quite where she is. So she will make her noises and stare up at the ceiling, and finally she will fix her eyes on me and start to smile.

I'll take her in the bedroom and put her on the bed, right between Susan and me. I'll pull the covers up so that she's like a real person in a real bed; I'm not sure she knows what this means yet, but she seems to like it.

For ten or fifteen minutes I'll talk softly to her; even if she's hungry again and ready to cry, she'll hold off at least this long. I'll talk to her and tell her stories, and although she has no idea what I'm saying, apparently she likes the sound of the words—she looks at me as if to encourage me. I'll stick my first finger out and touch her hand, and she will grasp it tightly and grin with the exertion.

When Susan wakes up she will roll over; we're past the point now where it's really shocking when we realize Amanda is with us, so Susan will just say, "Well, who do we have *here*," and now Amanda will turn toward her and give her the smile.

I'm sure this is no different from the way things have been in a hundred million households over the centuries. But it's new for us, and I can't compare it to anything I've experienced before. Things change daily for Amanda; every day something different comes into her life, and because of that it's as if every day is her birthday. And morning is the time we feel it; morning, in that hour before the world begins, as in the quiet of the new day she lies between us, is when my good fortune shakes me so hard I almost feel weak.

July 20

Susan had a new theory last night.

The problem has been this: Amanda has been crying again, virtually all day some days, and it is wearing Susan out. But when Amanda goes to bed at ten-thirty or eleven at night, it is not unusual for her to sleep all the way until morning.

Which would be fine for an adult, but doesn't make too much sense for a baby. Babies are supposed to sleep off and on; the whole idea is that the payoff you get for staying up all night with them is that they let the mother sleep for a while in the daytime.

Not Amanda.

So last night Susan set an alarm. She figured that if she woke Amanda up twice during the night and fed her, that might help get her on a more normal schedule. Amanda would be a little tired from getting up twice during the night, and would thus drift off to sleep during the ensuing day.

That's what the theory was.

It didn't work. Susan was, indeed, up twice with her during the night. It took her more than an hour to get Amanda back to sleep each time. And today, when Amanda should have been sleeping—under the new plan—she was still awake, fussing and crying, as Susan rocked her.

"If I could just get a nap once in a while," Susan said.

She is working on a new plan.

Today the television was on; a talk show was on the screen, and Susan, as usual, was holding Amanda and trying to persuade her not to cry.

On the show, a woman was complaining about the rigors she had faced in raising her family.

"For twenty-two years I was a slave," the woman said. "I wasn't a person of my own for twenty-two years."

Susan looked down at Amanda.

"Do you hear that?" she said. "Are you going to keep me in this room for twenty-two years?"

But Amanda just cried. I left for work, feeling Susan's eyes boring into the back of my head the whole way out of the apartment.

July 21

I RAN into a woman I had known several years ago. She was single then; now, I found out, she is married with two children.

She asked me what I had been up to, and I told her about Amanda.

She was enthusiastic about it, but within a few seconds she asked me if we were going to have another baby.

I told her I didn't know; I changed the subject, but she kept bringing it up.

Finally I said to her, "Why are you so anxious to know if I'm going to have another baby?"

"Because it's really important to have two children," she said.

"Why?" I said.

"Because when they grow up," she said, "you need two so that they can go lock themselves in a room and tell each other how much they hate Mommy and Daddy."

July 22

YESTERDAY'S entry was supposed to be funny. But it got me to thinking.

Earlier in this journal, you may recall, there were several references to Helen, my cat. Lately Helen's name has not been appearing here.

Before Amanda was born, Helen was extremely important to me. She gave my life a little symmetry; in the morning I would get up and go into the bathroom to shave, and Helen would curl up in the sink and watch me. Helen was a constant in my life; if I had to recall the last ten years, many details would escape me, but Helen would always be a part of the memories.

Since the birth of Amanda, though, it is as if Helen doesn't exist. We feed her in the morning and at night, but I know that we don't talk to her like we used to, and we don't look at her and ask ourselves stupid questions like "I wonder if she knows who we are." Helen, it must be said, has become not quite as important.

And I think she knows it. Every night she would sleep on the bed, curled up between us; in the morning she would get up with the dawn and stand up and mew us awake.

She doesn't do it anymore. Now she sleeps on the floor; she waits until she hears us getting up, and then she goes to the kitchen and stands there while we get her food. Somehow, instinctively, she knows that someone else has come into the house and has displaced her. She's still there; it's just that she knows we don't look at her as much.

And my question is this: if another baby were to come into the house at some point, would we treat Amanda in any way like we're treating Helen? I know you can't make the precise analogy; but the fact is, a new baby made us devote all our attention to her, and is it not logical to ask whether another new baby might not do the same thing?

If I've learned anything from Amanda, it's that a baby in the house takes precedence over everything. Today it seems impossible that any factor at all could make me think of Amanda less. But of course it's possible; if Amanda were three or four, and suddenly there was another baby in the house, I don't know what would happen.

I guess there's no reason to think about this right now. But some mornings I get up, and I see Helen over by the doorway, where she's been all night. She hasn't come onto the bed to awaken us; she knows that we're really not thinking about her. And it makes me wonder about a lot of things.

July 23

AMANDA had her regular doctor's appointment again today. At first I was surprised that babies were supposed to go to the pediatrician so often, but I guess it makes sense; babies can't tell anyone when something is wrong, so at least at first it seems to be a good idea to let them get seen all the time.

Dr. Scheinberg had her on the examining table, and was moving her arms and legs. He thought he heard something. He moved her leg a few more times, listening to the hip joint.

He said he wasn't sure—but he thought he might be hearing a faint popping. If it was there, it meant that the bone wasn't fitting into the hip socket exactly the way it should. He asked Susan to make an appointment with an orthopedic specialist to check it out.

Dr. Scheinberg said that we shouldn't overreact; he said that even if something was wrong, it was relatively minor, and could probably be corrected by something as simple as double-diapering Amanda for a few months. The pressure of the additional diaper would push the bone into the joint more firmly.

So now we have to make the orthopedist's appointment for Amanda. It's not that I'm nervous about it; it's just that this points out, once again, how tenuous all of this is. It seems to me that something can go wrong at every turn. If it's not her skin it's her navel; if it's not her navel it's her hip bone. And she's basically in good shape. The wonder of it all, to me, is that anything goes right any of the time.

July 24

Two new things:

She cries tears now. Before, while she was doing all that wailing, she remained dry eyed. Her little tear ducts hadn't developed enough for any fluid to come out. I didn't realize what was unusual about it when it was happening: she would be screaming and sobbing, and her face would be absolutely dry. Now I know what was missing, because just today small tears began to drop from the outside corners of her eyes when she cried. They're the littlest tears I've ever seen; but they're there, and when they begin to fall she seems just the slightest bit more human-like than before.

And she has begun to notice her hands. Actually, just her left hand. For all the moving around that she's been doing, she has shown no indication that she associated parts of her body with being attached to her. But now, sometimes when she's waving her hands around, she will see her left hand and stop it in midair. She'll stare at it for seconds on end; it's clear that she knows it belongs to her. I don't know why it affects me so much to watch her do this, but it makes me think about how far she has come in just the short time since she was born.

It's probably because Susan spends so much time alone with Amanda—but when I get home it always startles me to hear how much she talks to her, as if Amanda could understand.

"When you get a little older, I'll take you to Baskin-Robbins," Susan was saying to Amanda tonight. "And I'll say, 'What would you like, pink ice cream or white ice cream?' You can't have chocolate ice cream, because chocolate isn't good for girls as little as you. And one scoop only."

Susan caught me staring at this. But she doesn't care; she's planning some future that I'm only peripherally a part of. She knows that when the time does come to go to Baskin-Robbins, I'll undoubtedly be at work.

July 25

EARLIER I mentioned Neil and Linda Weiner, who had been in our Lamaze class. Linda came over one day last week with her baby to keep Susan company; they had made arrangements to pick us up for a Lamaze class reunion today, where all the mothers would bring their babies.

But Amanda sounded hoarse this morning; her crying had a raspy sound to it, and we could hear some congestion in her chest. We didn't know if it was the beginning of a cold or not, but we thought it was probably a bad idea to take her out among dozens of strangers.

Neil and I had been the lone iconoclasts at the Lamaze lessons; we seemed to be the only people there who weren't absolutely sold on Lamaze as the miracle cure-all for the pain of childbirth. And because of our work schedules, we weren't all that happy about having to go all the way to the other end of the city for three hours every week, either.

So when I called Neil this morning to tell him that we wouldn't be going to the reunion after all, I could almost hear the envy in his voice.

"It sounds like Amanda might be getting a cold," I said. "So I guess you shouldn't pick us up."

"If only Sharon had a cold," he said.

"I know what you mean," I said. "You're not looking forward to going back, huh?"

"I'd settle if she had a stomachache," he said.

July 26

THERE was a story about child abuse on the front page of the paper today. Like everyone else, I have been reading those stories for years, and I have always imagined that I have been as horrified as possible by them.

But now it's different. I read about how a man had systematically beaten his girlfriend's infant daughter, and had whipped her with a belt. The police had found the girl's body in an abandoned apartment.

I went in and looked at Amanda. It just seems impossible to me that anyone could bring himself to do that. Temper or anger seem to have nothing to do with it; certainly, when a baby has been crying for hours on end, it's enough to make you frazzled and edgy. But I looked down at her, in her pink terrycloth suit, and I tried to imagine how anyone could strike a baby.

The police officer who was quoted in the paper said that the man who killed the baby was "cowardly." That seems too easy. I've seen cowards. I've seen murderers. But I've never seen anyone who I suspected might have the potential of beating a baby in anger. And yet they're out there; they're all over the place. There are so many of them that their existence is not even considered abnormal anymore.

"I talked to a woman whose baby is ten months old today," Susan said.

"What did she say?" I said.

"She said that the baby hardly ever cries anymore," Susan said.

"And how does that make her feel?" I said.

"She said it makes her feel sad," Susan said. "She said it makes her realize that he isn't a baby anymore. She misses it."

July 27

AMANDA is working to turn over. She can't do it yet; her arms and legs aren't strong enough. But when she's on her stomach she presses against the bottom of the crib with her hands, and she grunts, and it looks like she's trying to do pushups. I wonder what's going on inside her head, to make her feel she has to flip over to her back. Everything in the world is done for her; this is the first and last time in her life that she doesn't have to try to do anything. And yet every time I look at her, she is struggling to turn. All I can think of is that it's the beginning of ambition.

I have to go out of town tomorrow; I have an *Esquire* assignment in California, and I'll be in Los Angeles for a few days.

Susan hasn't said much about it; she knew that eventually I would have to return to my normal schedule, and traveling around the country is part of that schedule. But just before we went to bed she said, "You'll miss Amanda's first bath."

Because of Amanda's trouble with her navel, the doctor had recommended that we give her only sponge baths until the infection cleared up. And we have. Now, though, it is time for a regular water bath. Tomorrow she'll get one. And I'll be on an airplane.

I lay awake and thought about it. The bath, of course, will go fine without me. As a matter of fact, it will probably be smoother without me hovering around and taking pictures. But it's the first milestone I'll be missing because I am somewhere else doing my work. It doesn't matter how hard I try to be there; the fact is, with the way the world works, there's a lot that I'm going to miss. I don't want to miss it; but none of us have any choice.

July 28

FLYING west to California was a new feeling for me. In the past, traveling has always been a welcome escape; no matter what is going on at home or at the office, I can pack a bag and pick up a plane ticket and, in three or four hours, be on another side of the country.

But now, with Amanda, it's different. After the plane took off and the flight attendants started serving lunch, I realized that this was the first time since the day she was born that I was unreachable. Out of beeper range.

In a way, it was a calming feeling. When there's nothing you can do, it tends to be relaxing. And Susan has certainly shown that she's up to taking care of whatever Amanda needs —certainly much more so than I.

Still, when we landed at the airport in Los Angeles, the first thing I did was to call home and make sure everything was all right. Tonight I sat out on the balcony attached to my room at the Century Plaza Hotel. Beneath me was the hotel's sprawling back terrace, with a meandering wading pool glowing blue in the night. Susan and Amanda seemed so far away.

Last year, when I was covering the royal wedding in London for "Nightline," I would call home and Susan would say how it felt as if I were in another world. I never quite understood that—I knew it was another world on the map, but I was just covering a story, like I always do.

Now I understand. I feel the distance. After the weeks of Amanda crying and us getting no sleep, it's a freeing feeling to know I will go to bed in a soundproof room tonight, and that no one will stir to wake me up until I'm ready. But already this is different than all my reporting trips before Amanda. I'm thinking of home much more than I ever did before. I know this goes away; I've seen enough businessmen who salivate at the thought of getting away from their families to know that, soon enough, this kind of travel will seem normal again.

But sitting on this balcony on a warm Los Angeles night, I think of the way Amanda looks up at the ceiling and opens her mouth, and part of me wishes I was back there already.

July 29

"I SUPPOSE I can imagine getting married and having children," Kristy McNichol said. "But I think it would be at least eight or ten years before I even started to think about it."

We were sitting in a health-food restaurant in Century City; I was interviewing her for *Esquire*, and this is where she had wanted to go to lunch. We had ridden around in a limousine her motion picture studio had provided for her; she had gone shopping for video equipment and for clothes, paying for everything with her American Express Gold Card. She is nineteen.

After lunch I had sat out in the sun at the Century Plaza; tonight I went to a restaurant in Beverly Hills with some people I had met. We had drinks, and good Mexican food, and in the morning I have an appointment to meet Kristy again.

And I think of Amanda and Susan, sitting in the apartment and maybe, if they get adventurous, going around the block for a walk. When I called home tonight I made a point of being vague about what I had been doing.

July 30

"ARE you going to call every five minutes?" Susan said.

I had gotten up from today's lunch with Kristy to check in at home. Susan doesn't exactly love it when I call; it means she has to put the baby down (and probably interrupt her nursing), put the baby somewhere where she's sure not to fall, and then rush to the phone before it stops ringing.

I, on the other hand, consider it a sign of utter devotion that I call so often.

"We had a bath today," Susan said. That's how she talks now; when Amanda is bathed, it's "We had a bath."

I went back to the table to rejoin Kristy.

"Where'd you go?" she said.

"Just had to check with my office," I said.

July 31

I FLEW home today. After all the roaming around Los Angeles, I walked in and there were Susan and Amanda, still on the couch where I had left them. The irony of this was not lost on Susan.

I went to pick Amanda up and hold her; there, on the top of her head, was a tiny speck of dried blood. I asked Susan what it was.

"From the fetal monitor," she said.

And it is true. When Amanda was having so much trouble being born, and they had inserted the fetal monitor into Susan to measure the baby's heartbeat, it had been attached to Amanda's scalp with a tiny wire. I felt myself shaking as they had inserted it then; I had not thought about it since.

Not it seems that there has been so much history among all three of us. Amanda smiled at me, and I ran my finger over the little speck on her head, and I realized that it hasn't been so very long, after all.

August 1

"MOST babies her age can't make sounds," Susan said.

I don't know if that's true or not. But Amanda definitely is responding by trying to make us hear her. What I thought of before as coos or gurgles really do seem deliberate on her part.

I will lean over her carriage and go "Hi." She will smile up at me—that much, there is no imagining. I will say it again. Still the smile. I will say it still again. And . . . something audible will come forth from her. It's nowhere close to a human word, but it is her trying to return whatever it is I am signaling to her.

I guess the thing that surprises me the most is that this should move me so much. Before, I was a little puzzled by the big deal people made over their babies' first words—the concept seemed so normal, so routine. And here I am, gazing in wonderment because she will try so hard to make a noise to match mine.

Susan thinks it's a case of Amanda being advanced. But I think it's just another case of us being swept away by miracles we were never even aware of.

We wake up before she cries. We don't know how it happens; it's something like the alarm clock in your brain that gets you up at the hour you want to rise, but it's even more mysterious.

Amanda will have gone to bed late the night before, and Susan and I will have drifted to sleep, and then at 4 a.m., or 5 a.m., or 6 a.m.—it differs every night—we will look at one another and realize that it has happened again: we are both suddenly awake.

And then, within five minutes, Amanda will cry from the other room. She will have just awakened, too, and we will be ready to go to her. I never heard of this before. It happens virtually every night.

August 2

Susan has seemed like she has had something on her mind. Tonight I got home from work; she was nursing Amanda on the couch. She said it:

"Do you realize that you never talk to me anymore?"

She said that ever since Amanda was born, I have been distant and reclusive. She said that she sits with the baby every day while I am at the paper, and that when I finally do arrive home I either pick up a magazine or watch the news or call one of my friends. She said it hurts her feelings.

I think she's wrong, but I also think I know why she's wrong.

For all the years of our marriage, Susan has had a job to go to. There were always people at the places where she worked with whom she spoke all day; her friends and business associates made up a great chunk of her working time.

And for all those years, I have been a fairly quiet person. That's just the way I am; I don't especially pride myself on it, but I don't say a lot when I think I have nothing monumental to express. It probably has something to do with the way I make my living; when you write a daily newspaper column, and you have to fill that space every morning whether you are feeling inspired or not, it does something to you. Often, by the end of the day, you subliminally figure you have said—on paper—all you have to say.

As far as I know, my quietness never bothered Susan before. But now it is compounded by the fact that she has literally no one to talk to. Except when someone calls, or on the rare occasion a friend with another baby comes over, she is alone with Amanda. Amanda, of course, can't talk. So Susan sits there all day hearing no voice other than the voices on the television. And then I get home, and I don't have much to say, and it builds up.

I tried to explain this to her, but she didn't seem satisfied with the explanation, and I guess she shouldn't be. I told her I'd try harder.

August 3

THERE'S something to be said for the confined life we've been leading. Susan has started taking Amanda out for short walks, and short sits in the park. But mostly, because of Amanda, we're shut in. We are home because home is where the baby belongs.

When we talk about it, we complain mildly that because of Amanda we can't really go out together at all. But there is a serenity in this—a safeness—that I think we will miss. In the years to come there will be enough nights when we wonder where Amanda is, and what time she's coming home, and who she's with.

So for now, to know all of those things for sure—and to be unable to change anything about it—doesn't seem so bad.

Speaking of the future, it's interesting for me to listen to Susan talk to Amanda. Often when she's holding the baby she will have long conversations with her; I'm sure she thinks she's just filling the air to soothe Amanda, but I get something else out of it. What I hear is Susan planning the coming years with Amanda—planning them out loud, even though she doesn't seem to realize it.

Tonight they were on the couch, and Susan was watching television, and suddenly I heard her saying: "Soon we'll watch 'Sesame Street,' and 'Mr. Rogers' Neighborhood,' and 'The Electric Company.' There's some shows we won't watch because they're not good for you, but the good shows will help you learn."

I looked over at them. By this time Susan was humming to Amanda again; had I asked her what she had just finished telling the baby, I don't think she could have answered. But it's important. I like it.

August 4

As Susan takes Amanda on more and more walks, she is noticing something. People stop her all the time, and look down into the carriage, and say nice things.

"They all say she's such a beautiful baby," Susan said. "They really do. Everywhere we go, everyone says what beautiful eyes she has."

I'm sure they do. Amanda's pretty. I'd have to say that many babies are very, very cute, and even the ones who aren't doubtless receive compliments everywhere they are wheeled. For the first year of a baby's life, he or she probably hears nothing but the sounds of approval.

This kind of bothers me. Not all babies grow up to be beautiful; if you walk down the street and look around you, you realize that the world is largely made up of people who aren't especially attractive. And I wonder what the procedure is in dealing with this. Your baby, for the first twelve months of her life, is beautiful. But obviously some of those babies end up as . . . not beautiful. What do the parents do when they realize that their child is one of those?

I just wrote a series of columns about something called a "Hot Legs" contest that was designed to find the woman with the best-looking legs in the Chicago area. Hundreds of women entered the contest; the ones I interviewed told me that being beautiful was an essential part of their lives.

The woman who won the contest—she was nineteen—said to me:

"I just don't think every woman has to be a super-brain and be super-smart. You can have a brain, or you can have other assets. . . . Women see someone who has something better than they do. Like good legs. They're insecure about their own looks; so they tell themselves that it's wrong for other girls to be proud of their looks.

"My family jokes that I started when I was born. The hospital where I was born had a contest to find the king and queen and prince and princess of the hospital—it was to pick out the cutest babies born there that year. I was chosen the princess of the hospital that year."

She told me that if she had to choose between being beautiful and intelligent, she would choose to be beautiful.

"Definitely," she said. "When you're smart, people don't really know it. But if you're beautiful and you walk into a room, people know it right away. Being beautiful is more of a thing that people can grasp and realize. Being beautiful is right there."

I fear that, despite all the changes that have happened in the way that women think about themselves, her attitude is not all that uncommon.

And now I have a little girl growing up in that world. I'm glad that people on the street think Amanda is beautiful. But I worry what will happen if someday they stop.

August 5

Susan had been carrying Amanda around all evening, and I said I'd give her a hand. I was in the bedroom; I told Susan to put Amanda down on the bed next to me, and that I'd play with her.

So Susan went into the kitchen, and I held hands with Amanda for fifteen minutes or so. When I got tired of it, I carried her back to her carriage, which was in the corridor between the living room and the bedroom, and I carefully put her down.

I went back into the room and phoned a friend.

In a few minutes I heard Susan calling out:

"What do you think you're doing?"

I didn't know what could be wrong. I rushed back out into the hallway. Amanda was still there.

"What kind of stimulation do you call this?" Susan said. "Leaving a baby in a darkened hallway?"

I thought she was kidding. But she had her hands on her hips.

"I mean it," she said.

It had never occurred to me that I was supposed to be stimulating Amanda at every turn. But apparently that is a part of a parent's duties. I don't know where you learn that; Susan had, and I hadn't, and now I was.

August 6

I was sitting in my office this afternoon, working on the next column, when suddenly I sensed something familiar. I looked up and Amanda was there.

Susan had been taking her for a walk, and had brought her by. People started to come by and look at her; I decided to hoist her up and walk her through the city room.

It's something to see what the sight of a baby does to people. I have never been a candidate for warm-employee-of-the-year honors, but people I had never spoken to were coming up and staring into Amanda's eyes and whispering to her. Copy editors and rewritemen were sticking their fingers into her palms so she could squeeze back. The editors of the newspaper were having a doping session for the Sunday edition; I carried Amanda in and everything stopped. Men I had never seen do anything but scowl broke into silly grins and spoke baby talk.

The workplace is an odd phenomenon. We spend most of our waking hours there, and yet we know very little about the lives our colleagues lead when they go home. We may have a few friends among our co-workers, but most of them—the men and women we say hello to every morning, who we see at the water fountain—remain mysteries to us. That is why it is always so shocking when you learn that someone you have seen in your periphery for years has committed suicide, or is discovered to be on heavy drugs, or has had a breakdown. That's the dark side of it—the idea that unseen demons haunt the men and women who populate your everyday world, and that you discover the existence of those demons only when it is too late.

The other side of it is something like today—when those same people light up at the sight of your baby. They aren't doing it for you; they aren't even doing it for the baby. They are doing it for all that a new life represents—maybe they don't even know that's the reason, but what else could it be? Ten minutes before they had been looking down at their desks, pondering the mundane problems that take up so much of all our lives. And now here is this infant among them, reminding them that—despite what goes on during our eight-hour shifts—life has another dimension, too.

I walked through that city room, and things actually got silent. Right on deadline, silence.

I carried Amanda back to Susan, who was waiting with the carriage in my office.

As she was preparing to leave, a young female editor came up and introduced herself to Susan. The woman had had a baby of her own several months ago, and this was her first week back at work. She played with Amanda and asked Susan questions.

Most of the questions were in the comparing-notes category. But then the woman said:

"Are you going to go back to work or not?"

Susan said she didn't know; at first she had thought she might, but now she was thinking she probably wouldn't.

"I don't know what to do," the woman said. "When I was pregnant I had it all planned out. I would stay with the baby for a few months, and then we would have someone with her during the days, while I was down here.

"But I've been back for five days, and it's making me crazy. I'm trying to do my work and all I can think about is the baby. I don't know how other women do it. It sounds so easy. But all day long I miss my baby so much."

August 7

EVERY day I run into something that challenges the notion that the modern father is automatically as close to his child as the mother.

Susan was about to take Amanda out for a walk. Amanda was on her back in the carriage; the part of the carriage that comes up to shade the baby from the sun was folded down.

"Aren't you going to put the top up?" I asked Susan.

"Not until we get outside," she said.

"Why?" I said.

She sighed. It was as if the question was so obvious it required no answer.

"Because Amanda likes to look up at the lights in the elevator," she said.

Oh.

August 8

I WENT to something called ChicagoFest today. It is supposed to be sort of a country fair in the city; it features lots of food and lots of musical acts.

The place was jammed with drunken teenagers. The boys were all bare-chested, and the girls seemed to be competing for some sort of Miss Lewd title. If they weren't showing off their chests, they were showing off their behinds. They were slopping beer all over each other, and sticking their tongues down each others' throats in the center of the midway.

As they sauntered along, their language—both the boys' and the girls'—was aggressively profane. The kids didn't seem to be aberrations; it just appeared to be the way teenagers act when they're by themselves. These are new times. A summer movie aimed at young people, just out, features an opening scene in which one high school girl gives her girlfriend lessons on how to perform oral sex on boys.

It makes me wonder all over again: How do you manage to make your own child turn out differently than this? Surely all the kids I saw today don't have parents who didn't care. Are the social forces of complete freedom—the social forces my generation helped make accepted—so strong that there is no longer a way to combat them? Is there no way to guarantee that in fifteen years, Amanda is not one of the girls on the midway?

August 9

MAYBE there is a way to guarantee it. Susan came home from the park today, and she said, "You wouldn't believe how some mothers are."

I asked her what she meant.

"They just walk away from their children and don't pay any attention," she said. "They just let their babies wander around."

I said that Amanda was certainly not in any danger of wandering anywhere.

"That's not the point," Susan said. "I keep my eye on her every second. That's what Dr. Scheinberg said. He said that you should never leave your baby unattended, even for five seconds."

Maybe if a mother can manage to maintain that attitude without going crazy, a kid won't end up drunk at ChicagoFest with her T-shirt rolled up to her chest.

On the other hand, maybe that attitude is exactly what causes a kid to do that.

I wish I had been through all this before.

August 10

THERE is one thing I vow never to do.

I got a long-distance call from an old friend of mine today. He had something he wanted to talk to me about.

We were in the middle of our discussion, and suddenly he said, "What is it, honey?" I assumed he wasn't talking to me.

I heard the voice of a little girl in the background. It was his daughter.

He returned to our conversation. I was saying something to him and he said, "What kind of bug, honey?"

I waited him out. He started talking to me again. He was in mid-sentence, and he said, "Was it a bug on our porch? Was it a bird? Was it an alligator?"

I have run into this syndrome with virtually everyone I know who has a small child. Men and women who would never dream of starting a conversation and then interrupting it to talk to another adult do it casually when their child is in the room. They don't even tell you they're going to do it; one second they're talking to you, the next they're talking to their kid. They expect you to understand.

I don't. I refuse to believe that it is being cruel to a child to make him be quiet while you are on the telephone. If you make a practice of stopping your conversation so you can talk to the child, it will only encourage him to talk to you every time he sees you on the phone.

"Are you done?" I said to my friend.

"Done with what?" he said.

"Talking to your daughter," I said.

"I'm not talking to my daughter," he said. "I'm talking to you."

August 11

HER hip is okay.

Susan took Amanda to the orthopedist today, and he listened to her hip joint and said it was nothing to get alarmed about. He said, if anything, there was a minor problem with the tendons. He said that for the next two months we should double-diaper her.

Which sounds fine, until you try to do it. We use disposable diapers on Amanda. Even using the smallest size, they look huge on her—she's still so tiny that it makes you laugh just to look at her with her diaper on. Double-diapering is out of the question, at least without some adjustments.

Susan has figured out a way to cut some material off the first diaper, put it on Amanda, and then put a full second diaper on. Then we pull her clothes on over that. Amanda doesn't seem to mind; she smiles all the while. But she looks absurd. Under her little blue suit it looks like she's wearing an inner tube.

August 12

SUSAN decided it was time for Amanda to sit up.

Since the day she was born, Amanda has looked at the world either from a lying-down position, or from being held in our arms. Today Susan bought her a cloth infant chair, with a strap to fit across her stomach.

What a sight. Sitting up, Amanda can turn her head and look around the room. In an instant, she became more of a grown-up. Before, she would look at shadows on the ceiling; now she can look at the same things we can.

I left the two of them alone in the living room while I went in the bedroom to make a call. When I returned, they were sitting there together—Susan on the floor, Amanda in her new chair.

". . . and you'll be in the chair," Susan was saying, "and I'll mash up your food for you. Peaches and baby peas. I'll bet you're gonna hate all this stuff. You'll go, 'ooooh, ick.' And I'll say, 'Oh, Amanda, *please* eat your peas. . . .' "

Susan looked up, embarrassed to find me watching. There are some things between them that I'm not supposed to know about.

August 13

TODAY, for the first time, my life was like it used to be.

I got up at 6 a.m. We were scheduled to videotape a "Nightline" interview in the suburb of Hinsdale; we were working on a story about white-collar unemployment, and I was supposed to talk to the wife of a fifty-thousand-dollar-a-year executive, a man who had been out of work for three months.

Betsy West, a young "Nightline" producer, drove out to Hinsdale with me; we met our camera crew there. We set up in the family's backyard, and I conducted what I thought was a satisfactory interview. We planned on taking the tape back downtown and screening it.

The wife brought out coffee for everyone, and we were sitting around the backyard drinking it when my beeper started to go off. I was alarmed; the first thing I thought of was Susan trying to find me in an emergency. I went into the kitchen and called the ABC bureau downtown to get the message.

Henry Fonda had just died. "Nightline" wanted Betsy and me to fly to Omaha immediately, to prepare a piece on Fonda's beginnings for that night's show.

I went outside and told Betsy. Within a minute we were back in the kitchen, passing the phone back and forth. I called Bill Lord, the executive producer of "Nightline," to see exactly what he wanted. Betsy called the ABC affiliate in Omaha to see what kind of file footage they had. I called the *Tribune* to try to arrange to delay the deadline for my column. Betsy called the Chicago ABC desk to begin making logistical plans.

It was just before noon. The first plane would get us into Omaha shortly after 4 p.m. We drove downtown; Betsy dropped me at the *Tribune*, and then went over to ABC to screen some Fonda footage the bureau had on hand.

I talked to my bosses and arranged to get the column in late. I went home and packed; I made my brief goodbyes to Susan and Amanda. I hurried to the airport, where Betsy was waiting with my plane ticket.

She filled me in quickly. Jim Mahoney, a free-lance cameraman, would be flying to Nebraska with us. A videotape editor would be flying in from New York and meeting us at the Omaha ABC affiliate. He didn't have editing equipment with him; an edit-pack was being shipped to Omaha from Dallas. Betsy had made arrangements for us to interview an eighty-one-year-old former colleague of Fonda's at the Omaha Community Playhouse, where Fonda had made his stage debut. On the plane, she wanted me to write the "bridges"—the portions of the script where I would appear on camera. The rest of the script would be written after the interviews were done.

We waited for Mahoney. Two minutes until takeoff, he wasn't there. If he missed the flight, we would be without a cameraman in Omaha. Just as the door to the plane was closing, he ran aboard with his camera—but with no soundman. The soundman he worked with had not made it to the airport.

We took off. Now Betsy would have to arrange to get a local sound engineer in Omaha. I sat in my seat and wrote the two bridges.

The first one was designed to be read outside, in an Omaha front-yard setting. It said:

"When you're from the Midwest, you learn early: don't promise—just do. Don't brag—just produce. Don't posture—just make it work. Simple qualities—qualities that millions of motion picture fans all around the world saw in Henry Fonda's face, and heard in Henry Fonda's voice."

The second bridge was meant to be read with me sitting in the seats of the Omaha Community Playhouse:

"He didn't dream of Hollywood . . . not at first. He started on the stage of a community theater right here in Omaha. The idea was to find out if he was any good—and there's no better way to discover that than to do your best in front of the people who know you the best."

The bridges written, I began trying to memorize them both. We wouldn't have time to do too many takes once we got to Nebraska.

When the plane touched down, Betsy and Jim went to the Hertz counter to rent cars. Jim waited for the baggage handlers to unload the fifteen cases of equipment he carried with him. I phoned our offices to see if there were any further instructions. I was told that "Nightline" was counting on us to provide the "mood" of the show; the Fonda piece out of Hollywood would be a fairly straight fan-reaction story, so any real feel of what kind of person Fonda was was going to have to be in our story.

Downtown Omaha was torn up with street construction; we

didn't get to the Omaha Community Playhouse until five o'clock. Fonda's elderly colleague was there; we set him up in the lobby, in front of a panel of pictures from the playhouse's history. He had a hearing problem, so I had to ask my questions in an unnaturally loud voice; but he was a lucid and lively interview.

A soundman from the Omaha ABC affiliate was helping Mahoney. We moved all the lights and equipment into the auditorium of the theater. The executive director of the playhouse, a man named Charles Jones, talked to me on camera about what it had been like when Fonda had returned home. Then we reversed the angle of the camera, and I sat in the seats and recited the bridge about Fonda's Omaha theater beginnings.

It was already after six; we were running late. But Betsy needed Jim to get some shots of still photographs of Fonda early in his career. We were short on video, and she needed everything she could get to cover the words I would write when we got to the station.

Then we went looking for a place to shoot the bridge about Fonda's Midwestern character. More minutes were lost; every neighborhood we drove into looked too expensive for our purposes. For some reason we seemed to be in the fanciest section of Omaha; it looked more like Beverly Hills than Nebraska.

Finally we found a perfect house. I sat on the front walk; a little boy who lived there seemed startled. Betsy told him who we were, and asked him if he could silence his dog, who was barking as if burglars were climbing in the windows. The boy did.

The sun was setting, and was causing strange-looking shadows to fall across me. So Mahoney had to go to his car and bring out a big metal reflector to place next to me—just out of camera range—and bounce harsh sunlight in my face. It was hard not to squint, but at least the lighting was even. I looked into the camera and said: "When you're from the Midwest, you learn early. . . ."

We packed up again and were at the station just after seven. A small crisis: the editor had arrived from New York, but the gear from Dallas was unsatisfactory. So Betsy begged the local news executives to let us use one of their editing rooms, and they said yes.

We quickly screened what we had. Basically it was going to be a story emphasizing how Fonda was shaped by the place from which he had come. My opening soundtrack was: "He made his name in Hollywood. He lived in fashionable Bel Air, California. But what made Henry Fonda Henry Fonda was the place from which he came—Omaha, in heartland Nebraska."

I quickly wrote the rest of the script, then went into the tiny editing room to read it onto tape. A few minutes later, Betsy came out. She didn't have the video to cover the lines about Hollywood and Bel Air. It would have to be shortened. We revised: "He was known everywhere. But what made Henry Fonda Henry Fonda was the place from which he came—Omaha, in heartland Nebraska."

By the time all this screening and tracking was done, it was 8:30 p.m., Central Daylight Time. Betsy would have to feed the piece to New York by 10 p.m.—which was 11 p.m. in New York, half an hour before show time.

She began to match pictures to words, dropping in the interviews we had conducted in the places I'd called for them to be. We had some file footage of Fonda talking about Omaha the last time he had been there; we were using that, too.

The clock kept moving. Nine o'clock, nine fifteen, nine thirty. Betsy called New York and said she might need an extra fifteen minutes. We were building toward an emotional final scene: Fonda is on the stage of the Omaha Community Playhouse during his final visit to the town. With him is his grandson, Justin. In a faltering voice, Fonda says that he wants the boy to take his first bow in the same place he had—"right here on the stage of the Omaha Playhouse." Justin bows, Fonda puts his arm around him, and they walk out of the spotlight into blackness.

Ten o'clock. Eleven in the east. In thirty minutes, ten million people would be watching. The videotape editor laid my voice over a shot of Fonda and Justin on the stage. My voice came out of the speakers: "What happened that night was pure Omaha, Nebraska . . . pure Henry Fonda." Then the scene with Fonda talking and the boy bowing. Then, over the applause, my voice again: "This is Bob Greene, for 'Nightline,' in Omaha."

We ran into master control to feed the spot to New York. The engineer cued it up and it flashed across a monitor. But there was a problem: something was wrong with one of the passages where Fonda was being interviewed during his trip to Omaha. The shot kept breaking up. The fault was on our tape; the master tape of the Fonda interview had been all right.

No time for us to fix it in Omaha. It was ten twenty; the show would go on the air in ten minutes. We fed them the raw original tape, with the Fonda interview on it; we told them what the in-cue and the out-cue were, and told them to splice it in New York.

It was ten twenty-four. We hurried back down to the station's newsroom. The local news was in its last minutes; it went off the air, and the "Nightline" theme music sounded, and then Ted Koppel was saying, "From Omaha, we have a report from contributing correspondent Bob Greene."

The piece flickered on the screen. Fifteen minutes ago we were still working on it here in Omaha; now it was being broadcast to every city in America. I heard my voice saying, "This is Bob Greene, for 'Nightline,' in Omaha."

I felt all the energy go out of me. Suddenly I realized that I hadn't eaten since breakfast. The producers in New York were saying that they liked the spot; all I wanted was some food and a bed. We drove to our hotel, the Red Lion Inn. The restaurant was closed. So I rode the elevator up to the bar on the top floor and, while a band played "Let's Get Physical," I drank a dinner of vodka gimlets. Home seemed very far away.

August 14

I GOT four hours' sleep. I had to catch the first flight back to Chicago so I could write my newspaper column.

In the Omaha airport, a girl of about two was walking

around. I was thinking about Amanda. The girl looked so cute. Then she toddled up to her mother and slugged her.

The mother said, "Don't hit! It's okay to walk up and love someone, but don't hit!"

Back to my new world.

I don't know who invented Snuglis, but they are definitely the eighties version of pacifiers.

Snuglis are those baby-pouches that mothers strap onto themselves. The straps crisscross over the mothers' backs; the babies fit into a carrying compartment in front, facing the mothers' chests. Susan wears one all the time when she is going to the grocery or out for a short walk; even if Amanda has been screaming, she is placid within a minute or so of being put in the Snugli. It's like a substitute for being back in the womb.

They were all over the Omaha airport. And of all the Snuglis I saw, not one baby in one Snugli was screaming. They were all snuggling against their mothers' chests and sleeping soundly. Somewhere there must be a baby who doesn't love a Snugli, but I've yet to see one.

August 15

I WENT into Amanda's room while she was sleeping this morning. She was sucking her thumb.

Another example of something I never would have thought about before. Of course babies suck their thumbs. But this was the first time I had seen Amanda doing it. And it took on a whole new meaning.

She was nursing; that's what I saw—she wasn't sucking her thumb, she was nursing. Susan wasn't there, and she had the urge to eat, and she had figured out that this was the way to do it. It was the beginnings of self-sufficiency.

I stood there and watched. As she progressed toward wakefulness, she began to suck harder; obviously her hunger was getting worse. She began to try to stick her whole hand in her mouth. And then, when she couldn't take the hunger any longer, she began to cry, and in a moment her eyes were open.

And in another moment Susan was there, with the real thing.

August 16

"WHAT a hard day you have ahead," Susan said to Amanda. "You have to eat, we're going to take a walk, you have to sleep. . . ."

I picked up my briefcase and headed for work.

August 17

AFTER dinner tonight we were sitting on the couch. Susan was holding Amanda and Amanda, as she is wont to do these days, was looking back and forth, from Susan to me, from me to Susan.

"Do you think she knows that we're related?" I said.

"What do you mean?" Susan said.

"I mean, do you think she realizes that you and I are related to each other?"

"Of course not," Susan says. "She doesn't even realize that we're people yet. She doesn't understand that she and I are separate people. She thinks that she and I are the same person."

She paused.

"So do I," she said.

August 18

Now she holds her hands in front of herself.

The same way she discovered that her hand was a part of her body, now she has somehow figured out that her hands were meant to clasp together. She will be waving them around, and then both of them will enter her field of vision at the same time, and she will put her hands together in two little fists and hold them in front of her eyes and stare at them.

I stare too. This is fascinating to me. Or maybe it's just that my mind is going.

The kitchen counter used to be the place where I would put Coke bottles after I had finished using them; where I would make myself peanut butter sandwiches; where I would store bakery bags of dessert.

No more.

Now the kitchen is where Amanda takes her baths. Her navel is okay now, so every other day she has a wet bath. Susan fills a yellow plastic tub with lukewarm water, and then puts a sponge lining into it. When the sponge is soaked through with the water, Amanda goes on top of the sponge. She pretty much hates it.

But it is always a shock for me to go into the kitchen and find Amanda, naked and dripping wet, where my Coke bottles used to be. Just another part of the house she has taken over; another part of my life she has changed.

If you ask me, a baby shouldn't take her bath in the kitchen. No one has asked me.

August 19

EVER since the day Amanda came to visit me at work, the other reporters and editors have been teasing me about it.

It seems that even though everyone else that day had been talking to her in the high, keening voice that people use around babies, I had refused to do it. I had spoken to Amanda in the same voice I use to speak to adults.

Today, someone at the office anonymously sent me, through the house mail, a story about a language called "Motherese." The story was from the Knight-Ridder newspapers, and it said that Motherese is a language used by people of both sexes to talk to babies.

The story gave the following example of Motherese:

"Hi, Sweetie Pie. Hello, Precious. Are you hungry? Do you want dinner? Of course, you want dinner. Okay, here comes dinner. Yum, yum, yum."

The story said that Motherese "comprises short sentences delivered in singsong fashion and usually in a higher pitched voice than conversational language exchanged between adults. Key words are repeated over and over. The voice tone is greatly exaggerated, which emphasizes the pleasure or displeasure of the adult speaking."

The story said that adults routinely switch between Motherese and regular English in the span of a few seconds. The adult might say to a baby, "Oh, we're getting very sleepy. So sleepy. See the big, sleepy yawn." Then the adult will turn to another adult and say, "Ever see a yawn like that one? His father must have been a hippo."

The person who sent me the story had underlined this paragraph:

"According to many psychological studies, Motherese is an easy language for babies to learn and mimic. It is rhythmic, repetitive, uncomplicated and usually telegraphs its meaning. The higher pitch may be more easily heard by babies than lower-pitched sounds. The singsong delivery style may serve to cue babies that, out of the jumble of sounds and language going on all around them, this particular message is meant especially for them."

Obviously whoever sent me the story felt that I was doing Amanda a disservice by talking to her as if she were an adult.

The person had no way of knowing that, when I'm at home, I speak exclusively in Motherese. To Amanda, to Susan, to myself in the mirror.

But I'll be damned if I'm going to do it in front of other people.

August 20

FOR the first time, she is scared of things.

If there is a loud noise next to her, or if something comes into her field of vision suddenly, she will wince and cry.

Like everything else that's been happening with her, I didn't notice fear's absence until I noticed its presence. For all these weeks we could walk into her room talking in a conversational tone, and she would continue to just lie there looking at the ceiling.

Now, if she's not expecting the noise, she'll jump. Well, not jump; but she'll jerk in place, and her face will show fear, and she will start to wail. Step by step, the world is becoming real to her.

August 21

THERE was a pre-season football game on TV tonight. One of the teams was the Cincinnati Bengals. Susan was holding Amanda and watching the television set.

"Your grandfather hates the Bengals," Susan said to Amanda.

The words didn't make any sense to me. Whose grandfather hated the Bengals?

Then I realized it. Susan was talking about her own father.

Mr. Koebel is a crazed Cleveland Browns fan. Half my life ago, when I first started going out with Susan, we would sit in the Koebels' family room in Columbus every Sunday and watch the Browns' games on television. The Koebels' Sundays were built around the Browns' games. When the Bengals came along, even though many Ohioans took them to heart, Mr. Koebel would have no part of them.

When I think back to when I first knew Susan, one of the most vivid memories is of those Sundays watching the Browns. We would watch the whole game, and than I would go home for dinner with my own family. I was a kid.

A lot of this experience has made me feel old. But I don't think anything has made me feel more ancient than that one sentence: "Your grandfather hates the Bengals."

August 22

I FIND myself wondering what she thinks of.

She's thinking of something; her eyes are always wide open, and she looks around the room and responds to light and to noises. She looks at us and smiles back when we smile at her; when she is displeased she will cry. There are thought processes going on.

But when I try to remember back to my own childhood, nothing comes into focus before I was four or five years old. It's as if those early years don't even exist.

Could that mean that they don't count at all? I can't believe that. Still, if you have no memory of something, does it exist for you?

I guess the thing I wonder the most about is if she will remember how attentive Susan has been to her. Amanda can't make a sound or move in her carriage without Susan checking on her, picking her up, talking to her. Is it really possible that Amanda will never recall any of this? She looks so comforted when Susan takes care of her. I can't help but think that this time is going to be very important in determining the kind of person she turns out to be—and how she thinks about us.

Still, though, I always come back to the fact that she won't remember any of this. Not one moment.

"What are you thinking about?" I say to her as she looks up at the ceiling.

She stares me in the eye and smiles so widely.

I know she's thinking something.

August 23

SUSAN and I seldom eat at the same time anymore. She has me watch Amanda while she makes me a sandwich or something; she says she will eat later, when Amanda is asleep.

Tonight I was doing some work in the bedroom, and I decided to take a break. I had eaten my dinner hours before. I walked back into the living room; Susan had Amanda cradled in her right arm, and had a plate in front of her. She was eating with her left hand.

I looked at the plate. I had no idea what was on it. I asked.

"It's mushed-up fish," Susan said.

Indeed it was; it was fish that had been mashed to the consistency of pudding.

"Why are you eating mushed-up fish?" I asked.

"So I can hold her with one hand and cut it with the other," she said.

My life is so much different from Susan's. I average one

restaurant meal a day; Susan has not been to a restaurant since Amanda was born. I at least get a sandwich for dinner; Susan's fish has to be mushed up so she can manage to get it into her mouth. She seems to feel it's all worth it.

As Amanda was going to bed tonight, I noticed that her little legs didn't stick all the way to the foot part of her suit.

"It's new," Susan said. "She's outgrown most of the old stuff."

Amazing. Day-to-day I don't notice it, but she is growing so much that her legs and arms were stretching the clothes she has worn since she got home from the hospital. I don't know why, but I hope Susan doesn't throw those first clothes away.

August 24

I WAS passing a colleague in the hall at work today. He is not someone I know well; I do know, though, that about six months ago he and his wife had a baby.

I heard a snatch of the conversation he was having with another man:

". . . and so we had to take her to the hospital last night. They say she'll be okay, but she has to be in there for at least a week."

It chilled me. The very thought of Amanda in a hospital, alone without us . . . it almost made me nauseous. I don't know how I could go to work, sleep, eat . . . there's no way that I could live my everyday life knowing that Susan or I wasn't with her all the time. Not knowing what the news on her was, and having to make the awful phone calls to find out.

I thought about stopping to talk to the man about it. But as I said, we don't know each other well, and it would probably have been an intrusion.

Still, when I got home tonight I was still thinking about it. I picked up Amanda and held her especially close.

Tonight she slept for ten hours—from the time we put her in her crib at ten until eight in the morning.

I wonder why? How does she learn that? During the daytime she won't sleep for more than twenty or thirty minutes at a spell. She continues to exhaust Susan by not taking naps. And yet something tells her that when we go to sleep, it is time for her to have a real sleep, too. I don't think it's as simple as getting her "on schedule," whatever that means. I think there's something inside her that makes her know that it's nighttime, and that it's time for her to sleep soundly.

But what? She can't know the difference between day and night.

But it's happening almost every night now.

August 25

I GET calls at work from people all the time; they have stories, and they want me to put them in the column.

Today a woman from the suburbs called. The story she told was not one I would use; in the past, I would have only half-listened to her. But today I was intrigued.

"Do you have any newspaper friends in Denver?" she asked.

I said that I knew a few people out there; I asked her what she needed.

"My daughter is in camp out there," she said. "And something terrible is happening to her."

She told of a series of letters she had received from her daughter. Her daughter said she was being picked on; she said that the other girls made fun of her, called her names, said she was ugly. She said the girls purposely kept her from sleeping, and woke her up in the middle of the night when she did manage to get to sleep. She wrote her mother begging her to come get her and bring her home.

There was no newspaper story in that. Kids have been being mean to other kids since the world began. But after we hung up (I did give her the names of some Denver newspaper people, not that it will do her any good), I found myself still thinking about it.

I understand why the woman was in a panic. Three months ago I wouldn't have.

If, ten or twelve years from now, we were to get the same kind of letter from Amanda, I think I might have the same emotions the woman is having. You think about the care you take in providing safety and warmth for your baby, keeping her away from anything that might hurt her. And then you realize that, once you send her off, anyone can do anything to her.

I tried to imagine what it would feel like to know that someone was being mean to Amanda, was preventing her from sleeping and purposely trying to make her life miserable. I can see why it was making the woman crazy; I'm afraid I'd be on the first plane to Denver to bring her home.

It was time for Susan to take Amanda for a walk.

She put Amanda down on the changing table and started to take off her little blue suit.

"Why do you always do that?" I said.

"Do what?" Susan said.

"Change her clothes before she goes for a walk," I said.

"I don't always do it," Susan said.

"But you're doing it," I said.

She sighed.

"If you must know," she said, "I put her in pink clothes before we go out because when she wears blue clothes everyone says what a pretty little boy she is."

August 26

My sister Debby came to town to see us. She is two years younger than I, but she has her own seven-year-old daughter.

Within minutes it became clear that she and Susan had much more to talk about than she and I. And 100 percent of the conversation had to do with children.

"Wait until her first day of kindergarten," Debby said. "Wait till you see what it does to you."

"How did you deal with it?" Susan said.

"I cried," Debby said.

And:

"I get so nervous when she sleeps over at a friend's house," Debby said.

"What does it feel like?" Susan said.

"The house feels so empty," Debby said. "You just want to get her back there so it feels normal again."

They are different than they were when I knew them in my previous life. Debby is still my sister, and Susan is still the person I married. But they are mothers now, and that redefines everything.

Tonight I was reading a book called *Jackpot!* by Jim Fixx, the man who wrote *The Complete Book of Running. Jackpot!* is the story of how Fixx—a self-defined "perfectly ordinary man"—became suddenly wealthy and famous beyond all reasoning, and how he tried to deal with it.

In one portion of the book, Fixx tells of a sound, wise piece of advice he got from his son, who was in college. It was a good anecdote, but it stopped me for reasons that failed to stop Fixx.

I thought: is this what's going to happen? Is this little girl in the crib going to be writing me notes of advice someday—

and is the advice going to be so good that I will revise my own thinking, and heed it?

Of course that's the way the world works. But I cannot yet comprehend the idea of Amanda someday being an adult—an adult who is concerned with my life, and who wants to help me. I'm trying to understand a lot, but that won't stick yet.

"You can tell she's growing," Susan said. "Look at her nose. "It has a bridge to it. That's new. When we brought her home from the hospital it was just a little bump on her face. The bridge has only been there for the last day or two."

If you pay close enough attention, you really can watch all of this happening.

August 27

Sometimes, very late at night, when I'm the most tired, something I can't quite explain happens.

Amanda looks a little like me. All parents think their babies resemble them, but there are parts of Amanda that really do look like me.

And late at night, when I'm so weary, I will look down into her crib, where she is crying, and because I'm so tired everything will be exaggerated, and she will seem to look more like me than she actually does.

And I will look down there, and . . . I don't know how to say this, but I will feel like I am looking at myself crying. Not me now; me as a baby. I will feel that I am somehow able to look back in time and see myself crying when I was only eleven weeks old. I will just stand there and stare; I'm perfectly aware that it is only an illusion, and that if I'd had a little rest I probably wouldn't be feeling this way. But it is such a special time; I will look at her and think she's me, and it will be like walking softly through a dream.

August 28

WHEN Amanda wakes up, it is not with a start.

We can see it coming half an hour before it happens. Her eyes closed, she will start to stretch. Sometimes her mouth will open and shut. She will extend her arms and legs.

Then, when it gets closer to the time, her face will take on a worried look. She will appear to be unhappy. She is hungry; not hungry enough to be awake, but hungry enough to feel the signals.

A few minutes beforehand, she will make sounds. It won't be crying yet. It will be more like "Uh . . . uh . . . uh." And then the cries will begin, getting louder and louder.

Susan will reach down, so gently, and lift her from the crib. Amanda will squirm; in a moment she will open her eyes, but she will not know what is going on yet.

"You're not awake yet, are you?" Susan will say. "You're still sleeping, aren't you?" And she will walk around the room with her until Amanda is fully alert, and is ready to eat.

And I wonder again . . . will Amanda ever know? Will something inside her ever let her understand how careful her mother has been of her feelings, right from the beginning?

August 29

IT's going to be a struggle to let her proceed at her own pace.

Above Amanda's carriage, Susan has hung a multicolored mobile. Various geometrically shaped pieces of plastic dangle from pieces of string; they are several inches above Amanda.

"She's supposed to know she can bat those things around," Susan said today.

I asked her what she meant.

"The books said that by her age, a baby should know she can bat those things around," Susan said. "She's still too young to actually bat them, but she should be noticing them and reaching for them. She's not."

This is the same woman who has taken such pride in how "advanced" Amanda is with her smiles and her sounds.

"I'm sure that when she's ready to bat them around, she'll bat them around," I said.

But it made me see something; it was like a distant early warning sign of the way so many parents are with their children. The Little League parents who get unhappy if their boy doesn't get a hit; the parents who have a need for their child to get all As in school; the dancing-school parents who want their daughters to get picked first by the boys every time.

Nobody consciously wants to be like that. But this must be how it starts; reading in a book that eleven-week-old babies try to bat at objects, and then letting it concern you when your baby gives the objects no notice.

"I wonder when she'll start," Susan said.

"I'm going to take the mobile away," I said.

August 30

"Do you think she knows this house?" I said.

"I don't know what you mean," Susan said.

"I mean, does she know that this house is where she lives?" I said. "If we were to move today, would she know that she was somewhere else?"

Susan laughed.

"Of course not," she said. "She knows hot, she knows cold, she knows wet, she knows hungry. She has no idea where she lives."

But again, that question . . . does that mean that all of this will mean nothing to her? I don't believe it. She may not know where she is in the way that Susan and I know where we are. But she senses something. She has to.

August 31

SUSAN'S single-mindedness is unwavering and even a little troubling. We were watching television tonight, and an actor on a commercial appeared to be reading his lines from inside a fish tank. I said, "Is that guy really in a fishbowl?"

And Susan, as if it were the most natural thing in the world, looked down at Amanda and said to her, "Maybe someday Amanda will have a fish."

Oh, well. That's the last thing on our mind now. Tomorrow Amanda is due to get her diphtheria immunization. Susan has been worried about it for days; she is picking up rumors on the mothers' grapevine that the vaccinations can have serious side effects. Today I talked to a woman whose son had developed a 105-degree fever following his first immunization; she had had to take him to the hospital, where they had bathed him in ice to lower his body temperature.

"Thanks a lot for telling me," Susan said after I had related that anecdote to her. "It's just what I need to hear. I'm falling apart just thinking about him putting a needle in her."

September 1

THE last thing Susan said to me this morning as I left the house was that I didn't need to show up at the doctor's office.

"I can take care of it," she said. "You'd just make me more nervous, anyway."

So naturally, when Susan and Amanda arrived at Dr. Scheinberg's, I was already in the waiting room. Susan just shook her head. Amanda gave me one of those big toothless smiles when she saw me, though.

I talked to Dr. Scheinberg about the immunization controversy. He said that, as far as he was concerned, it was absolutely necessary for a baby to have the shots; he said the risk of getting a serious disease was so much greater than the risk of bad complications from the shots that the arguments on the other side just didn't make sense.

He poked around Amanda's stomach for a few minutes.

"Is something wrong?" Susan asked.

"I'm just checking to see if I feel anything," he said. "If I could do only one type of examination on a baby this young, it would be an examination of the abdomen. I like to make absolutely sure that there's nothing wrong."

He told us a story about the time, at the beginning of his medical career, when he had been conducting this type of exam. He had been filling in for his older partner—the senior man in the office. The baby's parents had impatiently said that the baby had just had the same type of exam the week before. But Dr. Scheinberg had found something; it didn't feel right, and it turned out to be a tiny tumor. Within days the baby was in surgery, and the tumor was successfully removed.

"I just heard from that little boy," he said. "He just graduated from Tulane."

Amanda lay there on the examining table, wiggling and cooing. Dr. Scheinberg said that it was probably time to start feeding her solid foods; he suggested strained lamb.

I said I had a question about that, and he launched into a complicated explanation of why it was good to start a child on solids this young, and how doing it step-by-step could reveal any food allergies the baby might have. He had gone on for several minutes, when I said, "I trust you. That really wasn't my question."

"What's your question?" he said.

"My question is, how do you do it?" I said.

"Do what?" he said.

"Feed the baby strained lamb," I said.

"Now I'm not sure I understand *your* question," Dr. Scheinberg said.

"I mean, how do you feed her the food?" I said.

"With a very little spoon," Dr. Scheinberg said. "Is that what you mean?"

"Yes," I said.

He laughed. "You get a very little spoon," he said. "You take the strained lamb out of the jar, and you heat it up a little. Then you put the spoon in her mouth. When you're withdrawing the spoon, let the food rub against the top of her mouth. She'll spit some out, but she'll keep some in there. That's how you do it."

"Thank you," I said.

Then it was time. Dr. Scheinberg left the room for a moment. When he returned, he had a hypodermic needle in his hand; the clear vial was filled with fluid.

Amanda, naked, was on her stomach.

"This will just take a minute, Amanda," he said.

I put my finger in Amanda's palm, and she squeezed. Dr. Scheinberg leaned over and inserted the needle into her left leg.

I thought I heard singing.

I looked over. Across the room Susan was standing, looking the other way, her fingers in her ears, humming a song at the top of her voice so she wouldn't hear it when Amanda screamed.

September 2

No bad reaction to the shot the first day. But something else happened.

"Come look," Susan called from Amanda's room this morning.

I went in. Amanda was on her back, looking at the ceiling. We always put her to bed on her stomach. She had turned herself over during the night.

She is indeed getting stronger. This is just the latest manifestation of it. In the last few days, when she's been on her stomach, she has pushed herself up with her forearms, so she can raise her head and look around. It's nothing you would notice if you weren't watching her so closely every day; but it's given her a different aspect. Once again, in the smallest way, she is a little more independent. Now we don't have to hold her in order for her to see around the room.

The stress it takes is apparent. She will push herself up and see whatever it is she wants to see. But she can only do it for a few seconds at a time. After those seconds are up, she collapses back down onto her belly and just stays there. Her muscles won't do any more for her.

She seemed very pleased with herself after turning over; she looked up at us and laughed.

"She really isn't supposed to be doing that this early," Susan said.

"I know," I said. "So maybe you'll give her a break on not batting at the mobile."

September 3

Amanda must be becoming a real person, because Helen considers her to be one now.

I think it's the gurgling and the moving around and the laughing and the bringing her hands together. Whatever it is, Helen is very aware of Amanda now in a way she hadn't been before. She knew that something had changed about Susan and me; but I don't think she saw it in terms of a third human being in the house.

Now she looks at Amanda and it is clearly a cat looking at another person.

A routine is forming. When Amanda cries for the first time in the morning, I will vaguely hear it; Susan will get up, walk around with her, and then bring her into our bed to feed her. When I eventually do wake up completely, the two of them will be there together.

Today I rolled over, and Amanda evidently was fed and happy. She was smiling at Susan, and Susan was saying to her, "You're the only person in the world I'd get up for at five o'clock in the morning." I was about to ask if that included me, but I was afraid I knew what the answer was.

September 4

THIS is a little disturbing.

"Look," Susan said.

Amanda was on the living room floor, on her blue quilt. She was pushing herself up with her arms; the television set was turned on, and she was staring at it.

"Isn't that something?" Susan said. "Do you think she's really watching the TV? I think she is. She's like a real little person."

There didn't seem to be any getting around it. The flashing colors and continual sounds of the television were mesmerizing Amanda. Obviously she could have no idea of what the program was about; but with her mother and father in the room, she seemed completely captivated by the box.

That's sort of scary. I know so many people who are virtually addicted to television; they leave the set on even when they aren't really watching anything. I always assumed that this had something to do with a minor defect in their personalities.

But apparently TV's power is so overwhelming that it exerts a physical force. How else to explain this? Whenever it is turned on now, Amanda is constantly aware of it. Aware of it in a way she is not aware of me, for example; I can be in the room, and she is perfectly capable of paying me no attention at all. But when the TV is going, she is looking at it.

September 5

I SPEND time every day talking to her now.

"Hi," I will say. I'll be standing over her crib, and we'll be making eye contact. She will smile, and I'll do it again: "Hi."

Finally she will understand what I'm doing. And she will answer.

It won't be with words; she's got a long way to go before that happens. But she'll understand that I'm trying to communicate with her, and every time I will say "Hi" she will make a noise. It can't be a coincidence; she will be lying there quietly, and then I will say "Hi," and that's when she will make her sounds.

I didn't read about this anywhere. But it just seems to be the right thing to do. I don't know how a baby learns to have conversations, but it must come from getting used to someone talking to her, and then listening to her. At least that's what I think. There's never a day when I don't do it.

"We're not very happy today," Susan said to Amanda this morning. "You only slept from eleven to five. That's your worst night in a long time, Amanda."

I think Susan means exactly that: "*We're* not very happy today." She uses the first person plural so much that it can't be a slip of the tongue; when she thinks of Amanda, she thinks of herself; when she thinks of herself, she thinks of Amanda. As much as I love Amanda, the relationship is not the same;

in my mind we are still separate people. In this era of new attitudes on the part of men, I wonder if other fathers are different? And whether part of me is a throwback?

Somehow I don't think so. I think there's a built-in distance there that, if you're a man, you can never quite close. You can try all you want, but it won't happen.

September 6

I AM not the greatest son there ever was. For some reason, although I make my living by communicating through various forums, I am not very good at communicating with my own parents. When I visit them I often make excuses to go into another room and read a magazine, or put a record on the stereo; for whatever reason, I find it hard just to talk and sit around and be close.

I've been like this for so long that it's almost a joke in our family; my mother and father realize it's something about me that isn't going to change, and we all accept it. But I've always known that in a way it hurts them.

Before Amanda, I never understood exactly why they were hurt. But now I know.

If Amanda grows up to be like me—if, when she is an adult, she keeps to herself and favors silences whenever she can—I think it will rip me apart. And the reason is that I will always have the memory of these days.

Now, when she could not live without our care, we are feeling closer to her than we have ever felt to anyone. She isn't asking for this; we are giving it to her because of whatever magic the concept of family entails. There isn't a moment during the day we aren't thinking about her, and every time she smiles at us it's a new memory.

I can't imagine what it will feel like if this person we love so much grows up to be as distant toward us as I am toward my parents. It's not a lack of love; I think my parents realize how much I love them. But for some reason I have never picked up whatever social grace it is that allows you to demonstrate that love in obvious ways; and if twenty or thirty years from now I see Amanda walk through the room with just a nod, and close the door behind her, I hope I am smart enough to remember that I couldn't help it, either.

September 7

Amanda's not the only one being captured by the television.

"I found a discrepancy today," Susan said when I got home from work.

I asked her what she meant.

"On both 'Price is Right' and 'Wheel of Fortune,' they were giving Snark sailboats as prizes," she said. "But on 'Price is Right' the estimated price was seven hundred and fifty dollars, and on 'Wheel of Fortune' it was six hundred dollars."

She's got to start getting out of the house.

September 8

There's something about the sound of Amanda's laugh from the other room that's moving and important.

I will be on the bed reading; Susan will be in the kitchen fixing dinner. Amanda will be in her own room, in the crib.

And I will hear her laughing.

Something is striking her funny. We aren't there; she's all by herself. And in these last few days she has begun to be able to amuse herself. She's not reacting to anything other than what's in her own head. And it makes her laugh.

I like it.

September 9

"YOU'RE my best friend," Susan said to Amanda today.

Amanda, lying in her arms, looked up at her.

"We stay together all day, and we eat together, and we go everywhere together," Susan said.

"Someday you're not going to be my best friend. I'll tell you that I want to be with you, and you'll look at me and you'll go, '*Oh, mother. . . .*'"

She didn't know I was listening.

September 10

I'M in Atlantic City. I'm covering the Miss America Pageant for "Nightline" and for the newspaper; I'm staying with the crew at the Playboy Hotel and Casino.

In my room tonight, waiting for my producer to call to tell me it was time to go out and shoot the story, it struck me that it really does make sense that Amanda likes Susan better than she does me. Susan deserves it; she's not running off to write stories every morning, or getting on a plane every time some boss says to do it.

"I couldn't be away from her for a week," Susan told me the other day. She didn't mean it as a challenge; it was just a statement of fact. We are both Amanda's parents, but if someone called Susan and told her that she had to go somewhere without the baby, she would simply say no.

Me, I say yes.

But that doesn't stop me from thinking about her. There are casinos downstairs, and Miss America contestants next door, and showgirls in theater-dining rooms all over town. And I'm sitting here thinking about how Amanda looks when she opens and closes her mouth like a little blue-eyed guppy.

September 11

HOME again on a night flight. She was on the floor when I came through the apartment door; now she doesn't have to be in Susan's arms all the time. She's happy flailing about on her own soft quilt.

"I wonder what her voice is going to be like," Susan said.

It's something I hadn't thought about. I know what Amanda looks like, and what she smells like, and what she feels like. But the sounds she makes have nothing to do with any kind of real voice; the gurgles and sighs and laughs are only that. It's hard to imagine now that, one of these days, the thing that helps define a person most clearly—a voice—will be hers, and that we have no idea what it's going to sound like.

Amanda looking at me and asking me a question. . . . I can't even think about it.

September 12

I WAS in an elevator today, and a woman was riding downstairs with her daughter. The little girl appeared to be about two years old.

There was another man in the elevator. He looked at the child.

"Isn't she beautiful," he said.

He reached over and ran his hand over her arm.

The mother smiled.

"She really is beautiful," the man said. He rubbed the little girl's arm some more.

I don't know what it was . . . but I didn't like it. The guy showed no signs of being a pervert or a degenerate or a child molester. He seemed to simply feel that the girl was pretty, and his reaction was to stroke her.

But it made me feel odd. I don't want any stranger doing that to Amanda. What do you do in a situation like that, though? Do you say "Please take your hands off of her?" Do you yank her away? What do you do that isn't offensive?

I looked at the girl's mother to see if she was sharing any of what I was feeling. I couldn't tell. She was smiling a kind of chilly, distant smile. When the elevator ride was over, though, I was glad. One more thing to think about for the months to come.

September 13

"DID you ever really think about the future before?" Susan asked me.

I said sure.

"I mean *really* think about it," she said.

She said that before Amanda, she had only a vague idea of time unrolling ahead of us.

"I knew it was out there," she said. "But I had no idea of how to measure it.

"Now it all seems so clear. I think of a year from now . . . and I think that Amanda will be one, so that gives me some idea of what it will be like. And I think of ten years from now . . . and I think that Amanda will be ten, so that gives me another idea of what it will be like.

"It's as if the rest of our lives have suddenly been blocked out for us."

I don't know. For some reason, I avoid thinking about the very things that Susan seems to take such comfort in.

For instance, someone asked me today where I was thinking of sending Amanda to school. I said I had no idea. And I don't. She's only three months old.

"But surely you've thought about it," the person said. "I mean, you must be thinking about whether you want her to be in the public schools or a private school. And you must be thinking about whether you'll want to move to where there are good schools."

I haven't thought of any of that. I haven't spent a conscious second considering it. I don't know if that means I'm avoiding it on purpose, or what; but to my mind right now, Amanda is a baby, so all I have to think about are baby concerns. When she's a school kid, then I'll think about school kid concerns.

And Susan is already breaking the future down into years and months.

September 14

SHE saw her first televised killings tonight.

She was in her pink terrycloth suit. She was on her stomach on the blue quilt, which was on the living-room floor. Her little blue mirrored elephant was beside her, and her rattle, and her orange pig.

As has become usual, she was propping herself up on her arms, looking at the colors on the TV screen.

One actor shot at another. The second shot back. By the time thirty seconds had passed, three people on the show were dead.

I don't know if anything registered with her. Maybe I'm silly even to be concerned about it.

But I know this: when the gun went off, the sound made her flinch. I saw it happen.

September 15

She isn't bald anymore. When she was born she had just that little ducktail; now her head is covered with downy, soft, light brown hair. It happened so gradually that I didn't even see it. But now she is a baby with hair. She's still months—years—away from needing a haircut. Nevertheless, she is starting to look like a girl.

She's starting to eat solid foods, too. "Solid" should properly be in quotes; Susan mixes a little cereal with some warmed-up formula, and Amanda swallows two teaspoons, and that's it.

I don't know what nutritional value it has for her, but it has a certain psychic value for me. There are days when I start thinking of her as being very grown up; these three months have stretched into a long time.

But then I see her eat. *Two teaspoons.* And it fills her up; she is drooling and spitting some of it out by the end of the second teaspoon. I think of what I consider to be a meal. Then I watch her. My.

* * *

And when she plays on the floor, we've got to watch her. She scoots around so much that she's perfectly capable of scooting herself into trouble. She'll be on the quilt, and I'll look away for a couple of seconds, and when I look back she'll be facing in the opposite direction. And laughing.

September 16

I HAVE the flu.

I called my parents in Ohio. My father said, "How are you?"

"Sick," I said, looking for a little sympathy.

"You stay away from Amanda," he said.

Very nice.

September 17

ONE of the gifts of having Amanda is this: we notice things we never took time to notice before.

We were in the living room, holding her; it was a gray afternoon. Suddenly the sun broke through the clouds, and the streets below were flooded with light.

Susan held her up to the window. "Look, Amanda!" she said. "The sun's coming out! Look at it!"

The three of us looked together. I can't remember the last time, before Amanda, that we paid any attention to the sun and the clouds.

September 18

Susan is already worrying about things that hadn't occurred to me.

"I wonder if Amanda will be able to carry a tune," she said.

"I don't know," I said. "Does it matter?"

"I just hope she's not like me," Susan said. "It was one of the worst parts of growing up. I was so ashamed that I couldn't sing. I was in terror of the sixth-grade round-robin singalong. I didn't want anyone to hear my voice."

And:

"I hope you have lots of friends, Amanda. I hope the other kids like you."

She's not just saying the words. She's already agonizing over what it will be like for Amanda if she's unpopular. I almost wish she wouldn't do it. It makes me think about it, too.

September 19

Sometimes I think the frivolous parts of having a baby are overtaking Susan.

"I saw this great mobile at the store today," she said.

"Amanda already has three mobiles," I said. "She doesn't even know what they are. She doesn't need another mobile."

"But this mobile has a music box," Susan said.

"The mobile over Amanda's crib has a music box," I said.

"But this music box plays for ten minutes without rewinding," Susan said.

And sometimes I think the parts of having a baby that are entirely unfrivolous are overtaking her.

"Would you cut off your right arm for Amanda?" Susan asked.

"Come on," I said.

"Really," she said. "Would you cut off your right arm for her?"

"I'm not going to talk about it," I said.

"Just answer," she said. "Would you?"

"I told you," I said. "I'm not going to talk about it."

"I can't believe it," Susan said. "You wouldn't cut off your right arm for Amanda."

September 20

I HAVE never been a person who is very responsible about money. I know how much I make a year, but I don't take very good care of it. Generally, I let Susan handle the checkbook and all of the household finances.

Amanda seems to be changing my attitude a little bit. I got home from work today, and Susan said, "Do you have a check for us?"

That sounds entirely different than the old "Do you have a check for me?" "Do you have a check for me?" meant exactly what it sounded like—she was asking if it was payday; if it was, she wanted to deposit the check in the bank.

But now the money I make is earmarked for taking care of Amanda. I know I'm not the only new father who feels this way; a man the other day told me that for the first time in his life he was lying awake at night wondering if he had enough money stashed away. The reason was that he has a new daughter.

I think a lot of us are part of a generation that, almost on principle, tried to downplay the importance of money. It represented all the false weight that society placed on things that weren't, in themselves, very important.

Now it all seems different. The amount of money I am able to put away seems to correspond directly to the kind of life I will be able to provide for Amanda. Who will undoubtedly grow up scorning the idea of placing value on money.

September 21

I'm not sure what the clinical definition of postpartum depression is, but I think that Susan has at least a mild case. She's irritable and silent a lot of the time, and she manages to find fault with virtually every aspect of my attitude. Since my attitude is the same it's always been, I can only chalk it up to the physical and emotional changes that have come to her from having Amanda.

Tonight she was especially morose because Amanda was having trouble getting to sleep. Every time we would put Amanda in her crib, she would start wailing; after about an hour of this Susan was in tears herself.

I just didn't talk. The reason was, I covered a story today about a deaf young man on Chicago's South Side who had been robbed and murdered at his doorstep. His only crime had been to find a summer job that paid him a little money. Other men in his neighborhood found out about the job; they made a routine of shaking him down when he got home from work. Since he couldn't hear them coming, and he couldn't talk, he was the easiest of marks.

Last night he was shot to death. Whether he resisted them, or he just didn't understand that they told him not to run after they robbed him, is unclear. What is known is that, in fear, he tried to make it to his mother's door in a high-rise public housing building. The men who had robbed him followed him and murdered him.

I spoke with the mother today. She had raised him teaching him that there was a way to succeed despite the fact he could neither hear nor talk. Last night she opened her front door to find him dead.

I went home in a rotten mood because of it. When I heard Susan crying because Amanda was staying up an extra hour, a part of me felt resentful and angry. I thought of the life that South Side mother has had to lead, and now has to face without her son, and part of me was furious that Susan should be falling apart because Amanda was crying more than usual.

But another part of me knew how unfair my response was; no matter how tragic the incident on the South Side, it wasn't Susan's fault that the boy had been murdered. And I hadn't even told her about the story; she's depressed enough these days that I thought hearing the awful details would only make her gloomier.

So she grew angrier and angrier at me as I silently ignored her outbursts over Amanda. She thought I was being that way on purpose. And the angrier she got, the deeper I went into my shell. We went to bed without saying goodnight, and I still hadn't told her the South Side story.

September 22

ON the road again, this time in Charleston, West Virginia, for an *Esquire* piece. I think back to those days when it seemed to me I could never possibly leave Susan and Amanda for a mere story. Yet tonight my address, once again, is the Marriott Hotel, and I find myself wondering whether this is destined to be the pattern for the rest of my life.

September 23

I WAS the judge tonight for the Miss Kanawha County Majorette festival. It's an event put on each year by the Charleston Daily Mail, and I accepted the invitation to be the judge because it seemed to me it would make a good *Esquire* story.

In front of seven thousand people sitting in a stadium, I walked out onto a football field and, a clipboard in my hand, walked slowly down a line of a hundred high school girls dressed in short skirts, white boots, and spangled tops. My job was to pick the prettiest majorette in this particular county of West Virginia.

It was a chilly night that had followed a late-afternoon drizzle. After my initial inspection of the girls, I sat at a table with other judges and watched the majorette corps and the marching bands perform. The other judges were charged with selecting the winners of the talent categories; my duty, I had been informed repeatedly, was simply to decide which girl was the prettiest. I was given a pair of binoculars to use during the main part of the program.

At the end of the night the winners were named. The talent portions came first. Everything was leading up to my selection. I handed the name of the top three winners to the man in charge. The second runner-up was named first. Then the first runner-up. Then the girl who was the new Miss Kanawha County Majorette.

A cheer went up in the stadium, and the bands started playing, and the girl, crying, came running across the field. From the stands emerged her parents; her father was a driver for United Parcel Service. They embraced her on the forty-yard line. Of all the girls in Kanawha County, she was now officially the most beautiful.

I looked at the parents. Their dreams clearly rested in their daughter. Here I was, a stranger from out of town, and because I had found the girl attractive something inside the mother and father had been satisfied. Had I been drawn to another of the hundred girls, this girl standing in front of me now would be precisely the same person she had been before the night began; but now, because I had picked her, her mother and father were breathing irregularly, and she was still crying.

I handed her her bouquet of roses. I was vaguely ashamed of myself; it seemed that by my presence I was helping to perpetuate a sense of values—values based solely on physical beauty—that deserve to become outmoded. The world has changed in many ways in the last ten or fifteen years; I hope that by the time Amanda is a senior in high school, it will have changed in many others.

September 24

HOME on a packed Piedmont flight. Every time I am away from Amanda for even a night, it's a giddy feeling to see her again. I walked in and she was drooling down her chin and onto her clothes; I asked Susan if she could be getting a cold or something.

But Susan said that, according to all the books, this is normal; it's increased salivation, which is a prelude to teething. Apparently we're in for a long spell of Amanda spitting all over us—after which she will begin cutting tiny teeth.

I'm glad to know that now, because I'm going to spend that much more time concentrating on watching her smile. There's something about her smile with no teeth that I love; maybe it's that it somehow defines her being a baby. Once the teeth come in, she'll still be little, but not quite so much an infant.

The shoulders of my shirt are sopping wet. Amanda just laughs and drools on me some more.

September 25

AMANDA gets more exercise than I do. For the last few weeks, she has been unable to lie on her back without kicking her legs. It simply doesn't stop. She alternately laughs and coos and cries; but the legs are always moving. It's making her stronger. When I pick her up to hold her now, I have to hold on tighter. Given her own wishes, she would squirm right out of my arms.

September 26

Her first airplane ride. Susan put the Snugli on, and we took her to the airport for a trip to see the grandparents. After a lifetime of hearing the gate agent say, "We will now pre-board passengers who need assistance or are traveling with small children," it occurred to me that they were talking about us.

So we took off with Amanda in our arms. She didn't seem to think this was anything different than a stroll in her carriage. She got a little fussy fifteen minutes into the flight, so Susan unbuttoned her dress and began to nurse her. I didn't think this was such a great idea, but no one seemed to notice except the flight attendant, who saw Amanda in the Snugli and said, "Who is that little hamburger in the bun?"

As we left the plane in Columbus, the same flight attendant handed me a little metal pair of junior-aviator wings. I pinned them onto the Snugli, and out we walked into Port Columbus, with Amanda grinning and my parents and Susan's parents taking snapshots.

This is getting out of hand. The *Tribune* let me take a week of vacation so that I could take the baby to see the grandparents. So tonight I was relaxing with the two families, watching Amanda being passed back and forth, and the phone rang.

It was "Nightline." The National Football League players were on strike. They wanted me to go to Green Bay to do a reaction story.

I said I'd have to call back. I didn't tell my family what it was about. On the one hand, I had been looking forward to this vacation. On the other hand, the football story was a good one—just the kind of "Nightline" piece that I love to do. Going to Green Bay, though, counting the travel time and the story preparation time, meant four days out of the vacation.

I called the show back. I said I'd do the story if I could do it in Cleveland or Cincinnati. That way the whole thing could be done in two days. I argued that the Ohio cities were just as rabid about football as Green Bay was.

This time they said they'd call back.

They did.

I have to go to Cleveland in the morning.

September 27

BETSY WEST, camerman Ed Kita, and sound engineer Richie Frank met me in Cleveland. The Browns players were scheduled to have a team meeting at a suburban high school football field.

It was a cold day, and rain was coming down in sheets. The Browns ran through the downpour and into a dressing room in the high school stadium. Several dozen fans, despite the miserable weather, stood outside the grandstand just to get a glimpse of the football players.

We were inside with the team. I interviewed quarterback Brian Sipe and a couple of the other players; Betsy and the crew went out into the rain to get some atmosphere shots of the fans.

They came back in soaking wet.

"You got shots of the baby, didn't you?" Betsy said to Kita.

"What baby?" he said.

"You didn't see the woman with the baby?" she said. "Over by the fence?"

So they went back outside. When they came in again, they were shaking their heads. I was still talking to the Browns.

"I can't believe it," Kita said. "That baby is going to die."

A woman, they said, was holding a baby wrapped only in

a thin blanket. The blanket was soaked through. The rain was just pouring down on the baby. The mother showed no intention of leaving. The baby wasn't moving. With every second, the baby got wetter and colder.

"How old is the baby?" I said.

"I asked the woman," Betsy said. "She said five months."

I thought of Amanda. This baby was only a little more than a month older. I thought of how protective we tried to be all the time. I thought of all the nights we adjusted the temperature in the apartment so Amanda would not get too chilly or too warm.

"Betsy," I said, "make the woman take the baby home."

"What do you mean?" Betsy said.

"Go back out there and talk to her," I said. I was afraid if I did it, I'd kill the woman.

"What do you think I should say?" Betsy said.

"I don't care," I said. "But you've done your job already. You've got the video. We've just got to get that baby out of the rain."

"The woman thinks she's going to see the Browns practice," Betsy said. "That's why she's staying."

"Then tell her that the practice has been called off," I said. "Tell her she can go home."

Betsy opened her umbrella again and walked back into the storm.

When she came back she said, "They left. I told them there was no practice, and she went to her car."

"Thank you," I said.

September 28

WE worked two hard days. ABC flew in two more people—a lighting man from Washington and a videotape editor from Chicago. We were all over Cleveland—at Municipal Stadium, at a tavern in the suburbs, at a radio station where there was a Browns talk show, at a department store where Browns memorabilia was sold. We were dead tired, but we knew we had the basis for a fine story.

We called the show. They said they had been trying to reach us. Another breaking news story was taking precedence over ours. The football story was dead—had "gone away," in "Nightline" parlance.

So we went out to dinner, and then back to the hotel. I was kicking walls and throwing things across the room.

"Look," Betsy said. "You could have said no. When they called you you could have said you were on vacation with your family, and they wouldn't have put up any fuss at all. They simply would have assigned someone else to the story."

"I know," I said. "But you work two straight days on a piece, and it's going to be a great piece, and then you sit there and it's gone."

"You could have said no," Betsy said.

"I know," I said.

"So why didn't you?" she said.

I didn't say anything.

"You know why you didn't," she said. "On the one hand you had your vacation, and your hometown, and your family, and the people you haven't seen in years. On the other hand, you had a chance to tell a story on network television. And you came up here."

We talked about it for an hour or so. There is something so seductive about the work I do—a draw so strong—that at times it overwhelms everything else. I can't expect other people to understand it. I thought I would never again feel about my work the way that I had felt before Amanda was born. But here I was, in a hotel room in Cleveland, and I knew that if the story were airing tonight I wouldn't be weighing any of these doubts.

Betsy said that there was at least one good side to the story going away. Now she could get home to see her husband in Chicago. She had been on the road constantly for two weeks; she missed him.

Almost as if on cue, the telephone in the hotel room rang. It was Barbara Holzer, who is the secretary to Bill Lord, "Nightline" 's executive producer.

Betsy answered. Her face turned pale.

"Do you know why?" she said.

She shook her head at the answer on the phone.

"Okay," she said.

She hung the phone up.

"Bill wants me in New York tomorrow morning," she said.

I went back to my room.

September 29

I RODE back to Columbus and went straight to Susan's parents' house, where Susan and Amanda were staying. I rang the front bell, and Susan opened it, Amanda in her arms.

"Remember me?" I said to Amanda.

Her face lit up. She grinned and bobbed her head and started to move toward me.

"It's amazing," Susan's mother said. "She hasn't done that for anyone else. She really knows who you are."

I don't know whether to believe that or not. She's still so little—and Susan and I always tell ourselves that she can't possibly really know us, even with all the time we spend with her. But the look in her eye, and her reaction toward me, convinced me that she really might know. Can it be true? I go away for two days, and when I come back she knows that I'm her father?

I hope so.

September 30

I FIGURED I would knock off some newspaper columns while I was in Columbus; I called a woman for an interview, and she said she'd meet me for a drink when she was finished with work.

She was in her early thirties; she told me that her son, who was eight months old, went to a day-care center every day while she was at the office.

"You have that trauma to look forward to," she said. "I must have looked at twenty day-care centers. You don't know who you're leaving your child with. Some of the places reminded me of cages at the zoo."

Well . . . the fact is, Susan and I have not even entrusted Amanda to a babysitter yet. As much as Susan complains about not getting out of the house, she doesn't seem ready to let Amanda out of the immediate sight of either her or me. And I have to say that I agree; I can't imagine enjoying a night out knowing that one of us is not watching Amanda.

Amanda is almost four months old. This woman I met tonight has a son eight months old. Can I imagine, four months from now, leaving Amanda in the company of strangers every day of the week?

No. Not that we'll have to; at this point, Susan isn't planning on going back to work that soon, if at all.

But as we drank, the woman seemed calm and composed; obviously, leaving her son at the center every day is something she has gotten used to. Maybe I could, too. But I can't imagine it.

October 1

TODAY Amanda went to the senior citizens' residence where my grandmother lives.

There was a sign in the lobby. It showed a photograph of a baby and an elderly person; the caption was, "The ending of life is as important as the beginning."

Maybe, although I can't even guess what goes through the minds of these people when young children come to visit. Certainly it must brighten the place, in some way. But in others it must be vastly depressing. All these old men and women, living in small rooms with hospital-type beds, being bathed by attendants . . . the contrast between the sight of them, and the sight of Amanda squirming and twisting and laughing, is one that will stay in the memory.

My grandmother has been ill, and she didn't want to risk infecting Amanda. So we held Amanda in the doorway, and they just looked at one another.

As I was getting ready to leave, my grandmother said, "Thank you so much for taking the time to come over."

"I wanted to see you," I said.

"I'm just sorry that I couldn't hold the baby," she said.

"We'll be back soon," I said.

But of course, there is no guarantee that she will still be there. Each resident of the place has his or her name posted outside the room. But the name cards change regularly; you don't come here expecting a long stay.

We waved good-bye.

My mother, who had driven me over, walked down a long corridor with me.

"God," she said. "What must it be like to say good-bye to your grandson and know that you may never see him again?"

October 2

We flew back home. As nice as it had been seeing the relatives, this is where Amanda belongs; her room really is her room now, and I feel better with her sleeping in it.

Sleeping, though . . . that's still a problem. She was great on the airplane ride back; she was alert, and looking around, and paying attention to all the strange sights and noises.

When we got home, Susan put her on her quilt on the floor, and she gurgled and let out a friendly, high-pitched scream (that's new—she started it in Columbus) and seemed genuinely pleased to be back in a familiar environment.

When Susan took her in to put her to bed, though, she started wailing. She wasn't hungry or in pain; she does this every afternoon and every night when it's time for her to go to sleep. It doesn't matter how good a mood she has been in; she hits the mattress, and she falls apart.

"Why does she cry when she goes to sleep?" I said.

"Because it's not as much fun as being awake," Susan said.

Which, I guess, makes sense.

October 3

I WENT in to work, and one of the copy editors had his baby at work with him. It was a boy, just a few months older than Amanda.

He was wearing pants and a shirt; Amanda still wears only those zip-up one-piece suits. He was much bigger than Amanda. He seemed a lot more substantial.

I don't know if it's just the two-month difference in their ages, or whether I've become so protective of Amanda that she automatically seems small and fragile to me. This kid at work I could imagine fending for himself one of these days; Amanda still seems like someone you have to hold and shield against the world. Or does this have anything to do with the other baby being a boy, and Amanda being a girl? I'm not sure I want to think about the answer to that one.

October 4

"YOU'RE going to move to a bigger place, aren't you?"

A friend was asking me the question.

"I don't think so," I said.

"You watch," he said. "You'll get a house out in the suburbs."

"I really don't think so," I said.

And I meant it. I like living in the city; the condominium where I live is spacious and nice, and I like being relatively close to work, and I can envision living there indefinitely.

"You really think you can raise a child in that apartment?" my friend said.

"It hasn't been a problem so far," I said. "It really doesn't seem any smaller than it was before Amanda was born. That surprises me, because I was sure the place would feel like it had shrunk."

"You say that now," he said. "But wait until she starts to walk."

I had to concede that he had a point. When it's three people walking around the apartment instead of two, there will be a difference. And maybe that difference will result in us making a move—perhaps even a distant move. I have been so self-congratulatory that life still manages to go on with a baby in the house that I haven't given any serious thought to the time when there's not a *baby* in the house—but a third "real" person. It's like there's a whole second phase to having a child, and I haven't even begun to deal with that second phase. It's not that I don't know it's coming—it's kind of like when Susan was pregnant; we knew that pregnancy was a temporary condition, but it consumed us so much that we couldn't think rationally about what came next, even though we knew what was coming next.

I came out of the bathroom from taking my shower, and Amanda was on our bed. She was on her back, laughing, and with her left hand she was pounding herself in the stomach.

"What's she doing?" I said. "Isn't she going to hurt herself?"

"I don't know what to do," Susan said. "She seems to enjoy it. She's been doing it for the last two days."

I wonder how long that will last: this measuring of her activities by the days. Surely there comes a time when you stop thinking in those terms, but we haven't reached it. In a way it's sort of nice; it's a kind of reassurance that we're still paying close attention.

October 5

SUSAN'S lonely, and I don't know what to do about it.

I think that in the back of my mind I assumed that Amanda would be a foolproof antidote for loneliness; that because of my ridiculous work schedule she would be the perfect solution to the problem of me being called away so much, on such short notice.

But it doesn't seem to be working that way. All the hours alone with Amanda are just stressing to Susan how isolated this has made her become. We've been talking about it lately; it frustrates Susan to hear me say that I understand, because she doesn't really believe that I do understand, and even if I did that would be little consolation.

"You go out and lead your life," Susan said. "And here I am with Amanda."

"But I thought that's what you wanted," I said.

"I do want it," she said. "But there has to be some kind of change or I'm going to go crazy."

October 6

I CAME home late last night in a foul mood. I had been called in to the ABC Chicago bureau to do a "Nightline" commentary; the piece had read well, and I had delivered it well, and the videotape had looked good. I was anticipating the show with even more enthusiasm than usual.

And then the show had aired, and I wasn't on it. A second news spot had been added at the last second, and then they had committed the last few minutes of the show to a live feed from Katmandu, and my spot—which had been scheduled as the show-closer—was bumped.

Everyone at "Nightline" was quite complimentary about the piece, but I have learned that in television if it doesn't make the broadcast, then it doesn't exist. No one is interested in hearing how good your piece was that didn't make air.

So I was silent and angry when I got home, and I climbed into bed and stared at the ceiling until 3 a.m. When I finally did fall asleep, the sleep was fitful and troubled. I woke up still fretting about the show.

And then I heard Susan saying, "Things didn't go so well for your daddy last night, so you be nice to him."

She was carrying Amanda; she put her down on the bed next to me, and Amanda grinned at me and started to gurgle.

And despite myself I had to smile back and put my finger in her fist and hug her. This delighted her; she started to kick against me, and in a moment we were playing, and at least for that precise slice of time, the troubles went away. If this isn't what having a child is all about, I don't know what is.

October 7

AMANDA was on the changing table today, and I tickled her stomach while Susan put new diapers on her.

"I want you always to stay this exact age," I said.

I surprised myself by saying it out loud. I guess I have been thinking it to myself; it probably has something to do with the thoughts I had been having about whether we'll have to move when she gets older, and whether having a grown-up

Amanda in the house will change things. But I had never said it, not even to Susan.

What I meant is that she is so perfect now; she is a total joy to have around, and I can't imagine it ever getting any better. That's a terribly selfish thing to think, much less to express in words, but there the words were, hanging in the air.

"Say 'I can't help it, daddy,' " Susan said to Amanda. "Say, 'I keep getting bigger every day. There's nothing I can do about it.' "

"Sorry, Amanda," I said, and tickled her some more.

October 8

I HAD to fly to New York for a meeting with my *Esquire* editors.

I stayed over in a hotel. I woke up early in the morning; I knew it would be an hour earlier back in Chicago. Amanda would have awakened Susan already.

I called. "What are you doing?" I said.

"We're in bed," Susan said.

"What's Amanda wearing?" I said.

"Her Sweet Pea outfit," Susan said.

The Sweet Pea outfit is what we call this baggy yellow things she wears; her feet stick out of the bottom, and for some reason she reminds us of the character in the Popeye cartoons.

Two sentences: "We're in bed," and "Her Sweet Pea outfit." And yet across the miles I imagined them there, and thought of many things.

October 9

I WAS talking with a man who has a daughter just a few months older than Amanda.

"Have you been through the first cold yet?" he said.

I said we hadn't.

He rolled his eyes toward the ceiling. He didn't need to say anything.

"That bad, huh?" I said.

"Worse," he said. "There's nothing you can do. You can hear it every time she breathes, and you want to do something. You call the doctor and he tells you that it'll be over in three days. But you fall apart."

"Is there anything you can give her for it?" I asked.

"Just the Snugli," he said.

Four months ago I would have thought he was talking in a foreign language.

"The Snugli, huh?" I said.

"Yeah," he said. "It keeps her warm by keeping her close to her mother's body, but most of all it keeps her upright so she doesn't get so congested."

All of us out here, all of us fledgling fathers, in some sort of New Order of the Snugli.

October 10

AND two more new things:

When she sees the bottle of formula now, she makes sucking noises. That hadn't happened before; we would sense she was still hungry because of her crying, and we would bring the bottle to her mouth, and she would drink. But now as soon as it comes into her field of vision she starts the sucking.

Also, she reaches for me. It's different from when I put my finger in her fist. Now she looks up, and she sees it's me, and she lifts her arms toward me. If I'm close enough she grabs hold of my hand or my arm.

She does it for Susan, too, but she doesn't do it for strangers. She really is beginning to know us.

October 11

"SHE likes the rice cereal now," Susan said.

And Amanda was, indeed, eating the rice cereal as easily as if it were milk. She used to scream when she first tasted it.

"But look at this," Susan said.

She gave Amanda a spoonful of oatmeal. It looked almost exactly the same as the rice cereal.

But this time Amanda screamed and spit the cereal out.

"That's exactly what she did with the rice at first," Susan said. "Now I guess she's got to get used to the oatmeal."

I think of the signals going through her little mind. Rice, yes; oatmeal, no. And of all the decisions she will make in her life. Paying close attention doesn't make any of this any less of a mystery, or of a miracle.

October 12

ALL of a sudden her world seems centered on her mouth.

"Look at this," Susan said.

She held a spoonful of cereal near Amanda's mouth. Amanda hummed.

"She's doing that all the time now," Susan said. "She'll see the food on the spoon, and she'll start to hum and she'll open her mouth. She'll know it's coming."

I asked her why she thought Amanda was humming.

"All I can think of is that when I was feeding her, I always went, 'Mmmmm, that's delicious,' " Susan said. "She must be imitating me."

And:

Amanda was playing on her quilt, which was on the floor. There was a box of Kleenex on the table, and I pulled a Kleenex out and handed it to her. I wanted to see if she would grasp it.

"Don't do that!" Susan said. "She'll try to eat it!"

And sure enough, within three seconds Amanda was stuffing the Kleenex into her mouth, and we had to pull it out. Even a week ago she didn't know how to put anything into her mouth; now, it appears, we are into a new stage.

October 13

WE have a cleaning lady who comes in once a week.

This morning I was getting ready for work, and I heard Susan telling the cleaning lady that she would be going out for a few hours in the afternoon.

I pulled Susan aside.

"You're taking Amanda with you, right?" I said.

"No, I thought I'd leave her with the cleaning lady for a couple of hours," Susan said.

"You're kidding," I said.

"Just for a couple of hours," Susan said.

I went crazy. I said that if we were going to start leaving Amanda with other people, then it was something we should sit down and discuss—not something that Susan should just decide to do on the spur of the moment. I said that I, for one, was not ready for Amanda to be with someone I did not know all that well.

"It's been four months. . . ," Susan said.

"Your parents have been here, my parents have been here, you've been to Columbus," I said. "It's not like you haven't seen other people."

Susan ran into the bathroom and closed the door. I heard her crying.

"This is ridiculous," I yelled through the door. "If you want to go out, I'll come home, but I don't want to leave her here without one of us home."

When she came out of the bathroom she was furious. "How do you think the cleaning lady is going to feel if she sees we don't trust her with the baby?" she said.

"I don't *care* how she feels," I said. "I'm just not going to be comfortable knowing that Amanda's here without one of us."

So I went in to work, and at one o'clock I came home. The cleaning lady was feeding Amanda a bottle of formula. I don't think Susan really thought I was going to return; she looked at me, then left without saying a word.

For two hours I paced. Amanda started crying and wouldn't stop. The cleaning lady held her, then I held her, then the cleaning lady held her again. The cleaning lady kept giving her formula; I thought she was giving her too much, more than Susan would have. The cleaning lady walked Amanda around the room; I thought she wasn't being as gentle as Susan was. We put Amanda in her room so that she could try to go to sleep; she screamed like the early days.

"She's a mama's girl," the cleaning lady said.

And I guess she is. She is so used to Susan by now that being in the house without her becomes a disaster. When Susan returned Amanda was still screaming, and I was still pacing, and the cleaning lady was still standing there.

I went back to work. As soon as I got there, I called home. The line was busy. It stayed busy for half an hour.

"Who were you talking to?" I said when I finally got through.

"My mother," Susan said.

October 14

JIM SQUIRES, the editor of the *Tribune*, called me into his office.

The biggest story in the country has been the Tylenol cyanide murders, which have been going on in the Chicago area. So far there have been no arrests.

Squires told me that the head of the Chicago office of the FBI and the superintendent of the Chicago Police Department had visited him today. They had come to say they wanted our help in the investigation.

An FBI psychological specialist from Quantico, Virginia, had flown in to assist with the case. He was convinced that if the killer could somehow be made to identify with the victims, rather than to think of them anonymously, then the killer might show himself in some manner. The FBI and the police wanted something from me. They thought that because of the human nature of my column, I might be able to touch the killer in a way the news stories hadn't.

Squires and I talked about it for a while. We were concerned about possible conflicts of interest; since the antiwar days, the idea of the press cooperating with the FBI has caused a bad taste in many journalists' mouths. But we decided that if the FBI was not going to try to dictate what I wrote, we would be open to helping out; we would at least listen to them. We wanted the Tylenol killer caught; as long as the FBI was not asking us to print false information or anything like that, we would see what they had to say.

At five thirty an FBI agent named Tony De Lorenzo picked me up in front of the paper. The expert from Quantico—John Douglas—was waiting for us in a hotel room out in the suburbs.

The radio was on; all the way out, the news broadcasters reported on developments in the Tylenol case. De Lorenzo and I did not say much to each other.

I noticed a bag from a pharmacy between us on the front seat.

"What'd you get?" I asked.

"I have a three-week-old son," he said. "He has a rash on his stomach, and the doctor said I should take this home."

"You're kidding," I said. "Is it around his navel?"

"Yeah," De Lorenzo said. "It's all inflamed."

"My daughter had the same thing," I said. "Is the stuff the doctor gave you red drops?"

"Yeah," he said. "Some kind of liquid antibiotic."

"It works great," I said. "In a couple of days the rash goes away completely."

"Did you go to Lamaze?" he asked.

"Yep," I said.

"Wasn't that the worst?" he said. "And I had to go to prenatal lessons, too. If you don't go, the wives think you're some kind of terrible parent."

"I know my wife felt that way," I said.

"So did mine," he said. "And she's an FBI agent, too!"

"Other than the navel, is your boy all right?" I asked.

"Well, he's got pimples all over his face," he said.

I laughed. "They're horrible," I said. "But they only last for a little bit."

We kept talking, and I almost forgot the reason we were taking this drive, and then all of a sudden we were at the Holiday Inn. We went to room 215; John Douglas answered our knock, and let us in.

Basically, he was suggesting that I write anything that I thought might cause the killer to think about what he had done to human beings. Douglas said the FBI had psychological profiles that indicated such a killer might react to those kinds of emotions in a predictable way. He didn't tell me just what they were looking for; but he did say that they had several specific suspects in mind, and that they would be watching those suspects react to the column.

I said that my instinct would be to help out; I just wanted Douglas to understand that whatever I wrote would be a story I would write anyway, given the chance. What I wanted from the FBI was access; one of the victims of the Tylenol killer had been a twelve-year-old girl. Her parents had not talked to the press at all. I wanted to talk to them. If the FBI could get me inside their house, I thought we would both be served. I would get a legitimate story, one I could not have written otherwise. And the FBI would have the lure it was looking for.

Douglas said he would be in touch with the family. He said I would hear from the FBI in the morning.

De Lorenzo and I walked out to the parking lot and to his car for the ride back downtown.

Again, the radio was playing the Tylenol drama. Again, we rode in silence; we were thinking about what we were in the midst of.

About halfway home, De Lorenzo said: "Where do you get your Pampers?"

"We don't use Pampers," I said. "We use Huggies."

"What about Luvs?" he said.

"I don't know anything about Luvs," I said. "I just know we use Huggies."

"You really ought to think about Luvs," he said.

I hoped all of this wasn't being tape recorded. It would drive some poor FBI eavesdropper somewhere crazy.

October 15

THE FBI arranged for me to interview the family of the twelve-year-old girl. Tony De Lorenzo drove me out to a shopping center parking lot in the suburbs, where we were met by another agent, who drove me to the family's house. I knocked on the door and introduced myself. The father and mother and I went to the living room. We talked for about an hour.

I went back downtown to my office. Here is the story I wrote:

If you are the Tylenol killer, some of this may matter to you. Or it may make no difference at all.

If you are the Tylenol killer, your whole murderous exercise may have seemed beautiful in the flawlessness of its execution. You doctored the capsules, and the people died, and you put fear in hearts all over the nation. If you are the killer, the success of your mission may be sustaining you.

If you are the Tylenol killer, though, you may be harboring just the vaguest curiosity about the people on the other end of your plan: the people who were unfortunate enough to purchase the bottles you had touched.

If you are curious, come to a small house on a quiet, winding street in Elk Grove Village. The people who live there, Dennis and Jeanna Kellerman, feel you have already been inside, anyway.

Maybe the names don't mean anything to you. You killed their daughter. She was twelve; her name was Mary Kellerman, and her crime was that she had a cold.

You might be interested in hearing what you have done to her parents. They are still numb, alone in the house. Jeanna Kellerman blames herself. You see, she came home from work on the day before her daughter died, and on the way she stopped to pick up some medicine. Mary was a child who didn't like to take medication; she would go "Yuck" when her mother offered her cough syrup.

So on that afternoon Mrs. Kellerman purchased a new bottle of cough syrup with a flavor that Mary might like a little better. And she picked up a bottle of Tylenol, too. At first she was going to buy a small bottle; then, because she suffers from arthritis, and she thought that she might need a pill soon, she changed her mind and bought the next bigger size.

She bought your bottle.

You ought to see her now, crying, her eyes vacant, as she sits in the family living room and talks about what her life might be like if only she had stuck with the first bottle that afternoon.

You might be interested in Mary's father, too. He woke up the next morning and went into Mary's room. She told him that her throat was so sore. He said he wanted her to stay home from school for the day.

He remembers exactly:

"I heard her go into the bathroom. I heard the door close. Then I heard something drop. I went to the bathroom door. I called, 'Mary, are you okay?' There was no answer. I called again: 'Mary, are you okay?' There was still no answer. So I opened the bathroom door, and my little girl was on the floor unconscious. She was still in her pajamas."

You might be interested in knowing that when Mary's mother and father returned from the hospital—returned without Mary, who, as you know, was dead—they looked in the refrigerator. In the refrigerator was a brown paper sack with a sandwich and a piece of pie inside. Mary had packed her lunch the night before. She thought she would be going to school, so she made herself the sandwich. She could not have known about you.

On the front of that refrigerator are a number of funny, furry little animals with magnets fastened to their backs. They are used to attach notes to the refrigerator door. Maybe you would care: Mary made those for her mother. They were gifts.

If you are wondering whether Mary's parents talk about

you, you don't have to wonder anymore. They do. You have never been in their house, and yet they cannot walk into a room without feeling you are there. You don't know them, but you have changed their lives forever; they feel as if they can't get away from you. If you had only wanted to steal their car, they think; if you had only wanted to burn down their house. Anything; they would have said yes to anything. Anything but this.

Do you want to know what they are thinking about you? "I would pay anything if whoever did this would walk up to my door right now." That's what Mary's father said. "I would give everything I own. Because once he walks in that door, he's mine."

As it is, you should know, Mary's parents are too shattered even to visit the cemetery. Mary is buried at St. Michael the Archangel in Palatine, and they wish they could go to her grave. But they can't; the hurt is too deep, and you are keeping them even from that.

If you are the Tylenol killer, you should know one more thing:

Mary's mother can't have any more children. Mary was her only baby; you might be interested in knowing that Mary was born one month premature, and that as she entered the world her mother was scared because she was not crying. But the doctor smiled and said, "It's all right; she's only sleeping." And she was; she was a quiet child, and because the Kellermans knew she would be their only child, she was especially precious to them.

You should know that Mary's mother has not gone into Mary's bedroom since her daughter died. Her clothes are still there, and her school books and papers. The door is closed; Mary's mother and father have to walk past it every time they go upstairs. Mary's father has gone inside, but just once; he went in to pick out the clothes for Mary to wear at her funeral.

If you are the Tylenol killer, you might want to know that Mary's parents considered themselves to be overly protective. Mary always had to be home by dark; even when she was out with friends, she had to call home frequently just to say she was all right.

The reason Mary's parents were like that was that they knew something that a twelve-year-old girl couldn't know. They knew that the world can at times be a cruel place, and that parents have a duty to protect their child from dangers the child might not even know are there.

They thought they knew about every danger that could possibly touch Mary.

But they did not know about you.

I went straight home after finishing the column. I showed it to Susan.

"Do you think you could have written this before Amanda?" she said.

"I don't know," I said.

And I don't.

October 16

"Do you notice something?" Susan said.

"What?" I said.

"The dining room table," she said. "This is the first time in four-and-a-half months that it's been cleared off."

And indeed it is. If she means that as some sort of signal that we're on our way back to our old life again, we both know she's kidding herself.

October 17

I WAS reading a magazine on the bed. I heard a squealing that got louder with every passing second. I didn't even have to look up: Susan was on her way into the room with Amanda.

When they came through the door I looked up and waved, and Susan carried Amanda over.

"I wonder if she even knows that she has a servant like this," Susan said.

She looked at Amanda.

"Are you the queen of the world?" she said. "Are you queen of the world, being carried around like this?"

Amanda just grinned.

"You think it's normal, don't you?" Susan said. "You think it's normal for someone to pick you up and carry you anywhere you want to go."

In a way, it's too bad: by the time Amanda is old enough to remember anything, she'll also be old enough for us to tell her what to do, and for us to become annoyed when she doesn't do it. This part of her life—the part of her life when she runs everything—she is destined never to even know about. She really is queen of the world now, but she has no idea.

October 18

It was after dinner, and Susan said something about a person we know. I took exception to what she was saying. Before long we were bickering back and forth.

"Stop it!" Susan said.

"Why?" I said.

"The most important thing in a child's development is that her parents agree in front of her," Susan said. "We should never disagree in front of her."

"Huh?" I said.

"She can tell," Susan said.

I looked down on the floor. Amanda was completely oblivious to us. She was on her quilt, trying to slug a rattle.

"I'm serious," Susan said. "She can tell."

* * *

Sometimes I lose sight of the fact that Susan hasn't been a mother forever. She and Amanda are so linked all the time now that I often momentarily forget that this is still pretty new to her.

"Do you know when I felt the worst?" she said tonight.

I asked her when.

"The day my parents left us with Amanda, after they visited us that first week," she said. "I stood on the street and watched them drive away, and it was like when I was a little girl and they were leaving me at camp."

The Tylenol column apparently has had no effect. It has been several days since it ran; there still have been no arrests.

October 19

EVERY night after dinner we put Amanda in her crib and let her squirm around and look at the mobiles. The high scream she has developed is almost constant when she does this. It is clearly not a scream of pain; it is almost like a long, continuous laugh, and when we hear it we know she's having a good time.

So tonight we were watching television and talking, and we heard that happy scream from the other room.

"You know, we should really pay attention when we hear that," Susan said. "This is the only time in her life that she's going to be allowed to just lie there and scream out for joy."

And it's true; things are bound to get so complicated, and so soon. Before long she will begin to have people's problems instead of just babies' problems.

I got up and turned the sound down on the TV set. And we sat on the couch, listening to all that joy from the other room.

October 20

We were in the kitchen. Susan was making dinner, and I was listening to the radio, and Amanda was on her back in her carriage.

The radio station was having a sixties week; they were in the middle of a series of Beatles songs, and "I Wanna Be Your Man" came on.

Ringo's voice filled the small room, and I heard Amanda laughing. I turned to look in her carriage. She was moving like crazy to the music. She clearly liked the song; she had the beat.

I thought back to when I had first heard the song, as a junior in high school. And now here was my daughter, too young even to talk, responding to the Beatles in the most visceral way possible. Ringo kept singing, and she kept laughing and moving; I guess some things are universal.

I have a feeling that Susan is starting to feel the same way I do about Amanda at this particular age: she isn't particularly anxious for it to pass in such a big hurry.

"Think of Amanda as a teenager," she said.

"I have been," I said.

Amanda was on her changing table, looking up at us.

"What have you been thinking about?" I said to Susan.

"Teenagers are such smart alecks," Susan said.

Amanda waited for her diapers to be changed.

October 21

AMANDA was on our bed; Susan had to do some things in the living room, and she asked me to watch her.

"I'm watching her," I said.

"Don't even leave for a minute," Susan said. "She's really getting strong. She can roll over and scoot right off the bed while you're not looking."

And it's true; lying on her back, Amanda has learned to propel herself by pushing her legs against the floor. She can't really steer herself yet; she gets all excited and starts moving, but she has no idea in what direction she's heading.

"We're going to have to start babyproofing the house soon," Susan said.

"What's that mean?" I asked.

"We're going to have to get rid of all the loose cords, and plug up all the electrical outlets, and make sure there's nothing she can get her hands on," she said. "The time is almost over when we can count on her just lying in the same place."

Even as she talked, Amanda was using her legs to scoot toward the side of the bed. I scooped her up and put her back in the middle, and she immediately started pushing her way to the side again.

I looked over at my bedside table tonight, and I realized that I have not had to set the alarm clock since Amanda was born.

That used to be something that was part of my routine: I would set the clock before I went to sleep every night. Now I don't even think about it; I know that Amanda will be up before we wake up. Some mornings I sleep through her first crying; but when I open my eyes, there she is, lying between Susan and me, nursing and beginning her day.

It's a better way to wake up than the old way.

October 22

A SIXTEEN-YEAR-OLD high school girl came to see me at the newspaper late this afternoon. She has been coming around for about three years; she will disappear for months on end, and then show up with news about her life.

It isn't a very happy life, apparently. She has been involved with drugs and alcohol; her parents are wealthy people who are in the midst of a divorce, and she mainly seems lonely.

I was busy when she came in today; I gave her a quick hello and then went back to my work. About half an hour later the phone rang. It was her. She wanted to talk to me. Could she come back?

So she did. She came into the office and said that some street-gang members had been harassing her; one of them had threatened her with a knife, and she had told the police, and now other people in the gang were out to get her. I didn't know how much of this was true and how much was in her imagination; I told her that she really ought to talk to her parents about it if she was that concerned.

"They're not in town," she said.

She stood there staring at me.

"Do you like me?" she said.

"Sure," I said.

"That's not very committal," she said.

"Yes, I like you," I said.

"It's not like I have a crush on you," she said. "I used to, but now I just want to be your friend."

"Well, that's probably good," I said.

"What are you worried about?" she said.

"Well, for one thing, I'm thirty-five and you're sixteen," I said.

"That doesn't matter," she said. "I had a fling with . . ." And she named a famous young comedian.

She said that they had been in a club together, and that they had both been "really wasted," and that she went off with him. "It was no big deal," she said. "He was pretty nice." She started telling me more about her experience with drugs, and with liquor, and with the gang members she said were bothering her.

And in the middle of listening to her I realized that I don't necessarily want to be in Chicago anymore. I have a little girl who has to grow up in this world; I'm not sure I want her to grow up with the same diversions that this girl was talking about. Maybe you can't run away from the changes that have overtaken the world; but there must be a way to do your work and yet avoid an environment that offers readily available dope and booze and gang membership and one-night stands with famous young television stars. There must be a place where sixteen-year-old girls don't automatically turn for companionship to thirty-five-year-old men whom they've seen in their newspapers.

If there is a place like that, I'd like to find it for Amanda. The one thing that scares me is that such a place may exist only in my memory.

October 23

THE thing that's different about Amanda is that she has become so substantial. Even though I've been paying close attention every day, I can't pinpoint the moment that she stopped being a tiny, completely dependent infant, and started being a person with characteristics of her own.

We've always put toys around her when she is in her crib or on her quilt on the floor. Suddenly . . . she knows they're there. She looks at them and takes interest. She reaches for them. We squeeze them, and they honk at her, and she moves and laughs.

When we put her in her crib and wind up the mobile, she will stare at the flowers moving around above her, and follow them with her eyes. When we place a rattle within her reach, she will eventually grab for it and wave it around.

She's not the only thing in her world now; she has begun to recognize that there are things and people all around her.

The quilt was replaced tonight. It has been a soft, beautiful, baby-like thing. But events have overtaken it.

Specifically, Amanda drools so much now that she's like a little fountain. She must be getting ready to teethe; if we leave her alone for even a few minutes, we will find spit all over everything.

So the lovely down quilt is now a utilitarian vinyl drop-cloth. When Amanda's on the floor, that's where we have her lie now. It's not as luxurious; but at least when Amanda's done drooling on it we can wipe it clean with a wet sponge. Reality has pushed aside romance.

October 24

I called home from the office today, and I asked Susan where Amanda was, and she said that she was holding her.

"Put her on," I said.

"What do you mean?" Susan said.

"Hold the receiver up to her ear," I said.

She did. I closed my office door, so that no one could hear me. Then I started talking to her in the same baby talk voice I use at home.

"Amanda," I said. "Remember me? Amanda, remember me?"

"I don't believe it," Susan said when she got back on the phone. "She knew it was you."

"Are you sure?" I said.

"She knew," Susan said. "Her face lit up just like when you talk to her at home, and she started smiling, and then she stared at the phone. She knew it was your voice."

I choose to believe it is true.

October 25

IT was time for Amanda's walk. It's getting cold outside; Susan had dressed her in a blue wool suit and had put a little hat on her head. She was fastened in the Snugli.

"We're getting near the end of the time she'll be in the Snugli," Susan said.

"No, we're not," I said.

"We are," Susan said. "Pretty soon she'll be too big."

"I just read an article about Snuglis," I said. "The article said you can let the Snugli out as the baby gets bigger."

Susan laughed. "In case you haven't noticed, I've already been letting the Snugli out."

"You have?" I said.

"Yes," Susan said. "She's getting to the point where I can't carry her around like this anymore. She's starting to weigh a lot."

"She hardly weighs anything," I said.

"Then you carry her around in this thing," Susan said.

"What will you do without the Snugli?" I said.

"Use the carriage, or put her in a stroller," Susan said. "She's getting really good at holding herself in a sitting position once you help her up."

I looked at Amanda, her head sticking just above the corduroy top of the Snugli, staring at me.

"I'm going to miss the Snugli," I said.

"I know you are," Susan said.

October 26

HELEN seems to have given up. For so many years she ruled the house; anywhere she prowled around she owned, and if she felt like leaping up on the bed to wake us in the morning, she did it without compunction.

Now she knows it's Amanda's house. Tonight both of them were on the bed. There was a time when I would have worried about Helen jumping on Amanda; she's that kind of cat.

But tonight she just padded over and stared. She looked at me. She looked at Susan. She looked at Amanda.

Then she turned, jumped from the bed, and went off to play with her food dish.

It's sad when the great ones realize their time is over.

One of the nicest things about Amanda is that she notices everything. If there's an unusual movement in the room, she turns her head. If a window creaks in the wind, she looks toward it. If one of us coughs, she tries to see what's going on.

Part of it, of course, is just a baby's natural reflexes working. But part of it is something else; something that we all start with, and grow out of. It is a relentless fascination with the world around us.

The first time any of us enter a new situation, we pay attention to everything. The first time we work in a new office or visit a new city, everything seems fresh and memorable. It's like no one has ever seen it before. Time passes, though; pretty soon the things that seemed so special become mundane, and fade into the background. We don't even know they're there anymore.

With a baby, the whole world is something that has never been seen before. Everything that happens is a new thing. And I love seeing Amanda react to it. Soon enough she will pass through this stage, and start taking things for granted.

Right now, though, nothing is taken for granted. As I watch her, I feel as if I am seeing things for the first time again, too, right with her.

October 27

SHE exercises now.

We put her on her stomach on the vinyl dropsheet, and she arches her back and rocks back and forth. She kicks her legs, and waves her arms; she holds her head upright, and she's like a miniature hobbyhorse, going forward and back.

The touching thing is that she is already looking to us for approval.

"Bravo!" Susan will cry, and Amanda will light up and try to rock harder. If Susan looks away, Amanda will look at her until they make eye contact; then she will rock again, and when Susan says "Bravo!" Amanda will laugh and try even harder.

It's something; it was such a short time ago that I was wondering whether she even knew who we were. Now it's gone so far beyond that; not only does she know us, but it matters to her that we think well of what she's doing.

October 28

"HOW long are you going to keep nursing?" I asked Susan.

"Forever," she said.

It really has become an important part of her life. There are times I think she needs it as much as Amanda does. I think back to how I couldn't understand why it mattered so much to Susan that she nurse Amanda and not rely on the formula; now I know.

How could anyone not know? The first thing I see every morning is Susan and Amanda in the bed, Amanda feeding; the last thing I see at night is her feeding one more time. For all of the wondrous experiences that have been a part of this, the nursing is the one constant. And it is the endless reminder to Susan that she is essential to Amanda in a way that no one else could be.

October 29

I HAD lunch with an old friend. His daughter is two years old; he has been through all of this before.

"I've been thinking," he said. "In a way, I kind of hope that my daughter will be ugly and unpopular and the kind of girl that the other kids don't like."

He didn't seem to be kidding, and even if he had been it wouldn't have been a very good joke anyway. I asked him what he meant.

"I don't know," he said. "I think back to the kids who were great-looking and popular and great athletes when we were growing up. Doesn't it seem to you that they all turned out not so great?

"I've kind of got a theory that if you go through all the terrible stuff when you're a kid, then you'll be in better shape when you get older. Because you'll have already handled all the adversities, and you'll be tough enough and smart enough to take care of anything that life throws you."

I asked him if he had really meant that about his daughter.

"In a way I do," he said. "I really want her to grow up to be a good person, and I think that if she has it too good as a kid, she won't have a chance."

Maybe he has a point. I'm not ready to endorse it quite yet, though.

October 30

ON the bar that hangs across the top of Amanda's crib, there is a little bird with a wooden beak. A string hangs down from the bird; there is a ring on the end of the string. If you reach up and tug at the ring, the bird pecks.

She does it. She knows that if she grabs the ring, the bird will do its pecking. It is remarkable to me; it is a sign that her mind is working. It can't be mere chance that she reaches for the ring again and again; it can't be chance that she laughs with delight when the bird pecks.

She is so young and so tiny for this to be happening. At times it seems that we have to do virtually everything for her, that she is helpless and completely dependent. And then I will see her reaching for that ring to make the bird peck, and I will realize how rapidly things are changing.

Now her hands are wet all the time. It's another step in the process that started with her drooling. The drooling hasn't stopped, but she has figured out how to put her hands in her mouth, so the effects of the drooling are spreading.

I know this is normal. But the pleasure of putting my finger in her hand for her to squeeze is no longer quite the same. Now it's sort of like sticking my finger in a dish of not-quite-ready Jell-O. It's okay, though, because it's Amanda.

October 31

SOMETHING sort of disturbing is going on. After weeks of being fairly placid, Amanda is now crying all the time again. There doesn't seem to be any pattern to it; it doesn't matter if she has just eaten, or if she hasn't eaten in hours. For no apparent reason it starts up.

As soon as Susan or I pick her up, she stops. But when we put her back down, the crying begins right away.

There's another part to it, too. She gives out these little grunts the whole time she's crying. She goes "unnhh . . . unnhh . . . unnhh." And the crying continues.

"Do you think it's an attention-getting device?" Susan said.

I said I supposed it could be: I guess if a baby learns that she will be picked up and held every time she cries, she might cry just so we will come to her.

But my worry, of course, is that she is in some kind of pain, and that we don't know about it. We will go out of her room for a minute, and we will hear the grunting and crying from her crib. We don't know what the story is.

November 1

SHE can't roll over to her stomach when she's lying on her back. But now it's not a big deal for her to roll over to her back if she's been lying on her stomach.

This is a great source of amusement for us, but it presents one potential problem. Amanda sleeps on her stomach. Since the day she was born, this has been the position that has been able to lull her to sleep.

Now, though, doing her little pushups, she is quite capable of being put in the crib on her stomach—but ending up on her back a few seconds later. And as of now, she can't sleep while she's on her back.

We'll put her down for the night, and fifteen minutes later we'll hear her in her room. We'll go in, and there she will be on her back—exactly the way we didn't leave her. I wonder how long it's going to take her to learn to fall asleep while she's facing the ceiling.

* * *

The grunting and crying hasn't stopped. Susan called Dr. Scheinberg. He said that she was too young to be doing it to monopolize our attention; he said a baby her age isn't really capable of doing that kind of thing. He said she must be feeling some sort of discomfort.

He suggested that Susan change the kind of formula she uses to supplement Amanda's nursing. Maybe the formula is at fault; maybe Amanda has started reacting badly to it.

November 2

I WAS sent out of town for the day on a story. I was in a mall on the road, and I was wandering around killing time; I spotted a baby store, and walked in.

I do not buy very many things; I'm just not a very enthusiastic consumer. I'm happy with what I already have. But I found myself asking the woman behind the counter what they had that would fit a baby almost five months old.

She took me to a rack with tiny T-shirts; I found one that I liked, and the tag inside said that it was for six-month-olds. The one next to it—the same style, but just a little bigger—was for twelve-month-olds.

I picked up the six-month-old version and started to carry it to the counter. Then I went back and took the twelve-month-old version, too. Why give her something she's going to like and that she's sure to outgrow?

I can't believe this. I feel like my father, bringing us kids presents from a business trip.

I got home tonight. Amanda was in her crib, reaching up for the ring that makes the bird peck. There are three multicolored discs up there, too. They each have a different pattern. She kept reaching for a particular one of them; every time she would stop and start over, that would be the one she went for.

"She really likes that one," Susan said. "It's her favorite."

She said that it didn't matter which one was closest to Amanda; she would always reach for that particular disc. Another development that surprises and tickles me.

November 3

She can almost crawl. She will be on her vinyl cloth on the floor, and her legs will be kicking like crazy, and she will arch up on her stomach and wave her arms. She really wants to crawl. But I guess it's just not time yet; for all that rocking and waving around, she stays in one place.

The crying is almost constant. And the little grunts. Susan is taking her to see Dr. Scheinberg tomorrow.

November 4

Dr. Scheinberg says it's definitely not a bid to get our attention.

He looked at Amanda. He heard the "Unnhh . . . unnhh . . . unnhh." He heard her crying.

He found a little tear in the lining of her rectum; apparently it had been caused by her straining while she went to the bathroom. He thinks that she feels it. When she is ready to have a bowel movement, her insides tell her to exert pressure toward the outside; but the pain from the little tear tells her to clamp up. That's what the noise is all about, he says; she is grunting because she is frustrated that she has to go to the bathroom but is fighting the urge the whole time. And the crying follows that.

He said it is nothing serious; we're supposed to go back to the glycerine suppositories, and to use a special ointment. It should be healed within a week.

The whole episode made me think about what it must be like being a baby. Amanda has been in pain, but she has had no way to let us know about it; the only way has been to cry. I wonder, if Susan was not so attuned to every change in her, how long her pain would have continued with us not knowing about it. It makes me want to hover near Amanda even more; if she can only signal us this way, then I feel as if I ought to be paying even more attention than I am.

So many little things that can go awry. I guess the only defense is to be looking for hints every second.

November 5

NOW she will casually pick something up.

If her rattle is next to her, she will reach over and lift it. If we're on the bed together and I'm reading a magazine, she will reach out and grab it. If we're feeding her and we put the spoon down, she's likely to pick it up herself.

I don't know how much of this is even conscious; often she will seem not to be looking at the object as she grabs it. It's as if she's flinging her arms around and she happens upon whatever is there; I can't be sure if she is actually selecting things to pick up.

Regardless, Susan says that we have to start being careful about leaving small objects around.

"You're going to go on dates, Amanda, and it's going to drive me crazy," I said.

She was craning her head around.

"It's going to be nine o'clock, and ten o'clock, and eleven o'clock," I said, "and I'm going to be pacing around looking out the window waiting for you to come home."

"You're going to be terrible on everything," Susan said to me. "Dates, school, birthday parties. . . ."

"Why don't you just stay here and never go out, Amanda?" I said.

She dribbled onto her vinyl cloth.

November 6

Susan and I were eating dinner; Amanda was lying on the couch watching us when she spit up on the front of her terrycloth jumpsuit.

"Get me another suit for her," Susan said. "The blue one."

I went into Amanda's room. It occurred to me that I had absolutely no idea where the blue jumpsuit was.

Susan called from the living room:

"In the upper right-hand drawer."

I went to the cabinet and opened the drawer, and there the suit was, right on top.

I don't believe that Susan—for all her thinking about it—is even aware of how completely Amanda has changed her life. It's little things like this that bring it home to me. She knows without thinking where everything of Amanda's is. Not just the clothes; if Amanda is scratching herself because her nails are too long, Susan will say, "Will you bring me her nail clippers? They're in a red plastic case next to the changing table." In a way, her world is shrinking; I hope the joys of this make it worth it to her.

November 7

SOMETIMES the clicking will wake me.

It's that pecking bird from the rod on top of her crib. She likes it so much now that she will play with it all the time. I will be asleep—my unconscious mind half forgetting that Amanda is even there—and I will hear the bird pecking. I will remember that she is here—here and starting to be her own person.

I know I am not the first father to be struck by all of this. But everything seems to be happening so fast. We have gone from the point where she didn't seem to be aware of anything around her, to the point where she can look up, see the bird, somehow know that the bird brings her pleasure, and start making the bird peck.

It's quite a feeling. I wake up to the clicking, and I know that my daughter is making herself happy.

She's still grunting and crying. We've started with the medicine; so far, it doesn't seem to be doing much good.

November 8

IN three days, she will have been a part of the world for five months. So much has happened; it seems that every day my life is crammed full of things I had never imagined.

But of course, it always comes back to the fact that she will remember none of this. I find that so hard to reconcile; she is so alert, and yet there is no way that any part of what we have been through will stay in her memory.

"Maybe there's a chance she will remember this," I said.

"Not a chance," Susan said.

"But she seems to be taking everything in," I said.

"So did you when you were a baby," Susan said. "But try to remember back to when you were five months old—you can't."

She's right, of course. This whole first part of Amanda's life is destined to be a blank. But I stick with my contention that something inside her will know how she was cared for.

"Do you think she remembers stuff now?" I said. "Not that she'll remember later—but stuff she remembers from day to day?"

"At her age, she has a three-minute memory," Susan said. "She can remember anything that happened up to three minutes ago."

"Where did you get that?" I said.

"I read it," Susan said.

"Well, it's wrong," I said. "If she can only remember three minutes, how can she recognize us?"

"I don't know," Susan said. "I don't understand all this either."

She has to have orthopedic shoes.

Susan took her back to the orthopedist to check on her hip. He said we don't have to double-diaper her anymore; everything is fine.

But he looked at her left foot and he said she twists it too much. He gave us a prescription for little shoes that will make her foot form properly.

He assured us it's no big deal. "The shoes should do it," he said. "I can't remember the last baby whose foot I had to put in a cast for this."

Still, though, the idea of her little feet in orthopedic shoes twenty-four hours a day is a melancholy one. And it will be twenty-four hours; the orthopedist said that, for a while, she even has to wear them when she sleeps.

Susan asked him how this happened, and he said that Amanda's foot was probably pressed up against her wrong while she was in the womb. It got started wrong and never corrected itself.

He told us again that the shoes will make everything okay. It seems so long ago—while she was in the womb. And yet here she is, having to get special shoes because of it.

November 9

EVERY time she makes a noise that sounds remotely like a word, I start wondering about what it's going to be like when she talks.

I've been thinking in terms of what her first word is going to be. But that's not really the miracle. I was talking to a friend named Bill Brashler, who has a three-year-old son.

"The thing that kills you is when they say something and you wonder, 'Where did that come from?' " Bill said. "Like the other day, my son looked up at me and said, 'Don't be so stingy, Dad.' I laughed, but the point is . . . where did he get that? Where did that idea come from?"

Bill said that's the most fascinating thing about a child talking; not the individual words themselves, but the wonder of actually hearing your baby's ideas out loud. "The other day he said, 'I want to go in my room for some privacy,' " Bill said. "Do you understand what it's like to hear your child say that? Think of your daughter saying that."

I did. I can't imagine it.

The medication seems to be working a little. She still grunts; she still cries. But it's noticeably less frequent.

November 10

At times it seems like every day there's something new. That's one of the reasons I'm glad I'm keeping track; I think if I was just trying to store all this in my memory, I'd forget the details of how it has come about.

Today it's kissing. Whenever I go by Amanda, I kiss the air a couple of times. Just a little signal to her. I never knew she even noticed.

Tonight I came home from work, and I walked by her carriage and, as usual, I did it.

And . . . she kissed back.

They weren't real kisses; they were little clicking-clucking sounds she made in her mouth. But they were in response to what I did.

So I stood there. I kissed the air again. She smiled up and made her kissing noises again.

I walked away and came back in five minutes. I kissed the air.

She did it again.

"How long has this been going on?" I said to Susan.

"She just started this afternoon," Susan said. "I never heard her do it before."

"Do you think she's really trying to imitate what I do?" I said.

"I guess so," Susan said. "What else could it be?"

November 11

My parents went to New York for their anniversary, and I found my reaction rather instructive.

They were going to New York together before I was born; they used to go to see the Broadway shows, and when I was a child they would tell me stories about what Manhattan was like. I suppose my image of New York was formed by them as much as it was by movies and television.

Now, though, I am the one who is traveling to New York frequently. There's no getting around it: it can be a mean and unfriendly city, and there's an undeniable feeling of nascent danger when you're walking the streets. I generally have a good time there; nevertheless, I never have trouble reminding myself that I'm not in the Midwest.

My parents, of course, live in the Midwest; they have lived in Columbus since I was born. They are sophisticated people. Nevertheless, knowing that they were in New York, I found myself feeling a little concerned. They are in their sixties now;

they are not the same people they were thirty years ago, and New York is definitely not the same city it was thirty years ago.

So during their three days in New York, I found myself making excuses to call their hotel and check in with them. I always had what sounded like a legitimate reason to do it; but I called at least once a day, and I knew that my real reason was just to see that they were okay.

I didn't like the idea of them wandering around New York with no one to keep track of them. And—as I was calling them on the last day of their trip—it occurred to me that I finally am at that mysterious point we're all supposed to arrive at eventually: the point where a person is responsible for all the people around him. Every day I feel responsible for Amanda; I'm getting used to that. But for most of my life I have assumed that there are people who will look after me, too: my parents.

Their New York trip made me understand that finally this has changed, too. It wasn't so long ago that they would check up on me if I was on a distant trip. Now it would never occur to them. I don't know what they were thinking when their hotel room phone rang once again, and it was me; but I know that I was able to go to sleep much easier knowing that I had called, and that they were all right.

November 12

She has her orthopedic shoes.

They're white, with holes where the toes should be. She really only needs the one for her left foot. But the doctor said that we should have her wear both so that she doesn't look lopsided when she goes out.

She doesn't wear socks with them; they're designed to be worn right over the feet part of her jumpsuits. "These are awful," Susan said as the shoe salesman was fitting them on

Amanda's feet. He just smiled and patted her hand and gave Amanda a red helium balloon.

They aren't, in fact, that awful. They just make Amanda seem a little less baby-like. It isn't so much that they're orthopedic shoes; it's that they are shoes at all. She hasn't had any reason to wear shoes yet, because she can't walk or stand up by herself. Now, suddenly, twenty-four hours a day, there are these white leather things on her feet.

She doesn't seem to mind them. She smiles and plays just as much (and grunts and cries, too; that still hasn't completely stopped). The only real difference I can see is that she had begun to reach down and grab at her feet and play with them; she doesn't do that with the shoes on. Maybe she'll get used to them.

I can tell that the shoes bother Susan a lot. They're just a visible sign that everything isn't totally perfect with Amanda; and somehow their presence takes away some of the softness of looking at her, while emphasizing how innocent she truly is. She looks at us, and the orthopedic shoes disrupt the picture.

I tell Susan not to worry about it. I call Amanda's shoes her "orthos," and say that in a few days we won't even notice they're there.

But the fact is, I don't exactly love them, either.

November 13

SUSAN's mother came through town today. I got home from work, and she was holding Amanda.

"She's getting so big," Mrs. Koebel said.

The first thing I thought was that she was holding Amanda wrong. She seemed to be gripping her more tightly than I did, and I thought that when she stood up to walk with her she did it too abruptly.

Then I remembered back to that first week, when I thought

that Mrs. Koebel was the only person in the world who knew how to hold a baby—and when I didn't have the self-confidence to hold Amanda myself for more than a few seconds at a time.

"Let me have her," I said. She handed Amanda to me.

"My, you are getting good at that," Mrs. Koebel said.

I suppose she holds Amanda all right.

The medicine apparently has done its job. The grunting and crying seem to be over.

November 14

Every night when I get home I lie on the bed and try to teach her to stand up.

I hold her under her arms and lift her up so the bottoms of her feet rest on my chest. Then I loosen my grip. If I were to let go completely, she would fall; but when she senses that she's safe, she attempts to stand on her own.

I can actually feel the strength in her legs. She flexes them; when they are weak she exerts a little extra energy, and she straightens up again. She loves doing this; she laughs the whole time, as if it's a wonderful new game.

The orthos help; the bottoms of the shoes give her a flat surface on which to balance. When she's upright she almost seems to be a different person. I look at her trying to stand that way, and I can imagine the time when she'll be walking around and discovering things for herself.

This is one of the best parts of the day for me. I know I can't spend as much time with her as Susan does. But somehow this makes me feel useful. Here is something that belongs just to Amanda and me.

November 15

THE receptionist at the *Tribune* called my office and said I had a visitor. The visitor came in; she was a young woman who was in the Navy. She was in full uniform.

She said that she had grown up in southern California, where, as a high school girl, she had read my column in her hometown paper. Following graduation she had joined the Navy, and was currently assigned to the Great Lakes base, near Chicago. So she had come downtown to introduce herself.

Now I think it's fine for women to be in the service. But the fact is, most women don't even consider doing it. And as we sat and talked, I wondered what a parent does when his daughter comes home one evening and announces that she has decided to join the Navy. Or to do something equally unusual.

Because I guess the chances are good that such a thing might happen to me one day. All of this time we are spending with Amanda is going to count for nothing once she grows up and decides she knows what is best for her.

"What did your dad say when you said you were going to be in the Navy?" I said to this young woman.

"He hated the idea," she said. "He said that was the kind of thing that dykes did. But my mom was very supportive, and I think that by now even my dad is secretly proud."

We talked for about an hour, and I showed her around the paper. Then she left to go back to her barracks.

I went home.

"Amanda, you're never going to go to the barracks, are you?" I said.

She smiled and kicked the floor.

November 16

I WAS in an apartment building, riding upstairs in an elevator. There was a woman aboard with a baby in a carriage; there were also two or three other people.

"Oh, she's looking so beautiful!" one of the other riders said to the mother.

"Thank you," the mother said.

"Hi, darling!" another passenger said. "How are you, darling?"

"Can you say 'fine' to the lady?" the mother said to her child.

The mother and daughter got off at their floor. The elevator door closed.

The woman who had said the baby was beautiful spoke:

"That's the worst baby I've ever seen. I've never seen a child so spoiled and ill-behaved around this building."

The woman who had called the baby "darling" spoke:

"I know. The child is a devil. I don't understand why her parents can't do anything about her."

They were still talking when I got off the elevator. I called home and told Susan to watch Amanda's behavior in public.

November 17

SHE'S getting really good at scooting around on her back. She will be on the vinyl cloth on the living room floor, and in a matter of seconds she will propel herself all the way across it. I'll pick her up and put her in the middle; she will squeal and start kicking her legs again, and there she'll go.

I hadn't been expecting this. I thought all babies learned to move by crawling on their stomachs first. Still none of that; it's as if she thinks zipping along on her back is the most natural thing in the world.

Today she left the Snugli.

Susan broke out the stroller we had bought when she was born. She dressed Amanda in her winter clothes and put her in the seat. She fastened a restraining belt across Amanda's middle.

She had started looking sort of big in the Snugli, but all of a sudden she looked tiny again in the stroller. She can't really sit up straight by herself; so she kind of slumped in the seat and looked around her.

"This is it, then?" I said.

"She's really big enough," Susan said. "I'll still use the Snugli once in a while. But it's time that she learns to ride in this."

They headed toward the door, and their walk. I stood and looked at them.

Susan turned around. "I know you liked the Snugli," she said. "But Amanda's getting too heavy for it. It may look cute to you, but my back is starting to kill me."

November 18

ONE of those magic moments. She was on her back on the vinyl cloth in the living room; I came into the room.

I knelt down on the other side of the cloth. Her head was facing me; she looked backwards and I could tell I was in her field of vision.

"Come here, Amanda," I said.

And she did it. She started kicking like crazy, her orthos thudding against the floor, and she laughed and pushed herself and she zipped right across the vinyl until she bumped into me.

I thought it had to be a coincidence. So I picked her up and carried her to the other side again. Then I went back to where I had been. She tilted her head backwards again and looked at me.

"Come over here to me," I said.

And out came her high-pitched scream and her giggles, and she pushed herself over to me again. I picked her up and she looked as proud as if she had just won the seventh game of the World Series.

November 19

HELEN is turning out to be a bit of a surprise. She was a real worry to us in the months before Amanda was born; she had always been such a rotten, mean cat in the presence of other people that we assumed she was going to be a major problem with a baby in the house.

As we've learned, of course, that hasn't been the case. Mostly she's ignored Amanda and kept to herself. But in the last few days, something new has developed.

Helen will walk up to within a few feet of wherever Amanda is, and she will stand sentry. There's no other way to describe it. She has become Amanda's protector. I don't know what Helen's worrying about; Susan and I have been doing all right in looking out for Amanda. But now Helen wants in the act.

Tonight she was doing it again: just sitting there, looking around the room, making sure that no harm came to the baby.

"I think we've got a guard cat," Susan said.

I think it's a case of if you can't beat 'em, join 'em.

Every morning as I go off to work, Amanda is eating solid food. Usually it's oatmeal with some sort of strained fruit on top of it: peaches, prunes, bananas.

She seems to like the sweet taste of the fruit. And the effect is showing; when she's in her diapers, I can see that she's getting bigger. It's no wonder she does so well when I try to teach her to stand up; there's more of her there.

Eating and sleeping are still the main things she does while I'm at work. But in a way, the eating part is *her* work. She has to do it to grow up; just as my full-time job is done in order to make a living, her full-time job is done in order to gain weight and strength.

"What is it today, Amanda?" I said this morning. "Bananas?"

Someday she'll be able to answer. Today the answer was clearly visible on the front of her jumpsuit.

November 20

SOMETIMES the smallest things almost break my heart.

When she is startled, she smiles. There will be a sudden noise from outside; or I will walk into the room unexpectedly; or the phone will ring.

And she will turn her head toward the direction of the intrusion, and her immediate instinct will be to grin that toothless grin. It is as if she believes that whatever comes into her world, it is bound to be pleasant and happy. It does not occur to her that anything might harm her; every signal she has received so far has told her that whatever happens will be good.

And of course that will not always be so. The day will come when she learns to be wary; when she learns not to trust anything she does not know. I think about that when I see her jerk her head and smile; I make myself pay attention, for soon enough she will have changed.

I thought it was just me noticing this. But tonight Susan was staring at Amanda as she laughed; Susan said, "It's so sad.

She's eventually going to have to learn that the world can be awful."

I guess that's right. But for now, we can watch her face light up.

November 21

UH-OH.

Let the record show that at 7:21 p.m. on this date, Susan said it for the first time:

"Would you ever want to have another baby?"

November 22

THAT was too flippant yesterday. I know the reason that Susan brought it up. Every day, as Amanda grows, we are losing something. She becomes more of a person; but she becomes less of a baby.

And Susan must already be wondering what it will be like when Amanda's baby days truly are behind her forever. Less than six months ago we could not comprehend what it would be like to have a baby in the house; now, it seems, Susan does not want to think about what it will be like not to have a baby with us. Surely there are more wonders in store when a baby becomes a young girl, and then a young woman; but can it ever match this?

We certainly don't know. But from Susan's question it's obvious she has been thinking about it. I dodged the question last night; it's not that I don't want to talk about it, but I really have no opinion that's worth anything. Right now

Amanda fills the house, and my life, to bursting; right now I want to keep on thinking about Amanda.

I got a call from an old friend. He said that someone we had known well in high school had just had a heart attack, and was in the hospital.

The man in question was a year behind us in school. That makes him thirty-four now. This is a first for me. I have never known anyone younger than me who had a heart attack.

It scares me terribly. Before Amanda was born, I always had a kind of romantic notion about my own mortality. It just didn't matter that much to me. If I lived well, the length of my life was not that important a factor. I used to joke about it; I said that I was a believer in the Elvis Presley Theory of a Normal Human Life Span: forty-two and out.

Now, though, I wonder about the pace at which I live: too much food eaten too quickly, not enough exercise, high-pressured city existence. I don't want the romantic notion anymore. Susan and Amanda need me to be around. I think about the old acquaintance lying in his hospital bed. I can't imagine him at thirty-four. When I think about him, it is as a junior in high school.

That's my main problem. When I think about myself it's as a junior in high school, too. It's time to stop.

November 23

I'M afraid she really is becoming something of a mama's girl.

She has learned that if she cries, Susan will pick her up. Susan has spent so much time with her that Amanda is not happy unless she is in Susan's arms. And Susan has rushed to her so often that Amanda knows how to get her attention.

So if Susan puts her in her crib too early; if she leaves her to play on the living room floor; even if she puts her down with me and walks out of the room; Amanda will start crying.

It's different from a cry of pain. We know what that sounds like. This is just her way to make Susan come running. And Susan does it every time; even though we know Amanda is okay, neither of us can bear to hear her crying.

So tonight Susan was going to go into the kitchen to make my dinner. "Just watch her for a minute," she said, and put Amanda next to me on the bed.

Amanda took one look at me and decided she would rather be with Susan. And the wailing began.

Susan rushed back. "She's doing this on purpose," I said. "She knows what it takes to get you."

"I know," Susan said. But she picked her up and started carrying her toward the kitchen anyway.

"It's easier if I just take her," she called.

Maybe. But I have a feeling this could very easily get out of hand.

Susan and Amanda had gone out for a walk. I wandered into the living room.

I spotted something on the couch and went over to see what it was. It was one of Amanda's orthos—her tiny white left shoe with the hole where the toe should be. Apparently Susan had forgotten to put it back on her after she had changed her.

I picked it up and just stared at it. It fit in the palm of my hand. The moisture from Amanda's foot had made the writing inside start to fade away. I don't know why, but my eyes started to tear up and I found it hard to swallow. Just her shoe can do that to me.

November 24

I was doing an interview in Hamburger Hamlet tonight. At the table across from mine, a young couple was sitting with their baby. The little boy seemed to be a few months older than Amanda.

His whole face was wet from his slobbering. His mother was helping him drink a bottle of formula. He was half-sitting, half-lying in a high chair; every once in a while he would kick against the chair, and the sound would echo through the restaurant.

I watched him; I watched his parents try to eat their meal while continuing to pay attention to him every moment. It made me feel not quite so alone. Obviously, all over the country, uncounted thousands of young parents are going through the same things we go through every day, observing for the first time the same things we are observing.

When you're in the middle of it, it's so private; you feel you are isolated in your own little universe, facing problems no one has ever dealt with before. But of course that's not true; we're all out here—we just don't get to see each other very often.

The baby boy started to cry and his mother picked him up. I saw her reach for her blouse and then look her husband in the eye; the unspoken question was whether it would be appropriate for her to nurse in the middle of Hamburger Hamlet. There wasn't much I could do to help him stop crying, but at least I didn't have to add to their discomfort. I looked away, and hoped that everyone else in the restaurant would, too.

November 25

HER first Thanksgiving.

All week long Susan went back and forth, trying to decide whether to call Dr. Scheinberg with the big question. He had said it was all right to give Amanda fruit and strained *meat*; but he hadn't said anything about poultry, and Susan wanted to know whether it was okay to give Amanda strained turkey on Thanksgiving.

She didn't call him. He's a nice man, but she thought she might be testing his patience with a question like that. So she made a big Thanksgiving dinner for us, and Amanda had her usual milk and oatmeal and peaches.

Susan pointed out that our Thanksgiving turkey weighed almost exactly the same as Amanda; we looked at her and laughed about that. While Susan was cooking the dinner I went into the bedroom and read a book. From the kitchen, I heard Susan talking to Amanda as she got things ready.

And I realized: that's the difference, right there. Before Amanda, when I was home and Susan was in a different part of the apartment, there was silence. No longer. I read my book, and in the background I could listen to Susan trying to explain to Amanda why people eat turkey on this day. Amanda couldn't understand a word, of course, but it didn't matter. It was a joyful noise. And a nice Thanksgiving.

November 26

ANOTHER baby visited Amanda today.

Some friends from New York were in town, and they came down with their daughter Pamela, who is just a few months older than Amanda.

We sat around talking about the wonders of having your first child. I looked down on the living room floor; there were Amanda and Pamela, exploring each other.

Pamela was the aggressor; she can crawl easily and is starting to learn how to walk, and Amanda still can't do any of that yet. So their daughter moved around Amanda, just staring and checking things out. The two girls were very aware of each other.

They started to touch one another. First Pamela put her hand on top of Amanda's head; then Amanda reached out and poked Pamela's cheek; then Pamela put a hand on Amanda's shoulder. It was clear that they realized they were different from the rest of us; I don't know if they knew they were both "babies," but they instinctively knew that whatever the parents were, it was something separate from what they were.

We all stopped talking and watched them. Their eyes were locked on each other. It was the first time I had really thought of Amanda as part of a generation of babies. The other night in the restaurant it had occurred to me that there were parents all over America going through the same sets of experiences; but now, with Amanda and the other baby tentatively touching and exploring each other, I recognized that long after we are all gone, this new generation of babies will still be around, dealing with a world that is theirs. Each day they will interact with the other people in that world; some they will like, some they will hate. Dealing with others will be a normal part of living for them. Today I saw Amanda do it for the first time.

November 27

As usual we were awakened this morning by Amanda's first cries of the new day. And as usual Susan went into her room, turned on the lamp with the soft bulb, and said, "Well, what's this? Are you awake, pumpkin? Do you think you're still asleep? Ahhh, come here."

And then she picked her up and carried her to our bed, where we both spoke to Amanda and held her hand and eased her into wakefulness.

There are probably some lousy aspects to being a baby—since babies can't discuss them, we'll never know what they like the least—but I have to envy Amanda for the way she gets to wake up after every sleep. The pampering, the soothing, the gentleness—there can't be a better way to reaffirm your existence every day.

With the rest of us it's alarm clocks and ringing telephones and hurried breakfasts and appointments that must be kept. With Amanda it's as if she is being welcomed into the world anew with each new time she awakens. It's automatic; when she wakes up she is made to feel she is returning to a place where she is the most welcome, loved person who ever lived. Which in a sense, I guess, is the truth.

November 28

"Amanda!" Susan yelled.

She hurried from the couch and to Amanda's side. Amanda was on the floor, on the vinyl cloth.

Susan reached into Amanda's clenched fist and came out with a paper clip.

"Five more seconds and she would have eaten it," Susan said. "We just have to be more careful with what we leave around."

November 29

Sometimes, when I'm thinking what things will be like for Amanda in the future, I wonder how she will react the first time someone lets her down.

Because that's the thing right now: it hasn't happened to her yet. Virtually every waking act of hers is based on trust. The feeding; the changing of her diapers when she's wet; the hands that are there to catch her when she tries to remain in a sitting position; the rushing to her crib whenever she cries; she has come to accept all of it because she can trust us.

For all the meanness in the world, it's a pretty amazing thing that babies get by mainly on that trust—and that, for the most part, they aren't trusting in vain. This is the part of their lives when they have no self-reliance at all. Somehow, for some reason, adults who might choose to take the easy way out in almost any other circumstances come through when it's the baby who is at stake.

Tonight she spat up some milk; in a matter of seconds Susan had come over with a diaper to wipe it off, and Amanda was clean and happy once again. She may not even know that she's so trusting. I suppose the only way a child finds that out is when her trust finally goes awry.

November 30

"I USED to take you for walks in this when you were a tiny baby," Susan said.

She was carrying Amanda and walking past the carriage. In recent days, Amanda has been going out in the stroller, in which she can try to sit up.

So today Susan strapped her into the stroller, and they went out the door. The carriage stayed behind.

". . . when you were a tiny, tiny baby." She's still a tiny baby, of course; but it's clear that we have reached some sort of plateau. Not only is Amanda an accepted part of our lives now; she has a history with us. Susan can look back to a time in our past, and Amanda is a part of that time.

Granted, it's part of the very recent past; but there is something comforting in knowing that we no longer must reflect backwards and find only a world without Amanda. Now she has become included in those reflections; she is included in our memories.

December 1

WE talk to her all the time.

Susan will be watching television, and she will say, "This is a *silly* show, Amanda. Don't you think this is a silly show?"

I will come home at the end of the day, and I will say, "Well! Amanda Sue Greene! What have you been doing all day?"

She will be on her back, waving her legs and scooting off the vinyl cloth, and I will say, "Careful, Amanda, you're going to run right into the table."

In a way, this all seems useless; it gives us the illusion that she is a full partner in the household and should be included in our conversations, but we know that we make no sense to her at all.

On the other hand . . . I keep thinking that all of these words are going to her brain, and that something must be happening there. It's not happening yet; but of all the words we speak to her, some of them must be sticking. Maybe very few; maybe only one in a thousand.

When she does learn to talk, though, it will be because of these nonstop, one-way conversations we have with her. One of these days the flow of words from us to her is going to stop just long enough for her to return one. Some of these words are going to stay with her; we'll know which ones when it's time for her to give some back.

December 2

MOST of the time I tell myself that this isn't really changing my life. It's new, and it's fascinating, and it's something I've never done before; but I tell myself that I'm still the same person I always was, and that this is just a new aspect to things.

Other times that all seems like a delusion.

Tonight, for example. I have always been a person who likes to stay out at night. If I'm having a good time, and the company is enjoyable, I have few compunctions about calling home and saying I will be late.

Tonight I was, indeed, having a good time and the company was, indeed, enjoyable. And I was home by eight o'clock.

The lure just isn't there anymore. Whatever it is about being out on the town, it just can't compete. I'll look at my watch and start making excuses, and the next thing you know I'll be in the back seat of a cab heading home.

This is from a guy who used to think nothing of walking in the door at 4 a.m. Now, it doesn't seem to matter what's out there. When I take my coat off and hear Amanda squeezing her orange Mr. Pig, I know that I'm exactly where I'm supposed to be.

This is all subject to revision.

December 3

MORE and more, when I stand her up, she is starting to really try to stay up there.

Just a week or so ago, when I would lie down and hold her up with her feet resting on my chest, she would attempt to balance, and she would flex her legs, but that was about it. The desire was there, and the growing strength—but she didn't know quite what to do with it all.

Now she's figuring it out. I'll put her in place, and she will dig her toes into my chest. Sometimes she does it so hard that it hurts. She seems to sense that if she tries hard enough, one of these days she'll be able to stay up without my hands under her arms. She scrunches her face up and points those toes and *digs in.*

I don't know how much longer we should let Amanda keep coming into our bed.

It's part of our morning routine. When she wakes up Susan goes into her room to get her, and brings her back to our bed. She feeds her there; then Amanda fades back to sleep. When she wakes up again we talk to her and play with her; then Susan and she go out to the living room.

I've read that it's unhealthy for a baby to get used to being in bed with the parents; the baby starts mistaking the parents' bed for her own, and before you know it she doesn't want to sleep alone.

I asked Susan if she thought we ought to quit bringing her in.

"Of course not," she said. "She's still too young for it to matter. There's a difference between letting her sleep in the bed, and bringing her in in the morning."

"But she does go to sleep when she's in here," I said.

"If you think I'm going to get up at six o'clock in the morning and sit in a chair with her when I can bring her back to bed. . . ," Susan said.

She's probably right that it's too early in Amanda's life to make a real difference.

But when does the difference start? Do you find out on the morning that your baby cries and screams because you want her to go back to her own bed?

I don't know what I'm worrying about; I suppose I'll find out soon enough.

December 4

AMANDA still doesn't have a clue about crawling.

She continues to do her rocking horse imitation. She'll be on her stomach, and she'll lift her legs and her arms, and she'll exert herself. But the only thing that will happen is that she will rock back and forth on her stomach.

"No, Amanda," I said tonight. I got down next to her on the vinyl cloth and I started to crawl.

"Follow me," I said. I moved in front of her and started crawling forward. In a few seconds I looked back to see if she was imitating; she was just rocking like crazy on her stomach.

"Let's try it again," I said.

"That's okay, honey," Susan said to Amanda. "You do it your way." And as I crawled across the living room, Susan patted Amanda's rocking head.

This detente with Helen might be in danger.

Tonight Helen was standing guard over Amanda as usual. Amanda looked up, smiled, reached out, and grabbed a handful of fur from Helen's side.

Helen raised a paw and calmly swiped it at Amanda.

That may be more ominous than it sounds.

December 5

I WILL be quite happy when the ortho period is over. Today Susan took Amanda into a very fancy clothing store. The salesman looked down at the white orthos on Amanda's feet and said, "Oh, I know what those are. Those are Lithuanian peasant shoes!"

Her sleeping patterns are simply not like anything we have read in any book. We read that all babies her age are supposed to take morning naps; Amanda never takes a morning nap. We read that they are supposed to sleep away much of the afternoon; Amanda drifts off for a few hours at most. We read that they are supposed to go down for the night early in the evening; often Amanda stays up later than we would normally want to. We read that once they go to sleep for the night, they stay asleep until morning; as often as not, she's up several times during the night.

Her health seems to be fine. But this variance from what the books tell us is disconcerting. The books are great when your baby is doing what they say she should be doing. When she isn't, you wonder whether something is wrong.

December 6

She may not be able to crawl—if you define crawling as what a baby does when her stomach is toward the ground—but she keeps getting better and better at scooting along on her back.

"Tell your daddy where you scooted this morning," Susan said when I got home from work. Amanda flashed me the usual toothless grin.

"You scooted all the way past the wastebasket over to the air-conditioning vent," Susan said.

The limits and delineations of her world are confined to such a small area; I can't imagine it will be as comforting when Amanda's world becomes the real world.

A trip to Dr. Scheinberg's today. She is twenty-five and a half inches long; she weighs thirteen pounds, five ounces. Slowly, it's happening.

December 7

We had our first snowfall of the year tonight. I put Amanda over by a big window that extends all the way down to the floor. She peered out at the heavy, wet flakes floating down to the ground. It would be nice to say that she was enchanted, but that's not quite it. She was befuddled.

She stared and stared, and there was a look on her face of pure puzzlement. What were those things? She has been looking at things for almost six months now, and nothing before even vaguely resembled this.

I knelt down and watched with her. That's one of the nicest things about this: it lets you remember what so many things were like the first time.

December 8

TODAY a would-be terrorist drove a truck up next to the Washington Monument, said the truck was filled with explosives, and threatened to detonate the whole thing.

By the time I got home from work all three networks were on the air with live coverage. I sat on the floor in the living room and went from channel to channel, watching the drama.

Behind me, on the couch, Susan was nursing Amanda. I wasn't paying too much attention to them; I was going from anchorman to anchorman, trying to find the freshest developments.

So the room was filled with the somber sounds of the voices of broadcast journalists. And behind me I heard Susan talking to Amanda:

"Hey, look at the TV! We're going to get to see an explosion!

"An explosion, Amanda! Keep watching! An explosion!"

I didn't say anything at the time. But when the drama was over, and law enforcement officials had shot the terrorist dead, I gently tried to talk to Susan about the distorted reality that Amanda seems to have brought to her life. A guy is trying to blow up the Washington Monument; that translates now, in our household, to a pretty picture for Amanda to see.

I endeavored to be as tactful as possible about it. It didn't work.

"You try staying with her all day long," Susan said.

And then, in a second, she was back to her happy voice, talking to the baby.

"Okay, pumpkin, let's start winding our day down. Are we getting ready for bed?"

I probably shouldn't have said anything.

December 9

SUSAN burst into tears tonight. She had been trying to get Amanda to fall asleep for hours. Each time she put her in her crib, Amanda started wailing a few minutes later.

"I just can't take this!" Susan finally screamed. "She won't sleep!" And she began to sob.

I think she was prepared for it to be hectic the first few months. But Amanda will be six months old the day after tomorrow; I think that Susan was planning on having a perfect, placid baby by now. Amanda wailed, and I picked her up and held her, but she didn't want me; she wanted her mother.

"I'm here, sweetheart," Susan said, taking her from me. "Don't cry."

I stood there and watched.

December 10

I HAD to fly to Cincinnati today to make a speech. When the offer came in, I thought about it. Speaking engagements are a good way to pick up some extra money; but are they worth being away from home for yet another night?

I talked to Susan about it, and we decided that it was such an easy trip—in on Friday afternoon, speak on Friday night, back on Saturday morning—that it didn't make much sense to say no.

So here I am. The event was an annual dinner meeting of the Ohio Prosecuting Attorneys Association. There were about two hundred people in the audience. After we finished the meal I was introduced, and I stood up to begin my talk. From the back of the room I could hear a baby crying; I looked back there, and I could see that the baby's mother and father were sitting together at one of the tables.

To make sure the baby's crying didn't disrupt the speech, the mother carried the infant out of the room. I talked for about forty-five minutes, went briefly to a reception, then rode the elevator to my room to go to bed.

Lying awake trying to go to sleep, I thought to myself: that baby's father is out with his wife and his child on this Friday night, sharing the evening. I'm on the road at the Westin Hotel, by myself. What makes one person one way, and another completely different?

I called home. Susan said Amanda was crying again.

December 11

I FLEW home from Cincinnati. Today is Amanda's six-month birthday.

Susan was sitting on the couch with her. As I walked in, I heard her saying:

"When you're a mother yourself, you'll call me on the telephone. You'll say, 'Mom, I don't know what to do. My baby is crying and crying, and she won't go to sleep. What can I do?'

"And I'll say, 'Don't worry, Amanda. Some babies don't sleep as much as others do.'

"And then you'll start crying and you'll say, 'But Mom, she won't sleep at all.' And I'll say, 'I'm glad you have a cute baby, Amanda, but some babies just don't sleep.'"

"Hi, I'm home," I called.

December 12

WE were invited to Neil and Linda Weiner's home for Sunday brunch. The Weiners are the couple we became friendly with during Lamaze class; Linda and their new baby had been over to see Susan and Amanda once, but we had not all been together since the babies had been born.

It was interesting; at Lamaze class we had been four nervous, uptight people, not having the vaguest idea of what lay ahead of us. Now there were six; I held Amanda and Neil held Sharon, and the babies made exploratory gestures at one another, and everything seemed a lot calmer than it had back then.

As the afternoon wore on, I noticed an unfamiliar emotion in myself. Sharon is about a month older than Amanda, but she is clearly more than one month more "advanced." She's crawling like a turtle, and she's grabbing the sides of tables and pulling herself into a standing position—things that are clearly way beyond Amanda right now.

And I found myself feeling competitive. I wanted Amanda to be as far along as the other baby. No matter that there is a wide range within which babies are considered "normal"; no matter that none of this has any application at all toward what the girls will be like when they are older.

The fact is, Susan and I have been telling ourselves that Amanda is extremely bright and advanced. Today we found out that at least this one baby is more than Amanda's match in the precociousness department. As Amanda lay on the floor watching, and Sharon crawled briskly across the room and finessed herself into a standing position, I could just watch and be surprised at what I was feeling. I wanted Amanda to be doing better.

Something tells me that this may not be the perfect attitude.

December 13

AND then there are times when nothing could seem to be better.

After Susan changes Amanda's diapers, she always rubs some moisturizing cream into her own hands. Today she had just finished with Amanda, and was rubbing her hands together to soak in the cream.

Amanda started laughing like crazy. She looked at Susan, and she held up her own hands. It seemed to be obvious what she wanted.

So Susan put a little drop of cream on each of Amanda's palms. And Amanda, still laughing, began to rub *her* hands together, too.

I wonder if Sharon Weiner can do that?

December 14

MY mother came in to visit for a couple of days, which has given Susan a little moral support. It's one thing for me to be around; it's another to have someone who has been through all of this before.

So as Amanda continued her nonstop crying, my mom assured Susan that she isn't the first mother who has had to deal with this dilemma. She said that when my younger brother Tim was a baby, he cried even worse than Amanda.

"It would be the middle of the night," my mother said, "and I would hear Timmy crying in his room. And I was so exhausted, and I knew there was nothing I could do to make him stop. But I couldn't just stay in bed.

"So I would walk down the hallway to his room, and I would sit down on the floor outside his door and I would cry, too. If someone was listening they could hear the two of us crying."

As much potential comfort as that kind of story might bring to Susan, it wears off pretty quickly when she realizes she's back to the present. Amanda was crying, and my mother tried to give her a bottle, and that only made her cry more.

"Maybe she's not hungry," my mother said.

But when Susan offered her the same bottle, she took it and gobbled the formula down.

December 15

THREE more months of the orthos. At least.

Susan took Amanda to the orthopedist today to have her foot checked. We'd been hoping that he'd say Amanda was making great progress, and that she wouldn't have to wear them anymore.

He said she was making progress. And to keep them on until her next appointment, in March.

I think when I remember back to these times, it will be the little things that stand out.

Tonight Amanda was sleeping in Susan's arms, and she whispered to me that she wanted me to get her a red plastic case that held some tiny scissors. I did.

She took the scissors out and started to cut Amanda's fingernails. I asked her why she was doing it right now.

"It's the only time I can do it," she whispered. "If she's awake, she jerks her hands away. I have to do it when she's sleeping."

And Amanda snoozed away as Susan carefully moved the scissors from finger to finger.

* * *

Amanda had kicked one of her orthos off today, and was trying to eat it.

"She puts everything into her mouth," Susan said.

My mother said that was to be expected. She said my sister Debby used to do worse than that.

"One day I found her on the porch eating a dead fly," my mom said.

She sounded almost wistful as she said it.

December 16

WELL, I guess I'm going to have to stop referring to Amanda's "toothless grin" pretty soon.

Just before my mother left for home, she said she thought she had figured out why Amanda has been crying and fussing so much lately.

She said that she had stuck her finger in Amanda's mouth, and had felt a tooth beginning to jab through her lower gums. "It makes sense," she said. "If she's starting to teethe, that explains why she's been giving you so much trouble."

We tried to look inside Amanda's mouth to see the tooth, but she wasn't having any of it. Every time we would try to pull her mouth open she would twist her head to one side or the other; she didn't want us doing it.

She would let us stick our fingers in her mouth, though, and my mother was right. Right in the center of her lower gums, it felt almost like a tiny pin was sticking through.

"I wonder why we didn't think of that?" Susan said.

December 17

NOW that we know she's got a tooth coming in, her behavior is making much more sense. She's not just crying; she's drooling, too, and scrunching up her mouth.

It's so clear what's been happening. She's been uncomfortable because she's felt the tooth pushing its way in. She moves her mouth around all the time, in a natural reaction to the foreign feeling.

Susan called Dr. Scheinberg and asked him what to do for it. He said that the best solution was to get out a bottle of bourbon or a bottle of Scotch, then put a drop of the liquor on our fingertips. Rubbing it over the spot where the tooth was emerging, he said, should make Amanda feel better.

We did it, and it didn't seem to help. I told Susan I didn't think she should use that method anymore; I said we should ask the pharmacist if he had anything to suggest.

"What is it?" Susan said. "Are you afraid that using the liquor is going to turn her into an alcoholic?"

"I hadn't thought of it," I said, "although now that you mention it, it isn't such a ridiculous idea."

"Then why won't you do what Dr. Scheinberg said?" she asked.

"Because I just leaned down to kiss her, and I don't like the smell of whiskey on her breath," I said.

December 18

I FLEW down to Florida today to interview Ingemar Johansson, the former heavyweight boxing champion, for *Esquire*.

I spent part of the day with him, and then wandered around

the area. I was in Pompano Beach; I was staying in the hotel part of the Palm-Aire health spa and country club development.

For all my bitching about being on the road, there is something about getting out of town that relaxes me and lets me think and put things in some sort of perspective. In a way it's almost a tonic for me. Tonight I had a few drinks and dinner, and then I walked out onto the Palm-Aire golf course.

Back north there were freezing temperatures and snowstorms. Here it was a balmy night, in the seventies. I sat on a bench along one of the fairways. A brilliant moon hovered directly above. The stars were sharply defined against the sky. I heard a noise down by my feet.

I looked down. A family of ducks, shaking off the water from a nearby pond, was walking directly past me.

December 19

Back home on a late-afternoon flight. Tonight Amanda was trying to crawl again; she still can't get it right, and still rocks on her stomach instead of moving forward.

"No, Amanda," I said. I was talking in a gentle, happy enough voice. "You're really terrible at that. You're not doing any good at all."

"You know, you've really got to stop doing that," Susan said. I could tell she was serious.

"Doing what?" I said.

"You're getting in a very bad habit of talking down to her and putting her down," Susan said. "I know you're only kidding and that you don't intend to be mean, but who knows when she can start understanding what you're saying? It could be very bad for her self-image."

I tried to think of other things I had said to Amanda. When she spits up I guess I mention it, and when she makes nonsensical noises. But I have never said anything in an angry or even a mocking voice. I'm just kidding around. I pointed this out to Susan.

"I know," she said. "But I just wanted to bring it up now, because if you keep it up it could really be bad for her."

"I don't see how saying things like that is going to have any effect on a six-month-old baby who can't even understand words," I said.

"You're probably right," Susan said. "But we don't know when she *is* going to start figuring out what things mean, so I think it would be a good idea for you to stop saying stuff like that now."

"You're a great crawler," I said to Amanda, who was still rocking.

December 20

As much as Susan loves having Amanda with us, I can tell she is full of self-doubts about what it's doing to the person she used to be.

She was getting ready to go shopping with Amanda today; I was getting ready to go to work.

"The vacuum cleaner is back already!" she said. "I took it in yesterday to be fixed, and they had it back to me within twenty-four hours."

"Great," I said distractedly.

Susan sighed.

"I know I'm not the most interesting person in the world these days," she said. "But try to understand."

December 21

"NIGHTLINE" called last night. They needed me to fly east for some Washington duty. So here I am, Christmas week, in the Watergate Hotel. The place is virtually empty; no one with any sense is on the road at this time of year.

From my window, I can see Christmas lights across the way.

December 22

I DID a "Nightline" piece on deadline last night, four hours after arriving in Washington, and flew back home this morning. As always, even when I'm away for only a day, I noticed something about Amanda that seemed new to me.

Not only is she holding onto things now; she lifts them in front of her face, and turns them around, and *examines* them. Before it was mostly grasping—if something was within her reach she would clamp her hand around it, wave it in the air, and then drop it.

But genuine curiosity seems to be taking over. Tonight she had her orange Mr. Pig toy, and she was looking at it like a jeweler checking out a diamond. She looked at the front, she looked at the back, she looked at the sides—I have no idea what she thought she was seeing. But it meant more to her than simply something she could hold in her hand. She recognized it as an object that is somehow part of her world, and she seemed to be trying to understand what it might be.

December 23

SUSAN carried Amanda into the bedroom tonight and said to me, "It's a good thing I bought her her d-o-g when I did."

"Huh?" I said.

"I was at the toy store today, and they're all sold out," she said. "I'm glad I went shopping early."

"Shopping for what?" I said.

"I told you," Susan said. "Her d-o-g."

I began to understand. This will be Amanda's first Christmas, and Susan bought her a toy dog on rollers, designed for riding around the house. Amanda's still really too young for a toy like that, but she'll use it eventually.

"You don't have to spell it out," I said. "She's six months old. You can say 'dog.'"

"Shhhh!" Susan said, putting her hands over Amanda's ears and taking her out of the room.

December 24

AT this rate, she's going to have to keep wearing orthos forever. She has started to kick them off, all the time. She has figured out a way to press one foot against the top of the shoe on the other foot and push until the shoe comes off. It doesn't matter how securely they're tied; we put them on, and five minutes later we find them on the floor. And they aren't going to do her any good unless they're on her feet.

"Amanda, the one thing you were good at, you stopped being good at!" Susan said. Her voice was exasperated.

She was nursing Amanda, and Amanda was pulling away and refusing to eat.

"I can't believe it," Susan said to her. "You only knew how to do one thing right, and now you're not even doing that."

"Susan . . . ," I said. "Remember what you told me about not saying negative things to her?"

"When it's warranted you can say it," she said.

But she seemed to get the message, or at least consider it. A minute later Amanda wasn't eating any better, but Susan was saying to her in a gentle voice, "Do you think Santa Claus will be able to find you tonight? You weren't even here last year, so how will he find you? I wouldn't worry about it, though; Santa is very smart. . . ."

December 25

On her first Christmas the relatives all called; we held the telephone up to Amanda's ear and they talked to her. She knew something was going on; a quizzical expression came to her face, and she looked at Susan and me as if we could somehow explain it to her.

We gave her presents, including her d-o-g, which she seemed to enjoy. We made certain that we gave her something special: cloth books.

They're just what they sound like: short books printed on cloth. She has no idea what they are, of course; the only reason she likes them is that they feel soft in her hands, and they're colorful, and she can put them in her mouth.

Our theory is that there's a good chance they are good for her. If she can learn—even subliminally—that it's a positive thing to have books in the house, then it's a start. So many factors these days fight against a child's having any respect or reverence for reading; we figure that if we can signal to her, at this young age, that books are to be equated with pleasure, then maybe she'll continue to turn to them when she's old enough to really read them.

It was great to see her playing with her d-o-g on Christmas day. But it was even better to see her holding and examining her cloth books. Even though she did decide, after the examination, to try to eat them.

December 26

SHE wants to talk.

There's no doubt about it; there is enough urgency in the noises she makes that they are no longer just random sounds. We'll say something to her, and she will look straight at us and the noises will come pouring out.

They're still a long way from being words. But I listen carefully, and I can hear the distinct sounds forming. She is making "P" sounds and "F" sounds. I have no idea if she knows what she's doing; I can't imagine that she is really trying to say a word that starts with a "P" or an "F."

This has to be the beginning, though. I always imagined that one day a baby just popped out with a word—the first word. I'm finding out that the process starts way before that moment. I wonder whether it's frustrating for her, trying to say something and having nonsense emerge? Probably not; she may not even notice it.

But I sure do. I talk to her and our eyes lock and those sounds come tumbling out, one after another.

December 27

SHE seems to have decided that she is proud of her tooth.

All of a sudden she isn't clamping her mouth shut anymore. Up until today if I tried to take a look in there, she would lock up her jaws and turn her head and squeal and try to get away from me. I had just about given up.

But today I was holding her—and she grinned and opened her mouth up all the way. I thought it was an accident, but it was almost as if she was daring me to peer inside. So I did—and there it was.

It's on the bottom, on the right side. I could just see it coming up through the gum. It's so tiny; it looks like the beginning of a flower sprout pushing out of the ground. I pulled her bottom lip down to see better, and she even allowed me to do that.

When I put my finger in her mouth to touch the tooth, she snapped shut on me. It was the oddest feeling—there was the wet softness of her upper and lower gums, and then this one little pinprick in the bottom of my finger. Not even like a mosquito biting me; milder than that. But Amanda seemed to think she was being fairly ferocious.

December 28

THERE was a picture in *Time* magazine of Prince William—the baby son of Prince Charles and Princess Diana. He was born at approximately the same time as Amanda.

For his six-months' birthday, his parents had invited news photographers to the palace. The purpose, of course, was to give the world some idea of what the royal baby looked like.

But as I glanced at the color photograph, what struck me was not Prince William, and was not his mother and father. What struck me was the toy lying by his side.

It was a circular plastic tube, with colorful plastic rings hanging from it. It was precisely the same toy that Amanda plays with all the time. The photo was sharp enough that I could tell it wasn't just approximately the same brand—it was the exact same toy.

I have no idea how Charles and Diana choose what William plays with—whether they have a nanny go out shopping, or whether toy manufacturers send free stuff to the palace, or whether they actually purchase some of the things themselves. But however they got those rings, it was clear that William was as taken with them as Amanda is. I guess it doesn't matter if you are the next ruler of Great Britain, and you have all the money in the world; when it comes to some things, you just have to trust Fisher-Price.

December 29

It seldom fails. I may have had a bad day at work; the column may not have gone well, or I may not have been able to reach the people I was trying to interview, or the computer system may have broken down and caused delays in writing on the video terminals.

But as soon as I walk in the front door and into the living room, Amanda sees me and starts screaming and laughing. You'd have thought I'd been gone for a month; Susan will be holding her, and Amanda will wriggle in her arms and let that high-pitched squeal out and flail her arms in my direction; if she could fly she'd fly over to me.

It makes me feel like I'm the Beatles getting off an airplane.

I still do miss out on some things when I'm gone during the day, though.

Tonight—after Amanda's tumultuous welcome—I sat down with her and started handing some of her toys to her. I picked one up and said, "Here's Miss Rabbit."

Susan looked at me as if I had forgotten her own name. "That's not called Miss Rabbit," she said. "That's Baby Bunny."

"What's the difference?" I said.

"Less formal," she said.

December 30

IT doesn't matter what else has happened during the day or evening. There is one thing that has become a ritual.

At the end of the night Susan will take Amanda out in the living room once more to feed her before putting her to bed. This always makes Amanda drowsy. And just before putting her in her crib for the night, Susan will bring her into the bedroom where I'm watching the news.

"Say goodnight to daddy," Susan will say.

Amanda will be too tired to be paying any attention; most of the time her eyes will be half closed. She will be in the blue "sleeping bag" that she wears over her jumpsuit to keep her warm.

Susan will reach over toward me, and I will kiss Amanda on one of her cheeks. "Sleep good," I'll say. "See you in the morning."

We've never talked about why we do this. I suppose there's a chance that Amanda wouldn't know the difference, at this age, if I said goodnight to her or I didn't.

But I think we both believe that it has to be doing something good for her. Whatever part of her brain is retaining anything knows this: the last thing that happens every day is that her mother feeds her and her father kisses her goodnight and says something to her in a soft voice.

It may not end up making her a better person, but it certainly can't make her a worse one.

December 31

I HAVE had some fairly degenerate New Year's Eves in my life; the nadir probably came nine years ago, when I was working as a performing member of the Alice Cooper rock and roll band, doing research for a book about what it's like on the other side of the footlights. As midnight struck that night, I stood on stage with the band and watched an arena full of drunken, doped-up teenagers in Buffalo, New York, try to climb over barricades and fight past security guards in an effort to get to us.

Oh, well. Things change. Tonight we got out pointed party hats and put them on; we put one on Amanda and pulled the elastic string underneath her chin so it would stay on. We gave her a toy horn to hold. And we took pictures of her first New Year's Eve celebration.

The excitement seemed to get to her; she dozed off earlier than usual, and we found ourselves, for once, with no finicky baby to deal with late at night. We planned to stay up to watch the various celebrations on television at midnight. We didn't make it; we were asleep by ten-thirty.

I wonder what Alice Cooper did tonight?

January 1

WELL. My. Today is the first day she was officially able to crawl.

We had some friends over to say Happy New Year. They were holding Amanda, passing her back and forth; she was more amenable to this than she usually is with strangers, but I could tell that she still wanted to get back to Susan.

One of our friends handed her to me, and I put her down on the floor to see if she wanted to play. And . . . there she went. She saw Susan sitting on the floor about ten yards away, and she decided she was going to go to her.

Mainly she pulled herself with her arms. Her knees were getting into the act, too, but the strength was coming from her shoulders and arms. This was different from when she used to lie on her back and scoot across the floor as if she were doing the backstroke on dry land; today her stomach was toward the floor, like babies' stomachs are supposed to be in regulation crawling, and she was moving toward a target she could see.

Susan started to come forward to get her.

"Don't," I said.

And Amanda kept inching forward. It took her a few minutes, but she made it to Susan's lap.

Our friends didn't seem to think it was all that amazing; they don't have kids, and I'm sure they assume that babies crawl all the time. So we tried to contain our enthusiasm until they left.

And then Amanda really went to town. I went into the kitchen to play a radio we have there; she heard it, and she crawled all the way from the living room into the kitchen. (Well, not precisely *into* the kitchen. When her hands hit the cold linoleum, she decided she liked the carpet better, so she turned around and crawled back.)

It's a great sight to see. Already she has taken to pursuing Helen around the living room; luckily Helen is much faster than Amanda, and can get away at will. Every time Amanda is ready to reach for Helen's tail, Helen merely moves a step or two away. This doesn't stop Amanda. She appears determined to catch that cat.

All of a sudden, in the space of a day, she seems much older.

January 2

She's really feeling her oats. It must be the crawling that has given her confidence; tonight she hit me with another trick that's completely new.

I was eating dinner at the table; Susan was sitting across from me holding Amanda.

I absentmindedly tapped my hand on the table.

Amanda, still in Susan's arms, reached out and hit the table in front of her.

I looked up. She was staring at me.

I hit the table again.

She reached out and slapped the table.

I didn't do anything.

She didn't do anything.

I hit the table.

She hit the table and laughed.

"Is this happening?" Susan said.

I hit the table—twice.

Amanda reached out and slapped the table twice.

"No," Susan said.

I reached out and slapped the table twice again.

Amanda hit it once.

"Twice, Amanda," I said.

She started to cry.

"That's enough for one day," Susan said. "You're confusing her."

"Hey, who started it?" I said.

January 3

SHE was fussy all day. It didn't make sense; she has been in a great mood lately—showing us her tooth, crawling, hitting the table. But today she reverted to her crying, screaming persona.

We didn't know if she might be getting sick, if she was tired, if she was hungry. And then, as she was screaming, Susan saw it.

"Look in her mouth," Susan said. "See if you see another tooth coming in."

I reached to open up Amanda's mouth. Now, though, she was like she had been when the first tooth had originally shown up. Her jaws were clamped together. She didn't want me looking in there.

"This doesn't make sense," I said. "The other day she loved me looking at her tooth."

I waited until she opened her mouth. Then I took a quick look inside.

There was definitely another tooth coming in. It was on the bottom, just next to the other one—on the left side. I could barely see the white pressing through the pink.

She started screaming some more. "Amanda, are you going to do this with every single tooth you get?" Susan said. I tried to look again, but Amanda yanked her head away.

January 4

This crawling is already starting to change the rules. Susan went out and got little clear plastic stick-on gadgets, to place on the corners of our tables and chests that are close to the ground. The idea is that if Amanda is crawling along, and she sticks up her head to look around, the plastic things will cushion the blow if she hits a table. So far we haven't had to test their effectiveness.

Now that Amanda is free to seek things out on her own, one of the first things we're learning is that she doesn't necessarily seek out the things she's supposed to. For example, that rocking dog we got her for Christmas sits right in the middle of the living room; it's such a great-looking dog that we expected Amanda to take off in its direction right away.

She takes off toward the dog, all right. But it's not the dog that intrigues her. It's the snake-like black cords from the living room drapery. The cords lie on the floor about five feet from the dog, and Amanda is fascinated with them. No matter where we put her on the floor, she goes after the cords. We went to three different stores before we found a dog we liked; the cords, we never even noticed were there before. But apparently Amanda has been noticing them all these months, and now she's rejoicing in the fact that she can have them whenever she wants.

January 5

ANOTHER milestone; it's been a week for them.

Up to now, Amanda would play with whatever was closest to her. We were thrilled that she was able to pick things up and hold them; we took it for granted that she would pick up whatever her wandering hands bumped into.

Now that has changed. All of her toys are in a big open-topped plastic box in the living room. Starting today she crawled over to the box, and started going through what was inside—toy by toy.

She picked one toy up, looked at it, then threw it down. Picked another one up, looked at it, threw it down. She was going through a selection process for the first time.

We didn't bother her; we stayed off in the distance and watched. Finally she found something she liked. She put it down on the floor next to her and began to play with it. The other toys were forgotten; she had made her choice. I wonder whether she realized that she had never done this before?

January 6

I WAS reading through my old high school yearbook tonight. I turned to the section that contained our senior pictures; there I was, at the age of eighteen, and right next to me was my friend Tim Greiner. Because of the spellings of our last names, we sat next to each other in class all the way through Bexley High School.

On a whim, I picked up the phone and called him. I knew that he was still living in Columbus; I hadn't spoken with him in years. He answered.

We started to talk; he told me his wife was expecting their fourth child. One of his kids is already in elementary school—Cassingham Elementary, the same school I went to as a child.

Tim told me that he went to PTA meetings and open houses at the school. I asked him if it was weird to walk through those hallways again.

"That's not the weird thing," he said. "The weird thing is running into the other parents. They're not like the parents we remember. They're the same people we went to school with."

I understood what he meant. If I thought of going to a PTA meeting, I would imagine sharing the room with strangers whose only role in life—in my eyes—was being the fathers and mothers of children the same age as my child.

But for Tim, of course, it's different. He sees a father or a mother, and he is filled with memories. It's not just a father; it's a guy he used to play football with. It's not just a mother; it's a woman he went out with in tenth grade. And it's not just a school open house; it's a visit back into his own childhood, in a building that's as familiar as the house he grew up in.

I'm missing all that, of course. Whatever this adventure is that I'm in the middle of, it's completely different from Tim Greiner's adventure. I'm not sure which of ours is spookier.

January 7

I noticed something different about Amanda tonight. The knees of her jumpsuit were faded and worn; the designs on them were a lighter color than the designs on the rest of the suit, and they were getting threadbare in those spots.

"Are these starting to wear out already?" I said to Susan.

"It's not the material's fault," she said. "It's the crawling that's done it."

And, of course, that's true. Before, there was no reason for her clothes to show any wear; she wasn't doing much in them, other than sleeping and eating and being carried around.

Now, though, in the space of the last week, she's going places on her own, and her clothes are going with her. The knees are rubbing against the floor, and the cloth is wearing away. I guess this is the beginning of shoes that fall apart and shirts that tear and pants that give out. Amanda is a part of the world now, and the world shows on her clothes.

January 8

SHE had her regular appointment with Dr. Scheinberg this morning, but he was an hour late arriving at his office.

He said he had been down at the hospital. A woman who had had sixteen pregnancies and sixteen miscarriages had finally given birth to a child. But the baby was two months premature; Dr. Scheinberg had been trying to help save the baby's life, and he wasn't sure how well he and the other doctors had succeeded. The next forty-eight hours would tell.

Tonight we held Amanda especially close.

January 9

AT 4 p.m. I had finished my newspaper column for the day when the phone rang. It was "Nightline"; there was a new development in a story for tonight's show, and they wanted me to cover it. The development was in Chicago; a camera crew was on its way to the scene of the event, and I was supposed to get in a cab and meet them.

I knew that if I was going to appear on camera I should be wearing a coat and tie; at the office, I wasn't. So I hurried home to change. I walked in, and Amanda was crying, and Susan was pacing.

"She just won't sleep," Susan said, looking to me for help and sympathy.

"Is my blazer back from the cleaners?" I said.

I explained why I was in a hurry. Susan just looked at me. Amanda was still crying, and Susan was trying to quiet her, and I was putting a tie on.

"I'm really sorry," I said. "I know this isn't fair."

Susan didn't say anything.

I got to the story on time. We shot the videotape, then went back to the Chicago ABC bureau, put it together, fed it to New York, and watched it on the show.

When I got home after midnight, Susan and Amanda were asleep.

January 10

THERE'S a price to be paid for all this running around like I did yesterday.

Now that Amanda's crawling, what she does is no longer just a matter of us walking over to her and picking her up. She gets to determine her own agenda now; we watch her, and she goes where she wants.

Susan and I were sitting on opposite sides of the dinner table. Amanda was at the other end of the living room. She saw us, began to smile, and crawled in our direction.

When she was fifteen feet away, she realized she had to make a choice. If she veered to her left, she would crawl to me. If she veered to her right, she would crawl to Susan.

She looked around at both of us. And she crawled straight to Susan.

This is not the first time this has happened. Susan assures me that it's only natural; at this stage of a baby's life, she has spent so much time with her mother—especially during nursing—that she will always pick her mother out first. Her mother is just more familiar to her.

Maybe. But I can't help feeling that if somehow I could manage to find more hours to be at home, Amanda might at least think about heading toward me.

January 11

THIS is weird.

There's a commercial for the *Tribune* that's been running on television. The commercial features footage of several *Tribune* writers, including me; in the last shot of the commercial, I come floating into camera range in a paddleboat. I'm only on screen for three or four seconds.

There's a jingle that goes along with the commercial; the jingle goes "The *Tribune*, we give you . . . a better look." And as soon as that commercial and jingle come onto the screen —every time—Amanda stops what she's going and stares at the TV set.

Susan noticed this first. I didn't believe her when she told me, but since then I've been paying attention. Amanda will be crawling, or playing with her toys, or nursing. As soon as the jingle comes on, she will stop what she's doing and devote her full attention to the commercial. She will watch; I will come floating by in that boat. Then the commercial will end, and she will go back to what she was doing before.

I can't make myself believe that she really knows.

January 12

THIS is the first time I've dreamed about her.

I had to make a quick trip to Los Angeles; I was only scheduled to stay there overnight. And as I slept in my bed at the Century Plaza, I had a vivid dream about Amanda. In the dream, Susan was carrying her, and I thought that she was holding her too loosely, and I tried to take her away. I don't know what that symbolizes; the dream was so real that when I woke up suddenly, it took me a few seconds to comprehend that it had not been real life.

It's not the symbolism of the dream that strikes me, anyway; it's the fact that Amanda was in my dream at all. In all these months since she has been born, for all the days and hours she has been on my mind, I do not recall dreaming about her at all. That's probably because she has been such a new, jarring element in my life that she didn't belong in a dream; she was always in the forefront of my consciousness, and it has been my experience that I dream only about things that are in the back of my consciousness.

To be there—in the back of a person's consciousness—something must be accepted as a steady, constant part of that person's life. Something that's always present, whether the person is aware he's thinking about it or not. I guess that description now fits Amanda.

January 13

ON the way back home, I was on the same flight with Kris Kristofferson, the actor and singer.

Kristofferson was traveling with a little girl; I assumed it was his daughter. The social dynamics on the plane were interesting to watch. Virtually all of the passengers in the cabin took note of Kristofferson's presence; he is one of those people who is instantly recognizable, whether you are actively a "fan" of his or not. He was wearing a T-shirt and jeans; as he walked through the plane, a growing buzz of conversation followed him.

During the flight people left their seats and walked up to him for a few moments of conversation. He was cordial to everyone. But as I watched him, it was clear to me that the main thing on his mind was his daughter. He was solicitous to her; he went over the safety instructions with her, and asked her questions about the book she was reading, and never let more than a few minutes pass without leaning over and saying something to her. To the rest of the people on board, the most remarkable thing about the flight may have been that Kristofferson was a fellow passenger; the main thing on his mind, though, was clearly that his daughter was with him and that he was responsible for her.

That has to be the case for every parent, no matter how prominent or how successful. It didn't take a genius to realize that all of Kristofferson's talent and all of his money meant nothing when it came to determining what kind of a father he was; that had to come from another part of his being, and from what I was seeing he instinctively was aware of this—he knew that what the public thought of him was meaningless when compared to what his daughter thought of him. A man can be loved by millions, but that has to be no consolation at all if he can't bring his own love to his child. I knew nothing about Kristofferson's life, but it was apparent to me that he understood this.

There were two rest rooms at the front of the cabin. Kristofferson got up and walked to one; a few moments later, while he was still inside, his daughter got up and walked to the other one. When Kristofferson came out of his rest room, he looked at the seat where his daughter had been; she wasn't there. An expression of concern passed over his face; he said something to one of the flight attendants, and she pointed to the other rest room, explaining where his daughter was. Kristofferson nodded and smiled and sat down. I think I'll remember those few moments long after I remember any scene from one of his movies.

January 14

IT turns out I'm not the only one who's dreaming.

When I got home, Susan told me about a dream she had had. It emphasized to me how strongly Amanda's presence in the world has changed her life, and her view of herself. She prefaced it by saying it was a funny dream, but it made me kind of sad.

In the dream, Susan said, I had come to her and had told her I had a favor to ask her. I told her that the favor was for Betsy West, the "Nightline" producer with whom I often work. (Betsy calls the house all the time, but Susan has never met her in person.)

In Susan's dream, I told her that Betsy was so busy, with all of her traveling, that she never had any time to buy new clothes. Susan had a whole closet full of nice business clothes; since she wasn't working anymore, I said, why didn't she just give all of her office clothes to Betsy?

In the dream, Susan said, she had argued with me about it, but I had insisted. Susan didn't need the office clothes anymore, and Betsy did, and Susan would have to give them to her. But what if she went back to work someday, Susan had asked in the dream. Then she could buy new clothes, I had said, but with Amanda, she probably wouldn't be going back to work for quite a while, if at all.

In her dream, Susan had said to me: "All right. I'll give her my clothes. But I don't have to give her my peach gabardine suit, do I? That's my favorite."

And I had replied: "Yes. You don't need those clothes anymore. Betsy has to get everything."

Susan finished telling me the story about the dream. I didn't know what to say. Amanda, on the floor, began to cry, and we went to her.

January 15

AMANDA has a voice; she's not talking yet, but it's her own voice.

I was at the office today and I called home. When Susan answered the phone I asked, as always, how Amanda was doing. And, as she generally does these days, she said, "It's Daddy," and held the receiver to Amanda's ear so that I could talk to her.

I spoke to Amanda—the usual baby talk foolishness—and this time she responded. It was her routine half-sigh, half-coo; but I recognized her voice. I knew the tone and the sound of it; it wasn't just any baby—it was Amanda. If someone were to play me recordings of the sound of ten babies, I could pick Amanda out in an instant. There's only one of her in the world.

January 16

SHE was crawling around the living room today and she crawled right into a floor-to-ceiling window.

She didn't hurt herself; she didn't even act embarrassed at her mistake, the way she might if she were a little older. She was simply confused. There were things to see outside the window; she saw them; she tried to reach them; and suddenly there was some sort of mysterious barrier in the way.

She didn't understand. It was the first time in her life she has had to deal with the concept of a clear window. Starting now, that concept will be a given; almost every time she encounters a window she won't have to think twice about what it means, and on the rare occasion she bumps into one unthinkingly she will feel vaguely foolish about it.

Today, though, it was something brand-new; something that the rest of the world takes for granted, but that she had never experienced before. It seems as if every day she's coming across something new like that. It makes me feel the same way.

January 17

I TOOK Susan and Amanda to Columbus tonight.

Susan has been saying for months that she needs a break; she said that with all my traveling I get regular diversions, a luxury she doesn't have. She has no desire to take a vacation with me and leave Amanda with a babysitter or a family member; she would be thinking of Amanda and missing her every second.

What she did want to do, she said, was to go to Ohio and stay with her parents for a while. Her mother could help her take care of Amanda, and she wouldn't have to worry about cooking or cleaning—every time she thought about it, it sounded better to her.

She wanted to spend two or three weeks in Columbus; I told her that there was no way I could get that much time off from work. But I agreed with her; it would do her a lot of good to get out of the apartment, and to get some help, and to have someone to talk to all day.

So we agreed that she should do it. I didn't want her and Amanda traveling alone; I said that I would feel much better if I flew to Columbus with them, delivered them to her parents' house, and then flew back. When her stay was finished I would fly back and bring them home.

So we flew there tonight. Amanda was great on the plane; she slept almost the whole way, and she didn't cry. My own parents greeted us at the airport; my father was crouched just inside the terminal with his camera, like a paparazzo who feared his subject might bolt at the sight of him and get away before he had captured the scene on film. So as we walked into Port Columbus a flashbulb popped, and then my parents drove us in to Susan's parents' house.

I told Susan that I would be glad to come back and get them whenever they were ready. She said fine, but with all the commotion with the grandparents and Amanda, I'm not sure if she was really listening to me.

January 18–February 13

I SUPPOSE I was prepared to miss Amanda; I knew when I took her and Susan to Columbus that the apartment would seem empty without them.

But I wasn't all that concerned about it. Because I have traveled so frequently myself during the months she has been with us, I assumed that going home every night to the apartment would feel pretty much the way it feels when I am on the road in some strange hotel room.

I was wrong.

When I'm on the road I always know, in the back of my mind, that Amanda and Susan are at home waiting for me. In an airport or in bed at a hotel, I can envision the apartment, with them there. When I pick up the phone and call, it's not just their voices I respond to—it's my visual image of our home, and what it's like with Amanda there.

It's not like that now. I've been coming home after work,

and there's no one around. But the artifacts are all there, and that's what gets to me. Her Christmas rocking-dog, sitting in the living room. Her carriage in the hallway. Her box of toys on the floor. Her crib in her room.

The littlest things affect me. I was looking for a paper cup, and I opened up one of the kitchen cabinets, and there was Amanda's baby food—all the jars of strained fruits and vegetables, stacked up. And just looking at them made me teary. It really did.

What I'm saying, I guess, is that I knew I would miss Amanda while she was gone. But I really had no conception of how much she has come to mean in my life. Eight months ago she didn't exist. And now I find that, without her at home, there is a huge void in my life. I almost ache for not seeing her.

She and Susan seem to be doing fine in Columbus. I've been calling every day—several times a day, as a matter of fact—and Susan seems happy and relaxed to be getting help from her mother. Every time I call it makes me want to get on a plane and go there right away. Susan says that Amanda's top front teeth are coming in; it makes her fussy at night, but if you look carefully, you can see them starting to jut through the gums, just like her bottom teeth did. It's not that major a development, but I want to be there for it.

Susan's mother and father get on the phone and tell me, "You have a beautiful daughter," but that really doesn't help. It just makes me want to see her all the more. What makes it worse is that, near the end of the second week they've been gone, I was sent out of town on a lengthy reporting trip that took me in the opposite direction from Columbus. I had to be in six cities in the course of ten days, and there was no way to delay the journey. So that has added extra time to the days we have had to be apart, and now I'm starting to worry about things like whether Amanda will truly remember me.

I have to say that I'm glad we did this; Susan deserved a break from the apartment, and I'm just as happy that when my ten-day trip came up, she was in Columbus rather than back in Chicago. As long as I have to be on the road for that much time, it's better that she's with her parents.

But this trip is wearing at me in a way that the previous trips haven't—and I know it has less to do with the length of the trip than with the fact that our home is empty. This ends tomorrow; I'm flying into Columbus to bring them back home, and not a moment too soon. If I didn't realize it before, it couldn't be clearer now: she is literally a part of me.

February 14

MY plane was late; by the time I arrived in Columbus it was the middle of the evening, time for her to be asleep.

I took a cab from the airport to the Koebels' house. Susan had left a sign for me on the front door: "Knock softly—do not ring. Amanda sleeping."

So I tapped on the door, and Susan's mother opened it. When Susan joined her, I said, "Can I just go upstairs and look at her for a minute?"

We walked up together. Amanda was in a crib in the room where Susan's brother David had grown up. I stood over the crib and stared down at her. "Does she look any bigger to you?" Susan said.

I said that I wasn't sure; all I knew was that she looked like Amanda, and that was enough.

She opened her eyes and stirred for a moment. We were looking at each other. She seemed to figure out who I was; her face broke into that big smile.

Susan had been right. Two more teeth, right on top.

The biggest news came a little later, though, when she had woken up for a feeding.

"Da-da," she said.

I couldn't believe it.

"Da-da," she said again.

"That's right," Susan said. "Daddy's here."

"Da-da," Amanda said, and laughed.

"How long has *this* been going on?" I said.

"For about a week," Susan said. "She says it all the time."

It's definitely her first word. Like all the other developments, there's an aspect to it I hadn't expected. I always assumed that a baby's first word was "mama" or "dada" because the parents had trained the child that way; because they had constantly pointed at each other and said "mama" or "dada."

We never did that. She wasn't imitating us; there was no single word that we had emphasized enough for her to be trying to mimic it. The answer seems to be obvious, although I haven't read it anywhere: "dada" and "mama" must be the natural first sounds that any baby makes. They must be the sounds that are the easiest for a child to handle. The definition of "dada" as "father" and "mama" as "mother" must have come *after* babies began making the sounds. Enough babies in the long-ago must have said "dada" that the first generation of fathers began to call themselves "dadas"; same with mothers. At least that's the only answer that makes sense to me.

"So what have you been doing when she says it?" I said to Susan.

"Nothing," she said. "I've been waiting for you to get back so I could show her what she meant."

February 15

ON the airplane on the way back to Chicago, a flight attendant played peekaboo with Amanda. The flight attendant would put her hands over her own face, then remove her hands and say "Peekaboo!" Amanda would break up every time she did it.

It was the first time the flight attendant had ever seen Amanda, of course; so she accepted her as a fairly grown-up baby, at least developed enough to be enjoying this simple game. And the way Amanda looked around the cabin, shifting her eyes between whatever interested her, it was clear that she was aware of her world.

I kept thinking back to those not-so-long ago days when all she would do is lie in our arms and cry. Somewhere along the way she really did change; she's starting to grow up.

"Da-da," Amanda said.

Susan pointed to me, and made sure that Amanda looked.

"Da-da," she said again.

"There," Susan said. "That's dada."

Amanda scrunched her face up and showed us her teeth.

"Do you think she's learning that dada is me?" I said.

"You're asking me?" Susan said.

February 16

IF she realizes she's been gone from the apartment for a long time, it doesn't show. She was all over the place within minutes of getting back, crawling much faster than before and exploring all of her favorite corners and hideaways.

She's developed a real yen for Helen. Their relationship is entering yet another phase; now that Amanda can crawl around so quickly, she actually chases Helen. Before she just kind of lumbered up to her; Helen had plenty of time to see her coming, and to decide to walk away to avoid a confrontation.

Not now. Amanda will take off after Helen, and Helen will have to run to get away. Even when she does, Amanda continues her pursuit; it seems to me that Helen—being closer to

Amanda's size than we are—might, in Amanda's mind, appear to be the same species as Amanda. She isn't chasing her as a baby chasing a cat; she's chasing her as a friend, playing.

But every time she grabs for Helen's tail, I wince. Helen's good-natured attitude can't last forever.

There's another, slightly more disturbing trend. When Susan is holding Amanda, or Amanda is in a sitting position—as she often is these days—I will say something to her.

And more often than not, Amanda will crane her head so that she can look past me and stare at the television screen.

It happens a lot. There's no way she can be following any plot on the TV. I noticed when she was much smaller that she was mesmerized by the flickering lights on the screen. Now it's gone beyond that; it's obvious that, given a choice between me talking to her and the TV talking to her, I'm not guaranteed to be the winner. I've always known how powerful an influence television is; but it bothers me to know that it is already such a strong draw on my daughter. Susan and I laugh about it, but I'm not sure how funny it is.

February 17

SUSAN screamed.

I was closing the refrigerator door when she did it, and I immediately stopped what I was doing.

Amanda was on the floor, with her little hand on the edge of the door, near the hinge.

"It's all right," I said to Susan. "Her hand wouldn't have caught. Look. It's built with a space in between. Probably for that very reason."

And it was. But there's no getting around the fact that, with Amanda's newfound mobility, we have to be even more careful than we were before. Now that she knows she can get around at will, she becomes restless if we hold her for too long, or try to make her stay in one place. But it seems that every time she crawls away, she ends up doing something she shouldn't. If she isn't curling her hand around the refrigerator door, she's chewing on the hard metal buckle of my belt. If she's not chewing on the belt buckle, she's trying to pry the safety guard out of an electrical outlet.

There are good sides to this, of course. Susan lies on the floor now, and Amanda crawls over her almost effortlessly, like a little tank going over a steep hill. It's fine while we're watching. The problem is, we can never afford *not* to be watching.

February 18

Actually playing with her is great. Before, I used to fool myself into thinking I was playing with her; she would be on the bed or on the vinyl cloth, and I would do stupid things and pick her up and dance with her or whatever; but she had no real active part in it.

Now she does. Granted, it's not the most sophisticated form of play in the history of mankind. Today I sat next to her and made Bronx cheers with my mouth. She laughed and made Bronx cheers back. I did it again. She laughed and did it again. For about ten minutes we kept making the noises at each other.

Susan was at the grocery during all of this spitting, by the way.

After all the days of "dada," today she said "mama."

It didn't make Susan feel all that great, though, because Amanda was looking directly at Helen as she said it.

February 19

WHAT I've been trying to come to terms with in the last few days is the new fact that she *does* things; things aren't just done *for* her.

Today I was playing some music on our tape deck, and suddenly Bob Seger stopped sounding like Bob Seger and started sounding like Alvin and the Chipmunks. I was wearing earphones; needless to say, this was a little disconcerting.

I looked over at the tape console. Amanda had crawled up to it and had flipped one of the switches to a faster speed. She was just getting ready to fool with some more of the switches.

I picked her up and headed her in another direction, hoping she would lose interest in the tape deck. Gone are the days when I could know what she was doing just by knowing where she was. She has absolutely no interest in just lying in her crib and waiting for us anymore.

February 20

THERE is a story—perhaps apocryphal—about Jim Thorpe, the legendary old-time athlete.

According to the story, Thorpe, because he was known to be in such superb physical condition, was asked to take part in an experiment. Thorpe was supposed to get down on his hands and knees next to a growing baby. Everything the baby did, Thorpe was supposed to do. That's all. Simple.

The point of the story is that Thorpe allegedly gave up, winded, after a few hours. The baby, though, kept right on going, oblivious to the strain.

I thought about that story today. Susan said she was going to make some cole slaw in the kitchen; would I keep an eye on Amanda?

I did. She was in an exploring mood; she maneuvered all over the apartment, and just to test myself I tried the Thorpe experiment. I got down on all fours and tried to do everything that she did.

Needless to say, I am not in Jim Thorpe's kind of shape. It didn't take long for her to exhaust me. All the stretching, all the reaching up and down, all the rolling and leg-reaching and arm-bending—because she's so small, it doesn't seem all that impressive to watch. Until you try it. What a baby does in the course of a day is enough to put an adult in traction.

February 21

"Come here," Susan called.

She was in Amanda's room; it was early in the morning, and Amanda had cried to signal she was awake.

I got out of bed and walked into the room. Amanda was standing up in the crib, holding herself straight against the bars.

"She did it herself," Susan said. "When I came in here to get her, she was standing there looking at me."

Susan and I lifted the mattress out of the crib, then lowered its bottom a few notches, so that when she stands up she won't be in any danger of toppling out. What a long way we've come.

It didn't take her much time to put the standing-up-by-herself into her repertoire. After I went back to bed, I heard a gurgling noise. She had crawled in from the living room, grabbed hold of the side of the bed, and pulled herself upright. Now her eyes were peering over the top edge of the mattress.

"Can you say 'dada'?" I said.

Apparently not today. She let herself drop down to the floor, turned around, and headed back to the living room. I suppose I could have found out what for, but I didn't have a *TV Guide* handy.

Two steps forward, one step back. She crawls everywhere, she's beginning to talk, she pulls herself to a standing position. But tonight she woke up crying every hour from midnight until 6 a.m. It was the worst it's been since the first few weeks she was born, and we have no idea why.

February 22

IT turns out she's got great taste.

I was playing a tape with Buddy Holly's "Well All Right" on it; the tape was in one of those little hand-held recorders. Amanda crawled right on top of me and started waving her legs and arms in time to the music, laughing like crazy.

"You like this, wait till you hear 'You're So Square, Baby I Don't Care,' " I said.

I had been noticing a little yellow-colored patch on the skin right next to her nose. It was very small, and it was just a tinge of yellow; I was going to point it out to Susan, but I didn't because I thought I was being paranoid.

Today Amanda had her regular appointment at Dr. Scheinberg's. He was looking her over, and he said, "I see she likes carrots and sweet potatoes."

"As a matter of fact, she does," Susan said. "How did you know?"

"See that yellowish skin by her nose?" Dr. Scheinberg said. "That's what happens when a baby eats a lot of that."

Later, I told Susan that I had noticed the same thing.

"You did not," she said.

"I did," I said.

"Then why didn't you say anything about it?" she said.

"I didn't want to sound like an alarmist," I said.

"Right," she said. "You didn't notice anything."

February 23

It has happened so gradually that I haven't even thought to make note of it. But she has started to take morning naps. For all these months Susan has been concerned because Amanda didn't conform to the books; she slept only in the afternoon and at night. Now, suddenly, she gets tired at 10 a.m. On a good day, Susan can finally have three meals without having to hold or watch Amanda during any of them.

Another thing I haven't mentioned lately: the orthos. They're still with us. Getting scuffed, but still with us.

February 24

I came home and walked into the living room. Amanda was standing there looking at me.

That's so strange. She's begun to do it all the time now; she pulls herself up into the standing position, and she stays up. Susan or I don't have to help her; she does it all on her own. Without support she couldn't stay upright. Tonight, for example, she was standing by one of the bookcases, and she was grasping a shelf so that she didn't fall.

It gives everything such a different perspective. As ready as I am for her to grow older, it's shocking to walk into the apartment and to see Susan sitting—and Amanda standing. It just doesn't fit in with any of the attitudes I have built up about her.

Always she will fall. As soon as she lets go of whatever she's holding onto, down she goes. She doesn't hurt herself, but she cries frantically. It's from the surprise of it all; one moment she had been up there, and the next moment she's sprawled on the floor. It didn't occur to her that this was going to happen; she cries because she didn't expect it.

February 25

As great as it is to watch her physical development, if we pay close enough attention we can see signs that her mind is developing, too.

In the last few days, when she has dropped something she has looked down to the floor to see where it went. That doesn't sound earthshaking, but it's definitely new. There was that first long stage when she didn't pick anything up at all, and everything had to be handed to her; then there was the stage when she gladly picked up anything within reach, but then discarded it without paying any more attention.

Now it's different. If she is playing with a toy, and it slips out of her hand, she will follow it with her eyes; we can see her wondering what has become of it. A month ago it would have stayed on the floor, no longer a part of her consciousness; now, most of the time, she will return to it and pick it up again. She understands that even though it's out of her hand for the moment, it's still a part of her world.

February 26

"I'm going to have to take the baby carriage apart and take it downstairs to store it," Susan said.

The carriage has been sitting in our living room, unused. It had been a gift from her co-workers when she had left her office shortly before Amanda was due. Back then, it had seemed so out of place in our apartment; on the day Susan left work for the last time, she cleaned out her desk, piled all of the papers into the baby carriage, and wheeled it out.

Now Amanda is too big for it; she doesn't belong in a carriage anymore, and if she goes out it is in her stroller.

"You can keep it up here a while longer if you want," I said.

"No," Susan said. "It doesn't belong here anymore. That makes me sad."

February 27

We were in the living room; Amanda was taking a nap in her bedroom. She started crying.

Susan was reading a magazine; she said to me, "Will you go in there and lie her down?"

"How do you know she's standing up?" I said.

"From the sound of her voice," Susan said. "It sounds different when she's standing up than it does when she's lying down."

I went into Amanda's room. There she was in her crib, standing up and crying, holding the bars.

"I was hoping you were going to prove your mother wrong for once," I said to her.

But she just stood there crying.

February 28

I CALLED home from work today; I tried the number for about two hours, and kept getting a busy signal. I began to become alarmed.

Finally the phone rang in my office, and it was Susan. "I'm sorry if you kept getting a busy signal," she said. "Amanda knocked the receiver off the hook in the bedroom, and I just found out."

Things like that are starting to happen all the time. I have a shoehorn that I keep on the table by our bed; every morning I use it before I go to work. The other day I asked Susan where it was, and she said, "Amanda must have put it somewhere."

In the living room we have record albums stored on the bottom row of a bookshelf; now whenever I come home some of the albums are scattered about the floor, and I know without asking that Amanda has pulled them out and tossed them around.

In short, she has reached the point where she can lose things and mess things up. Just a few months ago, the thought that Amanda might be responsible for something like my shoehorn being missing wouldn't even occur to us. Now it's the natural answer.

March 1

AND now she crawls away.

She has become so good at getting around; she's always on the move these days. At first when she was doing it it was slow and filled with effort; each foot she moved from Susan or me seemed to traumatize her a little. Something inside her mind knew that it was essential to learn how to do this, but she didn't seem to relish the idea of her new independence.

That stage is over. When I'm on the floor with her and I try to hold her, she gets impatient. All she wants to do is crawl away and explore; when I reach out to keep her with me I can tell by the look on her face—and by the squirming in her arms and legs—that she considers it an imposition. I am preventing her from seeing the things she wants to see.

Susan says this is good; she says that if Amanda *weren't* so eager to be moving around and checking things out, that's when we should be worried.

Maybe I'm reading too much symbolism into it. But in a way it seems like sort of a demarcation point; she has learned that there are other places in the world to go than her mother's or father's arms, and that she has the means to get there. I can't help thinking about that every time I reach for her and she crawls away instead.

March 2

ON the other hand, there are times I feel absolutely necessary.

She can stand, all right; she does it all the time, and it's great to watch her grab onto the edge of a table or a chair and pull herself up.

But she has no idea how to get down. She doesn't have a clue. You'd think that would be the easy part. Every time she becomes tired of standing up, though, she looks around her, gets a puzzled look on her face, and then begins to cry.

"Don't be scared," Susan or I will say to her. We'll walk over, and we'll slowly lower her from a standing position until she's sitting on her butt; then we'll show her how to turn to the side and crawl away.

"It's easy," Susan will say to her as she lowers her.

So far Amanda doesn't seem to be catching on. "Show her the exact same way every time," Susan said to me. "If you change anything at all, it will confuse her."

Maybe the answer is to keep her standing up when she's with me. At least that way I know she can't crawl away.

March 3

IN the kitchen this morning, Susan was making herself a cup of coffee. The grinder was whirring away. And Amanda was on the floor, her mouth scrunched up, trying her best to sound like the coffee grinder.

"Is this the first time she's done that?" I said.

"She's been doing it for about a week," Susan said. "But this is the first time I'm sure that she's imitating the grinder. At first I thought it was just a coincidence."

"Are babies supposed to imitate coffee grinders?" I said.

"If you're asking me if any of the books mentioned it—no, they didn't," Susan said.

March 4

WHEN she was out in public, she used to smile at every stranger who came into view. If there was a new face in her field of vision, that face received a smile.

Now that's stopped.

If it's someone she's seen a lot before—clerks in the grocery store, the lady at the cleaners—she will light up and smile as widely as before. But now if someone new comes up and looks at her and says something, she will be wary.

It's her inhibitions beginning to develop. Something is telling her that everyone should not automatically be welcomed into her world.

March 5

The coffee grinder was one thing, but now she's trying to talk like Helen.

It's not unusual at all these days to find them chasing each other around the apartment. Actually, that's a little unfair to Helen; Helen has never done the chasing, only the running away. But Amanda is such a fast crawler now that it really has developed into a footrace. Before Helen could simply wait until Amanda had managed to lumber within a few feet of her, and then stroll away at her leisure. Now Amanda is almost as fast as Helen; there are times when it looks like some sort of Saturday morning cartoon at our house.

And when Amanda finally does come face to face with Helen, the two of them talk. Helen mews in a high cat voice; Amanda, not knowing any better, mews back.

"Is this normal?" I said tonight. I was trying to watch the news, and Amanda and Helen were over in the corner mewing at each other.

"I don't see how it could hurt anything," Susan said.

"I just didn't expect my daughter to think she's a cat," I said.

"I know," Susan said. "I think it has something to do with the fact that she's closer to Helen's size than to our size. I think that in a way she identifies with Helen."

Amanda looked over at me and mewed.

March 6

FOR some reason I looked at a calendar today and tried to think what I was doing a year ago.

Just about a year ago exactly, we started going to Lamaze class.

I know it was in March; thinking back to it now, it seems impossible to comprehend the innocence of our attitudes—all of us in the class.

We were all first time parents-to-be; every Sunday night we gathered at Michael Reese Hospital, carrying pillows, for our instructions and exercises. Looking back on it now, the amusing thing is that all of our efforts and all of our thoughts were aimed at that one day in the labor and delivery rooms—the day of our babies' birth. The woman who conducted the class tried to talk about what the weeks and months following the birth might be like, but when she started up on that our eyes kind of glazed over, and we didn't pay too much attention.

As far as we were concerned, once we got past the delivery, the hard part was over. The immediate trauma that lay ahead of us was getting that baby born; after that, we figured, everything would somehow take care of itself.

Of course, the day in the labor and delivery rooms was the one and only time when we had all the help on hand that we could conceivably need. I guess it's natural, though; when you have some tremendous, mysterious, frightening event looming in the immediate future, all of your energies go to dealing with that event. Everything else can come later.

But I looked at the calendar and smiled as I thought of those Sunday nights spent eating early dinners and gathering up pillows—as if that was somehow going to lead to the solution to everything.

March 7

IT was cold out today. Susan dressed Amanda in a blue snowsuit with a hood on it; she looked just like a little boy.

"What are we going to say when people say, 'What's his name?' " I said to Amanda. "What are we going to say your name is?"

Amanda stared at me.

"I guess I'll just say, 'His name's Arnold,' " I said. "I'll say, 'Our little boy's name is Arnold.' "

Amanda looked over at Helen and mewed.

March 8

AFTER all those days of lessons, she does this.

We must have showed her how to get down from a standing position five hundred times. Every time she stood up, we patiently lowered her until she was sitting, then rolled her to the side, then let her crawl away.

And every time Susan said, "Remember—the exact same way. Don't confuse her. Show her the exact same way."

So today, for the first time, Amanda got down from the standing position herself. She did it in a completely different way than we had been teaching her.

She was in the living room, with her hands on the coffee table, standing up. This time when she was ready, though, she didn't cry, and she didn't look to us. She merely flexed her knees, then lowered herself until her knees were touching the floor, then put her hands on the floor, and crawled away.

"Did you see that?" Susan said.

"I did," I said.

"What do you think?" she said.

"What happened to sitting down on her butt?" I said.

"I don't know," Susan said. "Did we ever show her anything about bending her knees?"

"Nope," I said.

But Amanda was already across the room. She put her hands on a chair and stood up. A few seconds later she flexed her knees and knelt down.

There must be a lesson here somewhere, but I don't want to think about what it might be.

March 9

SHE points now. She uses her first finger; if something intrigues her, she approaches it and points to it; then she touches it.

It means she's getting . . . *specific*. No longer is she just interested in sights and noises in general; now she lets us know precisely what has attracted her.

So if she crawls over to Susan, she doesn't stop when she gets to her; she reaches up to Susan's face and touches her nose. And we go "nose." If she points to my watch, we go "watch." She's catching on; she seems to know that if she points to something, we're going to tell her what that thing is called. It's almost like a game with her. When she's on a roll, she'll keep pointing to things and waiting to hear our response until either she or we get tired of it.

March 10

"Nightline" called me to New York; I was putting a piece together with Betsy West and videotape editor Donna Rowlinson, and we broke for dinner and went to a place on Columbus Avenue.

The three of us were led to a table. I had done my voice tracking just before we broke, so I was essentially done for the evening. I had three drinks in rapid succession; it had been a tense day, and it happened to be my birthday.

We were talking about office politics, and then Donna, out of nowhere, asked me what it was like to have a baby daughter in the house. I think what she said was, "Do you like it?"

Normally, I shrug that question off; it's so complicated and so consuming that I don't feel I can do it justice with a glib reply. I usually just say, "Yeah, it's great," and let it go at that.

But tonight—because of the drinks, because of my birthday—I felt like talking. I told Betsy and Donna that saying I "liked" having Amanda in the house was not even the beginning of it.

"I don't even know how to explain it," I said. "I've been spending time on the road ever since I started working for a living. I've complained about it a lot, but I've really liked the idea of it. Going into different cities, sleeping in hotels, meeting strange people . . . I've really liked it.

"Now, though, when I'm gone . . . I physically *ache* for missing my daughter. It never seems that any story is important enough to make me not see her for another day. I know I still go out on the road all the time—I wonder if I'm fooling myself—but missing her is not some vague concept in my mind. It actually hurts when I think that she's at home and I'm not with her. Sometimes I fall asleep thinking about it."

I babbled on some more, and they mostly listened, and then I said:

"I know it's supposed to be part of the mystique of this job, but being on the road on my birthday is particularly bad this year. Amanda's too young to know what a birthday is, but I just can't help thinking that I ought to be home with her tonight instead of sleeping in some hotel room in New York."

We finished up, and we walked back to the ABC building on Sixty-sixth Street. We went up to the second floor, where Donna's editing room is; she and Betsy closed the door and went back to work.

I walked around the building and talked to some people; when I went back to the editing area, Betsy looked out the door of the editing room and said, "Could you come in here for a second? We've got something for you to see."

I assumed it was a section of the story they had put together. I walked in the room, and they closed the door. There, among the editing equipment, was a huge bouquet of flowers the two of them had bought. They handed it to me and sang "Happy Birthday."

March 11

HOME again. To learn she has a favorite toy—a plastic telephone that rings and clicks.

We know it's her favorite because now, when she crawls over to the straw basket where all her toys are stored, she pulls herself up and searches around, moving all the toys, until she's found the phone.

She doesn't look all that much different than she did a month or two ago—she's a pound or two heavier, maybe an inch or so taller, and she's got more hair. But things like this—like seeing her purposefully crawl to that basket and look for the telephone—remind me that important changes are taking place every day, changes that we can't even come close to seeing.

March 12

SIX more months for the orthos.

"It doesn't depress me as much as it did last time," Susan said.

The orthopedist said that her foot was coming along fine; apparently the orthos are doing the good that they're supposed to. He said that she doesn't have to wear them at night anymore when she's sleeping. But he recommended that we buy her the next bigger size, and that we keep putting them on her in the daytime as a matter of course. He said to come back and see him again in September.

"It doesn't really matter so much now that she's getting a little older," I said. "At this age, all babies start wearing shoes."

"Not like these shoes they don't," Susan said.

March 13

SHE seems to have figured out a solution to a problem that has begun to apply.

The problem is this: she moves around freely, and she now has certain things she wants to take with her. For an adult, that would present no problem; you would simply pick up whatever item you wanted to transport, and carry it to your destination.

It's not quite so simple for Amanda, of course. Because all she can do is crawl, it doesn't make sense for her to carry something in her hands; she would just have to put it down every foot or so.

What she's decided to do is carry things in her mouth. She'll be playing with a cloth toy, and then decide to come visit with us on the other side of the room. So she'll put the toy into her mouth, chomp down on it, and then come racing across the room on all fours, the toy held securely in place.

She looks a little like a dog bringing the evening newspaper to his master. But that's okay; at least in this case we can be sure she's not emulating Helen again. Helen's never carried anything around in her life.

And we don't have a dog.

March 14

I ALWAYS assumed that, once a baby began to talk, she would talk every day, picking up words every few hours or so. But that's wrong.

Amanda still says "dada," and she says "mama," and occasionally she comes up with something new; when she's standing up and is ready to kneel down, the sound she makes comes very close to "down." But she doesn't talk all the time; sometimes a whole day will go by without her coming up with anything that can honestly be called a word.

One night it might be "dada" for hours at a time when she sees me; the next day it will be like she's never heard the word. I don't know why this should surprise me, but it does; it's just another example of thinking that things would be one way, and discovering that they don't work that way at all. I will try for twenty minutes to try to get her to say something; nothing will happen. Then, out of nowhere, it will be "dada" again.

The lesson, I suppose, is that a baby progresses at precisely her own rate. No faster, no slower. We're not here to speed things up; we're just here to listen and offer approval when they finally take place.

March 15

TODAY I did what I swore I'd never do.

Susan went out shopping, and I stayed home with Amanda. While Susan was gone I got two calls; one from my friend Paul Galloway, and one from Herb Holmes of ABC. Both were social calls; they just wanted to talk.

During the two calls I found myself saying, "Just a second . . . come here, honey . . . no, you don't want to crawl over there . . . no, I'll be there in just a second . . . sorry, what were we saying?"

It's precisely the thing that used to annoy me about friends with small children—the automatic act of interrupting a phone conversation to talk to the baby. I always used to think it implied that the caller was somehow much less important than the baby. Which, of course, is undoubtedly true, in a way. But that's not why you do it; you do it because the caller is grown up, and can wait a few seconds; the baby isn't, and if you don't tend to her she can end up in trouble by the time you finish a sentence on the phone.

So Herb was telling me about a story he had produced out in Wyoming, and I said, "I'm sorry, I have to switch to the other phone, she's crawled into the bedroom." When I had chased her down and picked up the other line Herb was still there; I apologized to him, but thirty seconds later I was chasing her back the other way.

I still think it's a rude thing to do. But it's a *necessary* rude thing to do.

March 16

WHEN I got home from work today, Susan was near tears.

"What happened?" I said.

It seems that she was out shopping, and Amanda was riding in her stroller. They were at a shopping mall, and a little boy of about two leaned over and kissed Amanda on the mouth. He did it so quickly that it was over before Susan knew it.

There have been stories in the papers and on the news about a meningitis outbreak in the area; doctors have been warning parents that the disease spreads by physical contact with other children.

"I don't know what to do," Susan said. "I know it's silly, but I keep thinking that maybe she's been infected. The little boy kissed her before I could even reach down to pick her up."

I said that, as far as I knew, there had been only six cases of the disease in the city; I was sure that if he had just given her a peck, there was really no danger.

"I know, I know," Susan said. "But I just feel like I should have protected her, and I didn't."

It's actually not that silly; it's another graphic example of the real world intruding on this private world we've built up with Amanda since she was born. It's symbolic of outside forces that are going to meld increasingly with whatever forces Susan and I bring to Amanda's world; ultimately, of course, the outside forces will have far more influence with Amanda than we do. Look at us and our relationships with our parents; that's the best example. Because of geography and time, they're pretty distant now. It happens to everyone. I think maybe Susan understands this; her being upset has more to do with that than with the meningitis outbreak.

March 17

AND something else along the same lines. Amanda was crawling in her room today; we were watching her. One of the doors on her chest of drawers was open, and she reached up to it and pushed it; it swung closed and one of the hinges pinched her thumb.

She let out a howl and then began to sob. We rushed over and picked her up; in a matter of a minute or so the thumb was red and swollen. We talked soothingly to her and washed the thumb with cold water. Amanda seemed confused by it all; every silent message we have tried to give her has been that as long as we're around, everything is going to be all right—but here we were, with her as usual, and she suffered sudden pain anyway. She knew that wasn't supposed to happen. So did we; but we couldn't stop it. Little boys give sudden kisses and doors slam in an instant, even when we're there; life really is beginning to have a way of intruding.

March 18

ANOTHER permutation of the favorite-toy development: not only does she have a favorite thing to play with—but now she seems to decide, on the spur of the moment, that she does, indeed, want to play.

We'll be watching her crawl around the living room, and all of a sudden she'll stop in her tracks and turn to the wicker toy basket. Once she's got it in sight, she'll home in on it; she'll head right for it and start searching for whatever it is she wants.

It's as if she has finally realized that her agenda does not have to be set by Susan and me; she knows she's capable of deciding what to do. A week ago if we carried her to the toy basket, she'd look for that toy phone; now it's gone one subtle step further. She's figured out that we don't have to carry her over there at all; why should we be the ones to determine when she should have her toys?

March 19

Amanda went to sleep around eight o'clock tonight; a few hours later, when Susan and I were getting ready for bed, Susan went in to check on her.

She came out of Amanda's room and whispered, "Come here."

I walked in. Amanda, in her crib, was hugging a red-and-white cloth doll named "Jolly Dolly." She has started to do it every time she goes to sleep; we keep Jolly Dolly in the crib, and Amanda gathers it up to her right before she fades off.

We stood over the crib and stared down. Amanda was hugging Jolly Dolly up against her. "I've watched her do it," Susan said. "She won't go to sleep now unless she's hugging the doll. Even if it's at the other end of the crib, she'll go get it before she lets her eyes close all the way."

A factual note: Jolly Dolly is not some name Susan or I made up. It's on the label that's attached to the doll. This is not the case, of course, with Mr. Pig or Baby Bunny.

March 20

For the first time this morning, Amanda woke up talking instead of crying.

Every morning since last June we've known that she was ready to get up because of the wailing from the other room. The sounds of her cries, which had alarmed and upset us so much at first, now were just another part of our early-morning atmosphere; Amanda's cries meant that she was ready for us to come get her.

Today, though, we heard her making her happy talking noises. No cries at all. When we went in, she was in her crib waiting for us. She seems to have figured out that, as long as she has learned to make these sounds, she might as well try them out on us. If we come to her when she makes them, then she doesn't have to cry every time anymore. It's a lot more pleasant for us—and I don't imagine it's all that much fun for her when she's crying, either. There was something rather adult about this morning; it seemed to be one step closer to her actually asking us to come get her.

March 21

Tonight she cried again—but something else changed.

For all these months, when she's cried in the middle of the night we've had to come in and pick her up. Sometimes she's required feeding; other times it was just a matter of rocking her and talking to her until she fell back asleep.

Tonight, though, even though she woke up crying three times, each time she fell back to sleep ten or fifteen minutes later. She seems to be picking up a little more independence every day. It may appear to be a small thing—but having her decide that she can go back to sleep without making contact with us seems to be a milestone of sorts.

And in the morning, she was standing up holding onto the side of the crib again when we came in. That's happening almost every day now.

March 22

NOW Amanda crawls alongside Helen when Helen is on her way to eat. We'll walk into the kitchen, and there will be Helen leaning into her blue dish to have her cat food—and there will be Amanda, on all fours next to her, getting ready to do the same thing.

"Amanda!" we'll go. "Blah! Bad food! Blah!"

And Amanda and Helen will look at each other and laugh. Really. Helen's laughing, too. I can tell.

March 23

AMANDA'S hair was all mussed up this afternoon; it was wild and disheveled and standing on end.

Almost without thinking about it, Susan said: "Where'd you put your brush?"

Which to me is sort of a major point: Amanda indeed *can* put her brush someplace. She can pick it up and carry it off and hide it. Which is precisely what she had done.

I think back to those early days when she would just lie there on the bed and wait for us to carry her to wherever she was bound next. It would never have occurred to us to ask her what she had done with her brush.

Or my shoehorn, which is missing again.

Now she's standing without her hands holding onto something. Only for a second or two, and always with great trepidation. But she's learning that she can do it.

March 24

SUSAN was out shopping this afternoon, carrying Amanda, and all of a sudden Amanda started shrieking and trying to talk. Susan didn't know what was going on.

Until she looked in the direction Amanda was staring. Across the aisle was the woman who lives in the apartment next to us. Amanda sees her all the time at home; now, out in public, she was excited to be seeing her again.

"That's so odd to me," Susan said. "The idea that she can actually recognize someone in the middle of dozens of other people. But she obviously can."

"I find it a little hard to believe," I said.

"I would, too," Susan said. "But I saw it. There can't be any other explanation for it."

March 25

TODAY that same lady came over to see Susan and Amanda. One of Susan's friends was over, too, with her own baby, and the neighbor made a point of talking to the other baby and making a fuss over him.

Amanda hated it. She crawled over, she made noise, she

pointed at our neighbor with her first finger—she did everything she could to make the lady pay attention to her, not to the other child.

The funny thing was, Amanda had showed no interest at all in the other baby; she didn't seem to care that he was in the room. But as soon as our neighbor started making a fuss over him, Amanda was clearly annoyed and anxious to change things around.

I guess it counts as another first; the first pangs of jealousy.

March 26

WHENEVER she hears music she likes, she dances.

It's taken me a while to figure out that that's what she's doing—because obviously a baby who can't walk yet doesn't dance in the traditional sense.

But when a song that pleases her comes onto the radio or the TV set, she'll freeze in her tracks, wherever she's crawling, and start to rock back and forth. Her hands and knees will stay on the floor, but she'll sway forward and back, and get this funny clench-jawed look on her face. She'll do it for as long as the song lasts. As soon as the song is over, she'll crawl off again.

She seems to be partial to the Who and to the theme from "$25,000 Pyramid" on TV.

March 27

WHEN I refer to her favorite toys, I mean her favorite things among the items we keep in her toy basket. But the truth of the matter is, there are certain objects she far prefers to whatever we have brought her home from the toy store.

The three that mesmerize her the most are a rubber disc we keep in the kitchen to help open jars with lids that stick; a cloth tape measure; and my belt, which I generally leave lying on the floor after I've undressed at the end of the day.

Amanda prefers these things to anything the toy companies have designed. The disc especially she is in love with; I can see nothing at all attractive about it—it's mundane even for a kitchen utensil. But whatever is going on in her head has convinced her that the disc is just about the most fun in the world. She plays with it and carries it around and chews on it; when she's got it with her, her toy basket might as well not exist.

Also: she has begun to hold different things in two hands at the same time. If she is grasping something in her right hand, it now occurs to her that she can also pick something else up with her left hand. That's new.

March 28

THIS is something I'm having trouble getting used to. I will be in bed reading a book or watching television, and I will look down at the foot of the bed—and there will be Amanda's head staring back at me.

Apparently, I have become one of the objects that fascinate her. So if she's in the living room with Susan and she hasn't seen me for a while, she will know that she can crawl into the bedroom and probably find me. And once she has reached the bedroom, she knows that if she pulls herself up, her head will stick up just over the level of the mattress—and there I'll be.

It's so strange. After months of having to go to her, now she is choosing to come to me. I don't know quite how to react. When she first started doing it, I would reach over and lift her up and put her on the bed with me. But she doesn't really want that; as soon as I do it, she generally tries to crawl away.

All I can figure is that she *likes* the idea of coming in and looking at me. She doesn't expect anything in return; I'll look back in the living room, and off she'll go again.

It's a fairly simple arrangement. Still, though, when I look over and she's there looking at me . . . I don't know. It's sort of hard to adjust to.

March 29

THE sound of her crying as she makes her way around the apartment has become more frequent. It's a product of her growing ambition.

She knows she can stand up; she knows that once she's up she can move along any surface that has an edge for her to grasp. But she's getting impatient; often she tries to move between two objects—say, a table and a chair—where there's simply too much open space for her. She'll start off, and she'll reach out for something to support her, and there will be nothing there—and down she'll go.

So she'll scream and she'll wail and she'll sob, and we'll pick her up and tell her softly that she really hasn't hurt herself. In a few seconds she'll calm down—and then it will start all over again, with her attempting to go places she shouldn't, and then falling, and then crying.

"We have to just let her keep doing it," Susan said. "It's the only way for her to learn, and we can't be telling her she can't do things all the time."

Which is true, I suppose. But it's nerve-wracking to know that every time we look away, she's likely to try something she can't handle—and that every time she tries something she can't handle she'll hit the floor and cry out. I wince whenever I hear her do it; I feel for her, but I've got to let her figure out her limitations for herself.

March 30

WE had to move our stereo system up two shelves; it had been on the shelf closest to the floor, and she had been crawling up to it and fooling with the dials and trying to chew on the wires. When we first put the safety plugs in the electrical outlets, I thought of it as kind of a cute, doting, parental thing to do—not something that was truly necessary. Now I see that it was.

Add my beeper to the non-toys that have become her favorite toys. No matter where I leave my briefcase, she finds it, unclips the beeper, and carries it off.

It's not such a bad thing, though. If I can't find her I can always call ABC and have her beeped.

March 31

EVERYTHING has to come *off* shelves: records, clothing, papers, magazines. It's as if something inside her is telling her that she must remove anything she sees put neatly in place. She doesn't do it helter-skelter; she's actually pretty methodical about the whole thing. If we have left a drawer open, she will crawl over to it, examine what's inside, and then carefully begin to lift everything out and place it on the floor.

"I wonder why she doesn't put things away instead of doing this?" Susan said as we saw her remove every magazine from a rack and throw them onto the carpeting.

"I don't know," I said. "Amanda, why don't you put things away for us?"

She tossed a copy of *Glamour* over her shoulder and went after this week's issue of *Newsweek*.

April 1

STARTING early this morning, I worked hard on a column about the upcoming Chicago mayoral election. I had to go to the far north side of town to interview a man; then, once I got back downtown, I had several hours of phone checking to do. Midway through the afternoon the editors decided they wanted to promote the story on Page One, so I had to meet with the graphics people to explain to them what the story was all about. There were some changes to be made after I had finished writing; it was well after dark before I was finished.

I was still buzzing from the nonstop reporting and writing; when I got home all of the elements of the story were still knocking around my head.

And Susan said, "Amanda learned how to drink from a cup today."

Amanda was proudly holding a plastic cup with a dribble-proof spout attached to it; while I had been doing the political story, she had—for the first time—given up her bottle and tried to drink liquids the way she had seen Susan and me drink liquids. It is something that, yesterday, she had never attempted. Today she did it, and she will be doing it for the rest of her life.

I went into the kitchen and watched her. I realized that, for all the adrenaline involved in getting and writing the story today, and for all the importance I placed in crafting it so that it read well, next to this it meant nothing. Nothing. What Susan and Amanda had accomplished at home today was so much more important; I watched Amanda drink from the cup, and nothing else mattered.

April 2

SHE seems attracted to doors—doors of any kind. The kitchen door, the doors on cabinets, the door to her own room—all of a sudden they take precedence over anything else in her world.

"I read something about this in one of those child-development books," Susan said. "It's not the doors she's interested in. It's the hinges."

"What do you mean?" I said.

"She's just about at the age where babies become fascinated by hinged objects," Susan said. "That's what's going on."

"You mean there are chapters about babies and hinges?" I said.

"Not whole chapters," Susan said. "But they definitely mention babies being attracted to hinges."

"I think she just wants to crawl through the door," I said.

"Nope," Susan said. "It's the hinges."

April 3

TONIGHT Susan put into words what I have been thinking.

"I was looking at her sleep," she said, "and I looked down at her . . . and she didn't look like a baby anymore."

"What did she look like?" I said.

"Like a little girl," Susan said.

And it's true. I've been noticing it, too. She's still a baby, of course, and will be for another year or so. But she's not the kind of baby we were getting used to. She's not a tiny infant.

She's growing, and her face is taking on its own personality, and her hair is growing thicker; it's butterscotch in color now. It's really happening; she's beginning to turn into a little girl.

No matter how much attention I pay to her, no matter how hard I try to notice every change in her life, there are certain things that happen during the moments I'm not watching. I suppose if I watched twenty-four hours a day, the changes would happen during the split-seconds when I was blinking. There are certain things so magical and so mysterious that no one sees them happen. But they happen, all right; you can see them once they've happened. Yes, you can.

April 4

She must be getting pretty self-sufficient; for the first time, I found myself getting angry at her.

I walked into the living room, and about a dozen of our hardback books were scattered on the floor. Some of the covers had been torn.

"Susan!" I said. "What's going on?"

"She's been pulling the books out," Susan said.

I felt myself burning. I'm funny about books; they're special to me in a way that other things aren't. I didn't mind Amanda throwing the record albums around, and I didn't mind her throwing the magazines around. But throwing the books around, and ripping the covers . . . I was genuinely upset.

"Look, you can't let her do that," I said. "These books are part of this house. It's just not acceptable for her to tear them up."

"All right, then you watch her every second," Susan said. "If you think it's so easy keeping her away from the books, then you try it."

I started to pick up the books and put them back.

"It's not really the books she's interested in, anyway," Susan said.

"What do you mean?" I said.

"It's the place where the front covers meet the bindings," she said.

"What about them?" I said.

"They're hinged," Susan said.

April 5

I WAS brushing my teeth and shaving this morning; I looked down, and there was Amanda, watching every move I made.

She was standing up, holding herself against the bathroom cabinet. She had a look on her face that said this was the most natural thing in the world for her; just standing around the bathroom watching her daddy get ready for work. I laughed and she smiled back.

She took a bath in the tub for the first time tonight. Not her little plastic tub, but the big one—the real one.

It was funny to watch. In recent weeks she had become the self-confident captain of her own tub; she's gotten big enough that it seemed small to her, and she would try to crawl or step out of it. It was clear that she considered it something she had mastered.

But in our big tub, she was dwarfed. We just poured a little water into it, and sat her down; Susan held her in a sitting position and I talked to her, but it was clear she was frightened and unsure of herself. She usually screeches happily and tries to talk a mile-a-minute in her little tub; tonight, in the big one, she sat silently, her eyes wide, her body tensed up, her face uncertain, waiting to see what would happen next.

"Not as tough as you thought you were, huh?" I said to her.

She craned her head around, having no idea what to expect, and we picked her up and dried her off.

April 6

I got home from work a little late tonight. In the front hallway, toys were scattered all over the carpeting. In the living room, magazines were spread everywhere. In the bathroom, the toilet paper had been completely unrolled and left on the floor. Near the stereo, all of the albums had been pulled out and discarded.

"Hi," I said to Susan. "I'd ask you what she's been doing all day, but I guess I know."

April 7

She's getting ready to walk.

I'll stand up and hold her under her arms, and she'll move across the floor. Every instinct in her tells her that this is now the way she should propel herself. She does not want to get back down on her hands and knees to crawl; she wants to stay upright.

She's like a tiny colt. Her steps are unsteady and quavering; her legs bend and give way with each step. But *she wants to do it*; suddenly she knows that the crawling will soon be something she used to do when she was a baby, and that she is supposed to get around the same way her mother and father do.

I'll get tired before she does. Holding her up and bending over and moving at her speed is an exertion. But when I'll relax my grip so as to allow her to get back on the floor and crawl, she'll resist; she'll look back up over her shoulder as if to urge me to keep going. She wants this very much.

April 8

I LEFT my briefcase on the floor tonight; I looked up and she was rummaging through it. She came out with a bottle of pills.

I quickly took them away from her, but it pointed out something else that, until now, had been an abstract thought but is now turning into an absolute rule. Of course I knew that parents were supposed to keep pills away from children. Up until very recently, though, Amanda didn't have the mobility to get to pills. She lacked the coordination to search for them and make trouble with them.

Now it's simple for her. I took the pills from her and zipped them back inside the briefcase, then put the briefcase on a high shelf where she couldn't reach it. Then I toured the house and made a pill check.

It occurs to me that she has begun to think of this as her own house. All she does during the day is move around it, exploring; on some levels she is undoubtedly more familiar with it than I am. She knows what rooms she wants to go to; she knows what corners hold items she can play with. It's more than a house to her, of course; in a sense it's her whole world. But the point is, it's become very specific to her; if we took her somewhere else and put her down, she'd know within moments that she wasn't at home.

April 9

EVERY day she shows more ways in which she is becoming her own person, setting her own agenda. I will be on the couch watching television, and she will very casually crawl over to the set, touch the buttons, and change channels.

And: she will be crawling along the floor, and she will get tired, so she will decide to stop and sit for a while. She'll do it; she'll switch from the crawling position to a sitting position and just rest for a while. A week ago she couldn't do that; if she was going to sit, we'd have to rearrange her.

And: when she wants Susan or me to pick her up, she will attempt to talk to us and then raise her hands in the air as a signal. If we don't catch the signal, she will keep reaching up until we figure out what she wants.

And: she will surprise us by what she is able to accomplish. Today Susan brought a six-pack of 7-Up home from the grocery. It was in cans, and they were held together by those plastic rings that encircle the tops of the cans. While we weren't looking, Amanda crawled up to the six-pack and removed two of the cans from the rings. "Sometimes I can't even do that," Susan said.

April 10

ONE of the things I like most about having her around is that she makes me notice things I had always taken for granted.

I was helping her walk again this afternoon; with my assistance she was wandering all over the apartment. As her legs bent and unbent, and I held her from under her arms, I looked at her feet. They were so small; I was surprised that they could hold her erect even with my assistance.

But it's not just her; I looked at my own feet. What an amazing concept. Think of how tall an average adult is; then think of how that adult is able to stand up and balance on something as relatively small as his feet. You talk about a miracle of engineering and balance; the very fact that we can stand up and walk around is pretty startling, once you look closely at us and think about it.

I tried to explain this to Susan. She glanced at me like she thought I was crazy.

April 11

ONE of the most vivid memories I have of my own childhood was when I was nine or ten years old, and Elvis Presley was making his initial appearances on the "Ed Sullivan Show." My little sister and I would sit with our parents, and we would watch Elvis; seeing Presley on the Sullivan show was something of a national pastime.

I was moved by Presley and his music in ways that I couldn't quite comprehend then, and still can't explain now. What he represented was so different, so jarring, so completely foreign to the safe and placid way in which I was being brought up—I found my eyes locked on the television set. I was in our house on Bryden Road in Columbus, but part of me was realizing for the first time that life offered possibilities and pleasures my parents had never mentioned.

The reason I'm thinking about this today is that last night a movie called "This Is Elvis" was broadcast by NBC television; the movie was a documentary on Presley's life, and the old Ed Sullivan footage was included.

I was with Amanda. We were on the couch in the living room; she was sitting up next to me—she really is getting comfortable and contented in the sitting position—and I had my arm draped around her, like a kid with his date at the movies.

Ed Sullivan introduced Elvis Presley, and Presley began to sing "Don't Be Cruel," and all these years later the impact was the same. Those bloodless words on paper—"Presley began to sing 'Don't Be Cruel' "—don't come close to capturing what happened when Elvis Presley started to sing with a television camera trained on him. So I sat there watching, and I looked down—and Amanda, who turns ten months old today, was staring at Presley with the same fascination I was. She can't have any idea of who he is—she will, of course, remember nothing of seeing him here with me on this night—but the music was affecting her, too. It was something beyond the rocking-dancing motions she makes when she hears any song that pleases her; it was a visceral, almost chemical reaction to what happened more than twenty-five years ago when those two phenomenal new American forces—network television and Elvis Presley—first discovered each other.

So we sat there together, my daughter and I, watching Elvis, just as I had sat with my own parents and watched him in 1956. I was going to call them and tell them about it. But I didn't know how.

April 12

THERE'S a woman who lives in the same building we do, and every time she sees Amanda she says, "Hello, Mandy."

Apparently she did it this afternoon, because when Susan came home she said, "You know, I hate it when people call her Mandy. Her name's not Mandy. It's Amanda."

I know what she means. It's a fairly innocuous error on

someone's part—after all, I suppose a lot of Amandas *like* to be called "Mandy"—but when someone says it, it just seems all wrong. I suppose you should be flattered that they even have any idea of what your child's name is; you feel like correcting them, but you don't.

"Did you say anything to the woman?" I said.

"No," Susan said. "That would sound stupid."

"I know," I said.

"And Amanda doesn't seem to mind," Susan said.

April 13

I WAS talking to a woman friend today—a woman who had had a son the October before Amanda's birth in June.

"They're going to be in the same class," the woman said to me.

"No, they aren't," I said. "They were born in different years."

"That doesn't matter anymore," she said.

"What do you mean it doesn't matter anymore?" I said. "If you were born in a certain calendar year, then you go to school with kids who were born in that calendar year."

She laughed. "You'd better start checking up on this stuff," she said. "Everything's changed. It was like you and I went to school a hundred years ago. Every school district has different rules. I checked, and they said that if my son was born after September, he had to go to school with the children who were born the next year."

Maybe she's right; maybe she's wrong. The thing is, it sort of gets me jittery even having to think about this stuff. Having a baby in the house—that's finally something I'm getting used to. But I had no intention of thinking about things such as what grade Amanda should enroll in at what time—and I suppose, if I had given it any subliminal thought at all, I had assumed that all the rules were going to be the same as when I was a kid. The rest of the world has changed, but somehow I guess I pictured Amanda going to the same kindergarten class as I did, in the same room, in the same building, with the same teacher. When I mentioned this to my woman friend, she laughed again.

"Kindergarten?" she said. "That's when you think she should start school?"

"Pre-school?" I said.

Another laugh. "How about mother-toddler groups?" she said.

I'm really not ready for this kind of thing yet.

April 14

WE'VE been buying books for Amanda; just short, read-aloud things with big pictures in them. I've started to notice something.

In many of the books, when the text is about children, the illustrations show white and black children in approximately equal numbers. If the story is about Billy and Jimmy and Sally and Mary, it's likely that either Billy or Jimmy will be black, and either Sally or Mary will be black, too.

So in the drawings of the children playing, you will often see whites and blacks together. I tried to remember whether this was the case when I was growing up. I don't think so. I think that almost always, all of the children we read about were white. If there was a black child in the books, it was only one black child.

I have no idea how much of this Amanda is taking in as we read to her, but I think it's great. Over the past several decades we've all read the news stories about how racist and sexist language and images were being taken out of children's books;

I always skimmed over those stories when I saw them. But now that my own daughter is ready for these books, I realize how important it is. It's a beginning; a beginning of the formation of her attitudes about other people. Maybe, right now, the drawings of the white and black children don't mean anything. But eventually they will; eventually something's going to click. She will start her life with some assumptions about other people that my generation just didn't have. It strikes me as pretty nice.

April 15

SUSAN brought Amanda to the newspaper office today. As I've done on Amanda's previous visits, I picked her up out of her stroller and carried her around the city room area. I noticed something about her—something that I want to believe she has inherited from me.

She's very vocal at home these days, and in the company of people with whom she's familiar. She chatters all the time—sometimes it's hard to get her to stop.

But today, around the strangers at the newspaper, she became very silent. She didn't cry; she just looked at them with a pensive expression on her face. They talked to her and cooed at her and held her hand; she just stayed in my arms, her head ducked low, and returned their gazes.

It's the same way I behave around people I don't know. As full of opinions as I can be around my friends, when I'm thrust into a new situation, with new people, I clam up. I listen and I watch, but seldom do I say anything. I suppose it's a social defect; but it's part of me, and it's something I've never been able to shake.

So today all of the reporters and editors gathered around Amanda, and tried to get some response. All they got was that silent stare. "She's her father's daughter," someone said, and they were right about that one.

At home tonight, she played her usual game of finding me no matter where I went. Now that she knows she can do it, she crawls after me through every room in the house. If I'm watching television, I'll look down and there she'll be, looking up at me. If I'm reading in the bedroom, I'll look to the foot of the bed, and there she'll be. It's gotten to the point that when I go into the bathroom I have to close the door until it clicks shut—and even then it's only a matter of seconds until I hear her knocking against the outside, laughing and trying to talk.

April 16

OFTEN, when I go out on stories and interview people, I'll end the visit by saying, "If you ever come downtown, stop by the *Tribune* and say hello." It seems more polite than simply putting my notes away and taking off.

Once in a while the people take me up on it. Today the receptionist called to say a woman was at the desk; I had interviewed her about six months ago while I was doing a story out in the suburbs, and I had said to drop in when she was downtown, and here she was, downtown.

It was the lunch hour; I went out to greet her, and I was hungry, so I asked her if she felt like having something to eat. She said yes; we went to the Marriott across the street.

She was married with two young children; it turned out she did not know that I was married, and she was full of questions when she found out that I had a ten-month-old daughter. At some point in the conversation she said, "Do you think you'll be a strict parent?"

That stopped me. I had never really thought about it. With Amanda up to now, it hasn't been a question of being "strict" or "lenient"; we've merely had to try to get her through this first part of her life, and the stringency of our attitude toward raising children has never really come up.

I explained this to the woman; I said, "Do you consider yourself strict?"

"Oh, very," she said.

"In what way?" I said. "How are you strict?"

"Well, if my daughter wants to go down to the Seven-Eleven store, I won't let her go unless she has a legitimate reason," she said. "If she just wants to hang out, I won't let her go. If she has something she really has to get there, she knows that she has to be home in fifteen minutes. And she knows I mean it; she's always home within the limit, because she knows if she isn't, I'll be down there to get her."

It sounds so far away. But I know it isn't. A "strict father"; what an image to have of yourself.

April 17

There are times when I think that Susan and I are not so much parents as air-traffic controllers.

With Amanda's constant movement around the apartment, we seem to do basically the same kind of work as controllers do: we each watch her while she is in our particular geographic area of responsibility, and when we see she is about to leave we hand her over to the next person.

"She's crawling out of the living room now; can you see her?" "Yes, she's just moving into the bedroom." "She's not in the kitchen anymore." "I've got her, she's crawling right past your bathroom."

Kind of like a 727 flying from Denver to Chicago. With a pilot who drools and wears pajamas with feet attached.

April 18

I WAS playing with her; I had a plastic ball, and I bounced it over to her. She closed her eyes and cringed.

That's new. I bounced the ball again; again her eyes closed and her face clenched up. Before, she had no fear of anything that came near her; now, for the first time, she senses that she is open to danger.

April 19

THE three of us were in the living room, watching a television show; a bride came onto the screen.

"Someday, you'll be a bride," Susan said to Amanda. "You'll wear the same dress that I got married in.

"And on your wedding day, your daddy will walk you down the aisle and give you to your new husband. And then later, the orchestra will play, and while everyone watches, you and your daddy will go out onto the floor and you'll dance together."

I just looked out the window, thinking.

April 20

HER regular appointment with Dr. Scheinberg was today, and he said that she can start eating table food.

"What do you mean?" Susan said.

"Well, when you're having dinner, if you think there's something she should have, you can give it to her and let her try it," he said.

"Like what?" Susan said.

"If you're having french fries, for example, you can give her a french fry," he said.

French fries? Amanda?

April 21

I WAS shaving this morning, and—as is becoming her custom —Amanda pulled herself up close to the counter, held herself upright, and stood next to me.

She soon grew bored with that, however; she started opening and closing the cabinet drawers that were within her reach. That didn't bother me too much; we had already gone through the drawers to make sure there wasn't anything inside she could get into trouble with.

But soon I heard a loud yowl; she had slid one of the drawers closed, and had jammed her finger.

Susan came running in and picked her up. "That's all right, honey," she said. "That's all right."

"Actually, it's probably a good experience for her to do that," I said, still shaving. "She'll learn what happens when she pushes a drawer closed while her hand is still there."

"Wrong," Susan said. "She does it while you're at work all the time. She never learns."

By this time Amanda had stopped crying and was reaching for another drawer to open.

April 22

I WAS working on a column at the office, making telephone calls to get the details of a story. The other line rang; it was a woman I knew, saying that her own daughter was going to have her third birthday at the beginning of June, and did Amanda want to come to the party? She gave me a few of the specifics.

I was preoccupied with the story, so I half listened to her and said I would tell her "yes" or "no" in a few days.

Tonight at home I was going over my notes for the column. Apparently I had not stopped jotting when the other call came in; right in the middle of the interview notes were the following entries:

"B-day party . . . Maggie the Clown will be there . . . three years too old for Amanda? . . . yes, will be youngest child at party."

And then the interview notes continued. If any artifact represents the way my life has changed from today's date a year ago, this notepad is it.

April 23

I WAS in the shower this morning, and I noticed I was out of soap. I stepped out; it was cold and I was dripping wet. I pulled at the cabinet beneath the sink to get some more soap; the door was stuck. I pulled again. It wouldn't budge. I tried to use both hands. Nothing.

I started kicking at the cabinet drawer, and in a moment Susan stuck her head in the door.

"What are you doing?" she said.

"These things are stuck," I said. "I have to get some soap."

She walked over, opened the cabinet door a fraction of an inch, unlatched a trick lock inside, and the door opened all the way.

"What was that?" I said.

"I forgot to tell you," she said. "I had a repairman come in yesterday and fix up all the low doors and drawers in the house. Now Amanda can't get in them."

"Well, apparently neither can I," I said.

"I'm sure you'll learn," Susan said.

Now, when I'm home alone and Susan and Amanda are out, I can hear Amanda's voice in the hallway.

I'll be in the living room or the bedroom, and in the back of my consciousness there will be a sound that I recognize. In a moment or two I will hear the door opening; the voice will have been Amanda trying to talk.

Not such a big deal, I suppose. But still, the idea of hearing my daughter coming home is something I had not foreseen.

April 24

THE stage of carrying things around in her mouth when she crawls apparently has ended.

She is so nonchalant about crawling now that she can carry something in one hand and still manage to crawl along easily. This is fascinating to watch; unfortunately, the object she chooses to carry in her hand most often is my watch, which she has learned how to snatch off my night table.

April 25

A SYMBOLIC moment. Susan brought Amanda into the room; Amanda was wearing a new outfit. She seems to be getting another new outfit every time I turn around; it's nice to see her dressed so well, but Susan knows that I think she is overdoing it.

"Amanda, Mom likes to dress you up like a Christmas tree," I said. Amanda laughed.

Half thinking, I turned to Susan.

"You really do like to dress her up, don't you, Mom?" I said.

"What . . . did . . . you . . . say?" Susan said.

"I just said that you really like to dress her up," I said.

"I don't mean that," she said. "I mean what did you call me?"

"Call you?" I said.

"You just called me 'Mom,'" Susan said.

I laughed. "I couldn't have," I said. "I don't call you 'Mom.'"

"You just did," Susan said.

"I couldn't have," I said.

"You did," she said. "Please don't do it again. I am not your mom. I am your wife."

"Well, you're Amanda's mom," I said.

"I may be 'Mom' to Amanda," she said. "I am not 'Mom' to you."

I can see where this might rile her.

April 26

I WALKED into the kitchen after dinner. Susan was doing the dishes, and Amanda was standing next to her, holding herself up against the wall.

I suppose this will start to wear off soon; maybe I will get jaded about it before too much longer. But I can't get over it; that one phrase—*Amanda was standing next to her*—puts so much distance between where we are now, and where we were when this first year of her life began. I keep thinking back to those first few weeks, when she was so small it hardly seemed she was real. Now here she is, standing around the kitchen watching Susan.

I guess I was staring, because Amanda looked back at me.

"Da-da," she said. "Da-da."

I got the ice tray out of the refrigerator, and she started reaching for it. Every time she stuck her hand into the tray and came in contact with a piece of ice, she immediately withdrew the hand.

"Cold," I said. "Cold."

She was fascinated. She would stick her hand in again, and every time she would be ready to touch another piece of ice, I would say "Cold," trying to teach her the meaning of the word. She seemed to love this game; I know I did.

I don't seem to stop at bars on the way home the way I used to.

April 27

THERE'S something going on in her head; there's a word she says, and it clearly means something, but we have no idea what.

"Gun-yay," she will say.

We will look at her and wait for her to point to something.

"Gun-yay," she will say. "Gun-yay."

We haven't a clue. As amazing as it is to have her say "Da-da" or "Ma-ma," and as exciting as it is to realize that those words really do refer to us, this is even weirder. Whatever "gun-yay" means, it's nothing we have taught her; completely on her own she has identified something, has decided that it is called "gun-yay," and is trying to tell us about it. And it's up to us to translate it.

"I think it's your glasses," I said to Susan. I pulled the glasses off and held them in front of Amanda.

"Gun-yay?" I said. "Is this gun-yay?"

Amanda, bored, looked away.

"We've got to find out," Susan said.

"I know," I said.

"Gun-yay," Amanda said.

April 28

On the other hand, the translatable phrases haven't lost their wonder, either.

Susan was getting ready to feed Amanda, and she was preparing to tie a bib around her neck.

"Watch this," Susan said. She held the bib up in front of Amanda. There was a picture of a cat on the front of the bib.

"Meow," Amanda said.

"No," I said. "I don't believe it."

"She does it all the time," Susan said. "She knows it's a kitty."

"She can't know," I said.

"She knows," Susan said. As Susan stirred her food Amanda went:

"Eee-aye, eee-aye oh."

"What's that?" I said.

"When I feed her, I sing 'Old MacDonald Had a Farm' to her," Susan said. "When she wants to eat, she does the 'eee-aye, eee-aye oh' part to let me know she's ready."

"Eee-aye, eee-aye oh," Amanda said, and Susan said, "I know. I know. You can eat now."

I'm sure this has been happening in precisely this way for uncounted centuries. But nobody ever told me.

April 29

Helen's getting old. It makes me sad; when Amanda was just about to be born we were so afraid that Helen was going to be vicious to her. But Amanda's first year has coincided almost exactly with Helen beginning to show her age. She's almost ten; she's a pretty old cat.

It almost seems as if the livelier Amanda gets, the tireder Helen gets. She sleeps much of the time now; she used to wash herself all the time, but now she doesn't do it as often, and it's not uncommon to see her fur matted.

I keep wondering if Amanda being in the house has anything to do with this. Has it accelerated the process? Helen was used to being the only one in the house, beside us; now she must sense how Amanda has changed everything, and I wonder how much those changes have made her feel a little extraneous?

We do everything we can to be nice to her and make her feel that everything around the house is still the same. But she knows it isn't; we can't fool her. I suppose the one saving fact is that Amanda likes her so much; the single thing Helen seems to get a kick out of is Amanda playing with her. Within minutes of when Amanda stops, though, Helen is over in a corner, asleep.

April 30

For some reason, Amanda has developed a fascination with the sound of my shower.

Every morning I will be taking a shower before going to

work; I always leave the door to the bathroom open a crack, so that the bathroom doesn't get all steamed up.

A routine has developed. I will see, through the glass of the shower door, the door to the bathroom being pushed open wider. I will hear, beneath the roar of the water, the sound of Amanda trying to talk. And then I will hear a scratching—as Amanda tries to get into the shower.

I will slide the shower door open. "Amanda," I'll say, "you wouldn't have any fun in here. It's hot and it's wet. I'll be out in a minute."

And then Susan will come rushing into the room. "Don't let her in there," she'll say. "Close that shower door."

"Sorry," I'll say.

Could "gun-yay" mean shower?

Nah.

May 1

"COME here," Susan said. She was feeding Amanda in the kitchen.

I walked over.

"I know that you don't believe me when I tell you what she knows," Susan said. "So I'll let you do it yourself."

She handed me a jar of Gerber's strained bananas. On the label was a picture of the Gerber baby.

"Hold the jar in front of her," Susan said. "But hold it with the back of the label facing her."

I did. Amanda just looked at it.

"Now rotate the jar until the picture of the baby is facing Amanda," Susan said.

I did.

Amanda took her finger and touched the picture. "Ba-ba," she said.

"That's right," Susan said.

Amanda kept jabbing at the picture. "Ba-ba," she said. "Ba-ba."

"That's right," Susan said. "That's a *baby*."

"There must be some other explanation for it," I said.

"Right," Susan said. "Mirrors."

May 2

THE thing that has impressed me and moved me the most this year has been how smoothly Susan made the transition from being a working woman to being a mother. My own transition to fatherhood has been filled with stops and starts and lurches; I'm still trying to figure it out. Susan, on the other hand, seems to have known instinctively how all of this is supposed to work out.

It shows up in the smallest ways. Amanda is still fascinated by hinged objects, for example. Doors, books . . . if there's a hinge, she wants it.

Today Susan said, "I went to the hardware store to see if they had a plastic box with a hinged top, but they didn't have any."

"What were you doing at the hardware store?" I said.

"I told you," she said. "Looking for a plastic box with a hinged top."

"What did you need it for?" I said.

"For Amanda to play with," she said.

"You mean the only reason you wanted it was for Amanda to play with?" I said.

"Yes," Susan said.

"What made you think of that?" I said. "You weren't in the hardware store in the first place? You just got the idea to go there to see if they had a plastic box with a hinged top because Amanda likes hinges?"

"That's right," Susan said.

"You didn't see an ad for a plastic box with a hinged top, or anything like that?" I said.

"No," Susan said. "I just decided to see if they had one."

You can dream up all the grand examples you want of a mother's love. That's a good enough one for me, though.

May 3

WE bought her a walker that looks like a giraffe. It's mounted on wheels that make a clicking sound as they turn; the point is for her to hold onto the giraffe's rear end, push the contraption, and walk along behind it.

It works very well. She thinks she's playing with a toy, but really it's a structure that's designed to hold her upright while she moves along. So for the first time, she's really walking, albeit with the help of this device; if the giraffe weren't there to support her, she'd fall down.

She's all over the apartment with this thing. She lifts her feet much higher than she has to; it's as if she doesn't trust herself to move forward unless she's really clomping along. It's a funny sight; there she is, jerking one leg high into the air, then the other leg, as she moves across the living room.

It struck me that I had seen this kind of motion somewhere else before, and in a moment it became obvious. In nursing homes, the old people who need walkers to move about have this same motion. I guess at the beginning of your life and at the end of your life you need help with the simplest things. What seems melancholy when the old folks do it is a delight when a baby's doing it.

May 4

WHEN I came home from work, Susan looked as if she had been crying. I asked her what was wrong, and she said, "Nothing."

But her gloomy mood persisted; I kept asking her about it, and finally she said, "Amanda's ready to stop nursing."

"How do you know?" I said.

"I was nursing her today, and she pushed me away," Susan said. "I started to hold her close to me, and she just took her hands and shoved. She's never done that before."

"Well, she's growing up," I said.

"I know," Susan said. "But it was just her total lack of interest that got me. We've been doing this together since she was born, and it's as if she suddenly decided she had no use for it."

"You knew you'd have to stop sometime," I said.

"But I didn't think she'd shove me away," Susan said. "It's like she's telling me she doesn't need me anymore."

"She needs you," I said. "She needs you."

"I know," Susan said. "But I'm really going to miss this."

May 5

AS I was shaving this morning, Amanda crawled into the bathroom and pulled herself up next to me. So I picked her up and held her in front of the mirror.

She looked at it. Then she took her finger, pointed it toward the mirror, and moved it until it was touching her reflection.

"Ba-ba," she said.

I couldn't believe it. The Gerber bottle is one thing, but her own mirror image?

"Ba-ba," she said, jabbing the finger against the mirror.

"That's right," Susan said. She was standing in the doorway. "You're a baby." Susan pointed at the mirror image of me. "And who's that?" she said.

"Da-da," Amanda said.

My, my, my.

May 6

AMANDA really is getting older; when Susan's not around, there are actually things that we *do* together.

The new game is laughing. We both lie on the floor. I'll laugh in a certain tone; say, a low, rumbling laugh. She'll imitate it. Then she'll wait a second, and when it's clear that she's supposed to go first, she'll laugh in a different tone—and I'll imitate it. We keep going back and forth. You'd be surprised how many different ways there are to laugh.

May 7

MOTHER'S Day is tomorrow, so I stopped off at a store to buy Susan a present. I got a little crystal bird; it was sort of pretty, and I asked the saleslady to wrap it up.

"Would you like a card?" she said.

I said I would, and she handed me a plain white one, and a ballpoint pen. I must have hovered over the card for three minutes, thinking what to write.

Finally I just put: "To Mommy. Love, Amanda and Daddy."

What the hell. She can either take the salutation in the spirit it's intended, or not.

May 8

There's something else new that Amanda and I have in common. For the last couple of weeks, there have been these really good-tasting crackers in the kitchen called Cracottes. I just assumed that Susan had discovered them at the grocery store, and had started bringing them home for us. So I've been nibbling on them between meals.

Tonight I walked into the living room, where Susan and Amanda were sitting. I was biting down on a Cracotte.

"So *that's* where they've been going!" Susan said.

I must have looked puzzled, because she said:

"*You've* been eating them!"

"Of course I've been eating them," I said. "What am I supposed to do with them?"

"They're for Amanda!" Susan said. "They're real soft, and she can chew them and eat them. I haven't been able to figure out why they keep disappearing so fast."

I handed Amanda the rest of my Cracotte. She smiled and crunched into it. I think she sort of liked the idea that at last we're starting to eat the same things.

Susan liked the Mother's Day card. Or so she said.

May 9

SUSAN was cutting some fabric and doing some sewing. That's not typical for her; I asked her what she was doing.

"It's for Amanda's birthday," she said. "Come here."

She showed me a little wooden cradle she had bought; she was making a quilt for it. Right now she was cutting out tiny cloth hearts to sew onto the quilt; later she would buy a doll.

Amanda's birthday. This has been such an amazing year for me that I had never stopped to think in terms of it really ending. But I guess it's almost over; when June 11 comes around, we'll have a one-year-old in the house.

May 10

THIS is getting ridiculous. I was lying on the couch, reading a magazine, and Amanda crawled over, pulled herself up until her head was level with the cushions, and started jabbing the back cover of the magazine.

"Ba-ba!" she said. "Ba-ba! Ba-ba!"

I flipped the magazine over. Sure enough, in the ad on the back cover, there was a four-color picture of a baby.

"Now how does she tell the difference?" I said to Susan. "How does she know that this is a baby, and a picture of a grown-up is a grown-up?"

"How do *you* tell the difference?" Susan said. "A baby looks different from a grown-up."

"Yeah, but to her?" I said.

Susan shrugged. "Amanda know's it's a baby," she said.
Amanda laughed. "Ba-ba," she said.

And Amanda's decided to nurse a little bit longer. Not as much as she used to, but she does it. I think this is sort of a compromise on her part; she sensed she was hurting Susan's feelings.

May 11

SUSAN'S sister passed through town today. She had her two children, Fanny and Benjamin, with her; they had a few hours between planes, so they came to the apartment.

Fanny's five and Benjamin's four; it was interesting watching Amanda interact with them. She instinctively knew that they had something in common with her—i.e., they were both kids—but still she was wary. On the one hand, they were close to her own size; on the other hand, she had never seen them—she knew us. She kept looking back and forth.

Benjamin disappeared for a few minutes. I walked around the apartment, and I found him. He had climbed up into Amanda's crib and was playing in it.

My response was curious. I didn't want him in there. He wasn't hurting anything; he was just looking around and fooling with the toys that were on the mattress. But my first thought was that the crib belonged to Amanda; it was the one place that was hers and hers alone. No one else had ever been in there. And no one else should be there.

A year ago that room was my study. Now I found myself subconsciously defending Amanda's territorial imperative, as if it had been her room, and her crib, forever. I didn't say anything. But when Benjamin got bored and finally crawled out, I was glad.

May 12

In my middle drawer at work I have a picture of Amanda. Susan gave it to me; it is a blow-up of one of the snapshots we had taken of her, and it is in a red heart-shaped frame.

The picture was taken before Amanda had any teeth; in it she is propping herself up on our bed and smiling that gummy grin directly at the camera. When Susan gave it to me she told me it was to be put on my desk.

But I haven't. It's in the drawer, face-up; several times a day I open the drawer a few inches and look down at it. The reason I don't keep it on top of the desk is simple; if it were there looking at me all day, I would never think of anything else. I would be on the phone trying to get the details of a story, and I would glance over at it, and I would melt.

May 13

She woke us up at five thirty this morning, and it finally occurred to me: this isn't a case of her waking up early because something's wrong. This happens to be her idea of when a person is supposed to get up.

Some days it's five thirty, some days it's six, some days it's six thirty. But it's always earlier than I would choose, and I had gotten so used to her crying in the middle of the night that I began to consider this a part of that habit.

It's not, though; often now she sleeps through the night fine. She just happens to be an early riser; she's like a steelworker whose shift begins at 7 a.m. She's not grouchy, and she's not testy, and she's not ill-tempered at that time of the morning. She's simply ready to start her day.

And the fact that I'm not exactly ready to start mine doesn't seem to bother her in the least. I guess that's one of the perks that comes with being the baby in the house.

May 14

AMANDA looks different when she's wearing pajamas than when she's wearing real clothes.

In her PJs, which are soft cotton and have booties attached to the bottoms of the legs, she still seems like a small baby. Even though she's getting so much bigger, the pajamas make me remember the days when we first brought her home from the hospital.

In her real clothes—overalls, sweaters, little knit suits—she does seem like a girl who's getting older. If you saw her for the first time, and she was wearing real clothes, you'd know that she'd been around for a while.

This morning she was wearing a denim overall suit, and I said to Susan, "If you're just going to be around the house with her, why don't you leave her in her pajamas?"

"Because the day's started," Susan said. "Why should she stay in her pajamas all day? When she gets up, it's time to put her clothes on."

"As long as she's just going to be here, I like her in pajamas better," I said.

"Don't do that," Susan said. "You can't keep her as a tiny baby just by the force of your will."

May 15

MY first memory of my younger brother Tim is when he was a few months old, and my father was trying to take a picture of him, my sister, and me.

Timmy was propped up on the seat of a chair; Debby was on one side of the chair, and I was on the other side. My father stood a few feet away, ready to snap the shutter.

But Timmy's head kept flopping to one side or the other. We'd get all set for the picture, and his head would sort of plop in one direction or another. He was so small; he wasn't ready to sit up straight yet.

I thought of that tonight. Tim's wife Caryn, who is a flight attendant for Pan Am, was passing through town. I met her at the airport and rode to her hotel with her. We had dinner in the hotel restaurant.

We talked as we ate, but my mind kept wandering, and I kept thinking about how rapidly everything changes. Timmy sitting in the chair with his head bobbing seems as if it happened three weeks ago; now here I was with his wife, and he was out on the road somewhere, making his living. So much eludes us in the passage of time; it makes me glad that I've been paying such close attention to Amanda's first year.

May 16

TODAY Dr. Scheinberg said that she weighs seventeen pounds, seven ounces, and that she is twenty-eight and a half inches long. And we've reached another landmark: he said that she should stop drinking formula. When she's thirsty now, she can have real milk, just like a regular person.

May 17

I HAD to fly to Grand Rapids, Michigan, for an *Esquire* assignment. I had dinner with some reporters from the local newspaper, then went back to my hotel room and called Susan.

"She's looking for you," she said.

"What do you mean?" I said.

"She's crawling around the apartment going 'Da-da,' " Susan said. "She's looking everywhere. I keep telling her that Da-da went bye-bye, but she thinks you're here somewhere."

That's new. I'm used to the fact that she knows I'm "Da-da," and that she calls out the phrase whenever she sees me. But this is the first time that she's gone looking for me; before this, it always seemed that she was conscious of me when I was around, but that she forgot about me as soon as I left the house.

"She keeps going into your bathroom," Susan said. "She thinks you must be in the shower."

I changed my reservations to get an earlier flight home tomorrow.

May 18

HOME on an afternoon flight. And it's apparent that Amanda's getting stubborn.

If we pick her up and she wants to crawl, she yells. If we put her in her high chair to feed her and she's not hungry, she yells. If we leave the room and she wants to come with us, she yells.

"This isn't so great," I said.

"I know," Susan said. She sighed. "I was feeding her her

lunch today, and as soon as she decided that she'd had enough, she spit a mouthful of the food back in my face."

"She did?" I said. "What did she do after that?"

"She laughed at me," Susan said.

May 19

SHE'S moving right along in other ways, too. When we take her out in her stroller, she's becoming very nonchalant about the whole thing. She'll lift one leg up and drape it over the stroller's restraining bar, like a high school kid coolly hanging his arm out the window as he cruises in his father's car.

When I'm ready to leave the house in the morning she'll wave her hand frantically at me and call, "Bye-bye." When she catches my eye, she'll clap her two hands together and wait for me to do the same; when I do, she'll smile and clap some more.

So far, she hasn't spit any food at me.

May 20

IT'S interesting to watch her mind working. It seems to have become much more sophisticated than it was even a month or so ago.

Today she was playing with one of her dolls, and she tossed it onto a table in the living room. The table has a large surface; the doll was beyond her reach from where she was standing. So she started yelling—a signal for Susan to fetch the doll for her.

"No, Amanda," Susan said. "You figure it out."

Amanda yelled some more.

"I'm not going to get it for you," Susan said. "You figure out how to get it yourself."

So Amanda stopped yelling, and started looking at the doll and trying to think how she could get it back.

She saw that it was much closer to one edge of the table than it was to the other three edges. She pulled herself up to the table and, with her hands supporting her, started to inch her way around it, until she was on the side closest to the doll. Then she reached out and pulled it to her.

"Very good!" Susan said. "You did it!"

And Amanda threw the doll to the floor and crawled away. Having mastered the task, she had completely lost interest.

May 21

"CAN you say 'grocery'?" I said.

Amanda made her mouth into an oval and said "Gro-gro! Gro-gro!" She's been doing that for a couple of days now, and it cracks me up.

"You have to stop doing that," Susan said to me.

"Why?" I said.

"Because every time you say 'grocery' to her, it makes her think that I'm going to take her to the grocery. And when I don't, she gets confused."

"Grocery!" I said to Amanda.

"Gro-gro!" she said back, and started crawling rapidly in the direction of her stroller.

"Now, see?" Susan said. "She's going to the stroller because she thinks it's time to go to the grocery. I'm not kidding. Stop doing it."

She walked over and picked Amanda up. Amanda was clutching the arms of the stroller.

"We'll go to the gro-gro later," Susan said.

"Gro-gro!" Amanda said.

"Not now," Susan said. "Later."

I stood a few feet away, silently saying "grocery" with my mouth.

"Damn it, stop it!" Susan said.

"I can't help it," I said.

"She's more grown-up than you are," Susan said.

"I can't help it," I said. "I love to watch her try to say it."

"Then you take her to the grocery the next time you do it," Susan said.

Amanda squealed. "Gro-gro!" she said.

May 22

I HAD a "Nightline" story today; it was one of those pieces that had to be put together in one day, so I was up and out of the house by 6 a.m., and I ran around all day; we fed the piece to New York just before showtime. I didn't get home until midnight.

I walked in the front door. Susan was asleep in our room. Amanda was asleep in her room. I threw my coat on the couch and loosened my tie; I went in and looked at both of them.

There's something about this that makes me feel . . . *complete*. It doesn't matter how nuts the day had been. It doesn't matter that I didn't eat and that I didn't get to make all the calls I'd scheduled for the afternoon and that, thirty-five minutes before the broadcast, we were ordered to trim forty seconds out of a piece we'd carefully crafted. It doesn't matter that all of this starts all over again in seven or eight hours.

All that matters is that when I come home, this is waiting. It's a notion as old as mankind, and yet on nights like this, it strikes me like the newest and clearest vision on God's earth.

May 23

SLOWLY Amanda is starting to develop a life of her own that has nothing to do with me. I know that's natural, but it takes some getting used to.

"Tell Daddy how you laugh when Steve goes to get the meat," Susan said.

I asked her what she meant; she said that when she and Amanda go to the grocery, the butcher has a game he plays.

"Tell Daddy about Steve," Susan said. "Tell him how he sticks his head behind the glass in the meat counter, and he makes faces at you and you laugh."

Amanda, of course, can't tell me about anything. But if she could, I think I might be jealous of being left out of her life, even when I'm only being left out a little bit.

May 24

SHE was pushing herself along with that giraffe walker tonight, and every time the walker would come to a stop against a wall, she let out a scream. She would stop screaming only when we turned the giraffe around.

"She really is getting spoiled," I said.

"That's not spoiled," Susan said.

"What do you call it?" I said. "From the moment she got the giraffe, she's screamed every time it hits a wall even for a second."

"She just doesn't understand the concept of something stopping," Susan said. "It's completely foreign to her. As far as she's concerned, as long as she pushes the giraffe, it will move forward. She doesn't know how to deal with the idea that something can make it stop."

"What if I screamed every time something didn't go my way?" I said.

"You know," Susan said, "I'm not sure how healthy it is to compare your own emotional development with the emotional development of an eleven-month-old child."

May 25

THEY came to see me at my office today. On Amanda's previous visits, I picked her up out of her carriage or her stroller and walked around the premises with her. But today Susan took her out of the stroller, put her on the floor, and let her crawl around and explore.

It was so disorienting. Here's the room where I work every day—the one place that has had nothing to do with my home life. And all of a sudden Amanda is pulling herself up to the keyboard of my video display terminal; Amanda is sitting underneath my desk and looking up at me; Amanda is peering into her own reflection in the glass wall.

She stayed for only a few minutes; she was fussy, and Susan said it was time for her nap. But the change had already happened. Now, as well as being a part of the rest of my life, Amanda is part of my office, too. I'll never be able to walk in there again without thinking of her cruising around the floor.

May 26

THE shower routine has become a daily occurrence. I will get up in the morning and start to get ready to go to work; I will step into the shower, and about five minutes later I will realize that the door to the bathroom has been pushed open again, and that Amanda is in the room with me again.

It doesn't matter where she is in the apartment; Susan says that as soon as she hears the water running, she scrambles off to find me. She's come such a long way—from this little bundle we brought home from the hospital, to this *person* who wants to come looking for me as soon as she hears the shower running, and who knows just where to find me. What a feeling; I look out of the shower door, and there she is.

May 27

I WONDER why she has to cry before she goes to sleep? For all that's changed, that hasn't; it happens virtually every time.

It doesn't matter if she's visibly tired and yawning and rubbing her eyes; or if she's been up far too long; or even if it's merely her nap time. As soon as we carry her into her bedroom and lower her down into her crib, she starts wailing. She'll keep howling as we leave the room; usually, within several minutes, she has stopped, and she is snoozing away. But always, for those first few minutes, she cries, and cries hard.

I can understand why she cries when she wakes up; it's her way to let us know she's ready to start the day. But what's the reason for the bedtime crying? I can't figure it out.

May 28

I STOPPED off at a bar after work tonight; as I've noted, it's something I haven't been doing nearly as often as I used to.

So I pulled the stool up to the bar and ordered a drink. The bartender brought it. I began to drink it, and then I thought of Amanda crawling around the apartment calling "Da-da." Susan says she does it every day now; in the middle of the afternoon, when I'm not there, Amanda will start searching for me.

So I thought of her calling my name; I thought of her looking in the bedroom for me; I thought of her figuring out that I must be taking a shower, and crawling toward the bathroom.

I was finished with my drink. The bartender asked if I wanted another.

I said no. I headed home.

May 29

SHE walked.

I was supporting her in an upright, standing position; she was clutching onto my hands with her own fists. She was balanced on her feet.

Slowly, I uncurled her fingers so that she wasn't connected to my hands anymore. She didn't fall; she was standing on her own. I moved backward.

She started to bend her knees, as if she wanted to get down and crawl. "No, Amanda," I said. "Come here. Come to me."

I was perhaps five feet away. She looked me right in the eye.

"Come to me," I said.

She lifted her right leg, and moved it forward. She still didn't fall.

"That's great," I said. "Now the other one."

She lifted her left leg—really lifted it, much higher than she needed to—and brought it level with the right.

"A little bit more," I said.

She brought the right leg forward again. Then—much quicker this time—the left.

There was a combination of fear and excitement in her eyes. She stepped forward one more time with her right leg, and then fell into my arms. We just stayed there hugging each other.

May 30

IT'S cold outside for this time of year; people are still wearing heavy jackets.

Susan was getting Amanda ready to go out, and she said, "I have to get your hat out again. It's chilly out there."

She went to the closet to find the hat, and I thought once again that I wished Amanda could know about this some day. It would have been just as easy to take her for a walk without the hat; it's not snowing or anything. I'm a person who never even wears the right clothes in the rain; it always seems like too much trouble to deal with.

I watched Susan slipping Amanda's white knit hat over her head, then tying the strings underneath her chin. Of course she wouldn't take her out without the hat. I just hope something inside Amanda tells her how lucky she is to have a mom like that.

May 31

I WAS sleeping this morning, and I was dreaming that two people were whispering. When I woke up, I found that it wasn't a dream; Amanda and Susan were on the floor, whispering to each other. Susan was whispering real words, and Amanda was saying the real words she knows, and the word fragments she uses, in a hushed voice.

"What's that?" I said.

"I'm teaching her," Susan said. "I tell her that when daddy's asleep, she has to whisper."

"And she does it?" I said.

"Sure," Susan said. "She's been doing it for a couple of days now."

Amanda looked at me. "Da-da," she whispered.

"That's okay," Susan said. "He's awake now. You can say it loud."

"Da-da," she whispered again.

June 1

THE walking seems to be like when she first started to talk; I had expected that once she took her first step by herself, there'd be no stopping her.

But she won't do it. I stand her up and let her become sure of her balance. Then I back up a few feet and motion for her to try to walk to me. She just sits down and crawls.

Maybe that was just a false alarm the other day. Maybe she isn't really ready to walk.

June 2

BOY, was I wrong. Today she's been walking all over the place. It's as if it's the most fun thing in the world for her to do. We can't stop her; no matter what we want her to do, she wants to walk.

She'll take eight steps and shriek for joy. She's so obviously proud of herself; there's a look on her face that tells us she knows she's accomplished something great, and that she's done it by herself. I'll look at her, and she'll look back, kind of biting her lip and grinning; finally, she seems to be saying, I can do something wonderful without anyone helping me.

She holds her arms out to the sides, like a tightrope walker who has to keep adjusting his weight so that he doesn't fall off. Her steps are high and ginger, like a lady walking through mud puddles. So there she'll be—arms spread, feet lifting much too high—and she'll maneuver the whole length of the living room.

And when she finally does tumble down, she crawls away so fast—it's as if she's a little humiliated for falling, and has to prove something by stepping on the gas. We applaud every time she manages to go for a while before falling—we want her to know that she doesn't have to be ashamed for hitting the floor.

And the next thing we know, she's up again, heading straight for us, her mouth fixed, her eyes bright.

June 3

THE walking isn't the only thing that's new. "Watch this," Susan said tonight as Amanda was sitting on the floor in her diapers.

"Where's your toe?" Susan said.

Amanda took her first finger and touched her big toe.

"Does she really know?" I said.

"You try it," she said.

"Amanda," I said. "Show me your toe."

Without hesitation, she touched her finger to her big toe again.

"Where'd she learn that?" I said.

"What do you think we do all day?" Susan said.

I was on the phone talking to a friend tonight, when all of a sudden the line went dead, and I got a dial tone.

For an instant I thought that the phone might be broken, and then I looked next to me, and Amanda was standing there laughing.

She had walked across the room, come up to the table, put her finger on the telephone's button, and pressed it down. Walking, it seems, may not be all roses and light.

June 4

TOMORROW is that birthday party she's invited to; the one with the three-year-old kids and Maggie the Clown.

So today Susan came home from the store with a box; she opened it, and inside were dainty little-girl shoes, cut low and with white buckles.

"What are those for?" I said.

"The party," she said.

"But she already has shoes," I said.

"I'll be damned if I'm going to let her meet all those other children while she's wearing her orthos," Susan said.

June 5

WE went to the party; the orthos stayed home, and the new shoes looked ladylike and fine on her feet.

She was out of place as soon as she arrived. I had thought that it wouldn't make much difference that the other children were two years older; I thought it would be fun for her to be around other little people.

But the others walked with confidence, and talked to each other, and were fascinated with Maggie the Clown, who greeted each of them. Amanda just stood between Susan and me, each of her hands holding one of ours, puzzled and disoriented and a little scared. She kept looking at the other children, and then looking up at us; who were these people, and where were we, and what did this mean?

So while Maggie the Clown did her act, Susan and I took Amanda into another room, where she practiced her walking. She had been hesitant about trying it in front of the older children; but alone with us again, she was okay.

One of the other mothers came into the room. "It must be hard for her," she said. "I think three is probably as young as children can handle a party like this."

"I didn't know," I said. We left early, before the other children were served their hot dogs and potato salad.

June 6

LAST night, just before bed, Susan and I discovered that we had been thinking about exactly the same thing.

It had to do with the party. When we had first arrived with Amanda at the people's house, Maggie the Clown had been standing right inside the front door, greeting the guests. Most of the children had arrived there before us; they were gathered in a little knot with Maggie.

So Maggie, in her full clown's uniform, had asked us what our daughter's name was. After we had told her, she had said, "Amanda, come with Maggie and meet the other children." And she had reached out for Amanda's hand.

Amanda had looked at us for a brief instant—and had then taken Maggie the Clown's hand, and had tottered off to be introduced to the other boys and girls. Susan and I were only a few feet away, but it might as well have been a hundred miles. Those moments when Amanda was holding Maggie's hand, with her back turned to us, lifting her legs up and down the way she had learned at home, but on her way not to us, but away from us—I felt something happening in my throat.

Now, it turned out, Susan had felt the same way. We know that this is only the beginning; her life lies out there, and we are not always going to be the only people in it. I said to Susan that I had half expected Amanda to refuse to take Maggie's hand, refuse to walk with her; Susan admitted that she had been thinking the same thing.

But Amanda went; and when I think back on all the moments of this first year of her life, that is one that will remain in my mind.

June 7

She was drinking milk from her bottle this morning; I was holding her in my lap. She was holding the bottle all by herself.

Suddenly she took the bottle from her mouth and offered it to me. I laughed and handed it back to her. But she shoved it back toward me again. It was clear she wanted me to take a drink.

I don't like milk. But I pretended to put the bottle in my mouth, and to drink. She smiled broadly. She took the bottle back and took a swig herself. Then she gave it to me again.

She wouldn't drink any more until I had some—or, more correctly, pretended to have some. And so it went for ten minutes—Amanda taking a drink, then insisting that I have a drink, then drinking some more herself. I don't know what gave her the idea to do this, but it made me feel very good about life in general.

June 8

After Amanda was asleep tonight, there was a story on the news about a space shuttle flight that is scheduled to be launched in the next few weeks.

"I wonder if Amanda will ever go on a spaceship?" Susan said.

It was not meant in jest; some time, in the not-too-distant future, regular people will be transported into space. Perhaps not soon enough that Susan and I ever ever be able to do it—but by the time Amanda is an adult, there will almost certainly be space flights available to the general public.

I guess there is a genuine chance that some day she will ride in a spaceship. She and her contemporaries will have the opportunity to savor and sample things that have not even occurred to those of us living now. That's all a part of a changing world that will evolve in the decades to come—a changing world that will belong to Amanda and her generation. Everything we're doing—the men and women of Susan's and my generation—will come to fruition when the children of Amanda's generation become old enough to inherit our world. But it won't be our world—it will be theirs. We'll be gone.

I watched the graphic representation on the television screen, depicting the astronauts being buckled into their spacecraft. I thought of Amanda orbiting the Earth. In my mind, she still looked like she looks now.

June 9

NOW that she's walking, she is turning into quite the fashion plate. She found a scarf of Susan's, and before she totters across the living room she drapes the scarf over her head—kind of like a bride's veil.

So I'll be sitting and reading, and I'll hear her coming—and there she'll be, an unsteady baby with a big grin that sticks out from beneath a lopsided scarf.

Of all the things she might learn to identify and say this early in her life, I wouldn't have predicted that the human navel would be one of the first.

She's always pulling up my shirt, sticking her finger in my navel, and saying "Belly button." She doesn't say it that clearly, of course; it usually comes out more like "Beww bumm." But she knows what it is. It seems to fascinate her.

"Beww bumm," she will say, poking me. Then she'll look at me for confirmation.

"That's right," I'll say. "That's daddy's belly button."

And she'll shriek with laughter, and lurch away, arms spread for balance.

Our television set in the living room has a series of buttons, lined up vertically, for channel selection. The numbers of the channels are illuminated, and you punch the button next to the number you want.

Our viewing these days is in disarray, however, because it seems the numbers were printed on a long plastic strip that was inserted in the console. The lights inside the set made the numbers appear.

Amanda somehow figured out how to remove the plastic strip; she took it and hid it somewhere. So now the buttons are still on the set, but there are no numbers next to them. When we want to watch a specific show, we have to start at the top button—Channel 2—and count down to the channel we desire. I'm sure Amanda will retrieve the numbered strip eventually. It's just a matter of when.

When I leave for work now, she follows me to the door. She stands and waves and says "Bye-bye, Da-da."

She doesn't say it like an adult would say it, with emphasis on certain syllables. Each syllable is pronounced in exactly the same slightly excited tone; something like "BYE!—BYE!—DA!—DA!"

It's not so much a farewell; it's a request that I not leave yet, delivered in the only way she knows. "Bye-bye, Da-da," she will repeat, over and over, staring right up into my eyes.

I find myself very slow to leave the house these days.

June 10

On the way home from work, I stopped in at a bar I used to frequent in the days before Amanda was born. I felt like a Friday night drink. The bartender—even though we hadn't seen each other much lately—quickly fell into easy conversation with me.

After a while he said, "So what are you going to do this weekend?"

"I'll be at home," I said. "Tomorrow is my daughter's first birthday."

"No!" he said. "It's been a year? I can't believe it. It seems like she was born just the other day. Does it seem like a year to you?"

I just looked across the bar at the mirrored wall. "I don't know," I said.

June 11

It's five o'clock in the morning. I'm in the living room; Amanda and Susan are asleep.

Today my parents and Susan's parents arrive for Amanda's birthday party. Susan has hung crepe paper and balloons; there will be gifts and picture taking.

I don't know why I couldn't sleep; but here I am, looking out the windows and trying to sort out my thoughts. I suppose it's a futile task; maybe some day, years from now, I'll be able to delineate what this year has meant to me. But not now.

All I know is that, here in my home, I have a completely different feeling than I ever expected I'd have. Everything has changed; I guess I knew that was bound to happen, but I couldn't have predicted in precisely what ways. Quite simply, I am a different person than I was a year ago.

I just went into Amanda's room and looked down at her. She never knew me as the man I was before; she may never be aware that, just by living, she has changed another life so much. Some day I can try to explain it to her, and she can try to understand; but she will be attempting to understand the words of a person she knows only as her father—and it will be too much to expect her to decipher who that person was before he became her father.

All that can be dealt with later, though. I should be getting back to bed—it's going to be a long day, and it doesn't make sense to start it exhausted. But something in me doesn't want to sleep; something in me wants to stay out here alone, in the darkness, and let the unfocused thoughts drift over me.

So I may still be out here when the sun rises. When I hear the first sound from my daughter's bedroom I will go in and lift her to me, as I have on so many mornings; as I hope to on so many mornings to come. There will be one candle on a cake today; I will accept that as marking the end of this particular story. But the story goes on; it is unlike any I have ever been a part of, and it goes on.